The Transitional Justice Citizen

To Daniel, Oscar, and Ayla

The Transitional Justice Citizen

From Justice Receiver to Justice Seeker

Briony Jones

Reader of International Development, Politics and International Studies Department, University of Warwick, UK

Edward Elgar
PUBLISHING

Cheltenham, UK • Northampton, MA, USA

Published by
Edward Elgar Publishing Limited
The Lypiatts
15 Lansdown Road
Cheltenham
Glos GL50 2JA
UK

Edward Elgar Publishing, Inc.
William Pratt House
9 Dewey Court
Northampton
Massachusetts 01060
USA

A catalogue record for this book
is available from the British Library

Library of Congress Control Number: 2023930163

This book is available electronically in the **Elgar**online
Political Science and Public Policy subject collection
http://dx.doi.org/10.4337/9781803925127

Printed on elemental chlorine free (ECF)
recycled paper containing 30% Post-Consumer Waste

ISBN 978 1 80392 511 0 (cased)
ISBN 978 1 80392 512 7 (eBook)

Printed and bound in the USA

Contents

Acknowledgements

Because this book is so many years in the making there are countless people to thank. These thanks will also be insufficient as words fail to express how fundamental these people have been to ensure that this book was finally written. Many people have helped me directly by offering comments, reading drafts, and making cups of tea. Many others have helped me indirectly, with warm and motivating chats in corridors, by providing intellectually inspiring community, and by enriching other parts of my life.

I have benefitted hugely from input by Sam Hickey and Sara MacKian, who started me on this journey quite some time ago, and the founding members of Oxford Transitional Justice Research, who inspired me to focus on the field of transitional justice. Phil Clark, Nicola Palmer, Teddy Harrison, and Julia Paulson all introduced me to the ideas which are fundamental to this book, and did so with openness and laughter. When I first dipped my toe into publishing my research, it was with Aoiffe Corcoran, who has been there ever since as a constant and irreplaceable friend. My time with the Dealing with the Past team at swisspeace helped me to develop and refine my ideas, and in particular Sandra Rubli, Julie Bernath and Ulrike Lühe were my steadfast companions throughout the projects which have informed much of the content of this book. Lately, my time with the Politics and International Studies Department of the University of Warwick has given me the practical support, fierce encouragement, and intellectual space needed to put words on paper. Members of the Global South Study Group offered comments and moments of comradery, thank you all. I have also benefitted hugely from the work of research assistants Bronwen Webster, Shreyanshi Upadhyaya, and Mohamed El-Shewy; and kind peer reviews from Daniela Lai, Miriam Salehi, and Adou Djané Dit Fatogoma. Last but certainly not least, the support of the editorial team at Edward Elgar as well as the detailed and helpful feedback of four anonymous reviewers helped me to reach the finish line.

Of course, this book could never have been written without the generosity and openness of all the interviewees quoted. My time in Bosnia-Herzegovina, Côte d'Ivoire, and Tunisia was rich with conversation and observation and I am forever indebted to those who sat patiently with me while I asked questions, tried to answer those questions, and then asked some more. Any errors in the book are mine and mine alone, but it would not exist without the words and interpretations of my interviewees, many of whom do not have the luxury of their own platform upon which to write and publish their own stories.

Beyond the world of this book, I am forever grateful to my family, Smith and Jones, for providing the supporting and encouraging environment that is necessary if one is to go out into the world, to try to make sense of it, and to in some way make a small contribution towards a better future.

This book is dedicated to three people in particular: Daniel, Oscar, and Ayla, whose love, company and support is all I really need.

Abbreviations

AU	African Union
CACI-USA	Committee of Actions for Côte d'Ivoire – USA
CDVR	Commission of Dialogue, Truth, and Reconciliation (*Commission Dialogue, Vérité et Reconciliation*)
CNRD	National Congress for Resistance and Democracy (*Congrès National pour la Résistance et la Démocratie)*
CONARIV	National Commission for Reconciliation and Compensation of Victims (*Commission Nationale pour la Réconciliation et l'Indemnisation des Victims*)
CSO	Civil society organizations
ECCC	Extraordinary Chambers in the Courts of Cambodia
EU	European Union
FBiH	Federation of Muslims and Croats
FPI	Ivoirien Popular Front (*Front Populaire Ivoirien*)
ICC	International Criminal Court
ICTJ	International Center for Transitional Justice
ICTR	International Criminal Tribunal for Rwanda
ICTY	International Criminal Tribunal for the Former Yugoslavia
IVD	Truth and Dignity Commission (*Instance Verité et Dignité*)
OHCHR	Office of the United Nations High Commissioner for Human Rights
OHR	Office of the High Representative
OSCE	Organization for Security and Cooperation in Europe
SCSL	Special Court for Sierra Leone
SDS	Serb Democratic Party
SFRY	Socialist Federal Republic of Yugoslavia
SR	Serb Republic

UN   United Nations
UNOCI   United Nations Operation in Côte d'Ivoire

1. Introduction: contextualizing the struggle for justice to learn from the citizen

1.1 LOOKING FROM THE INSIDE OUT

While conducting fieldwork in Bosnia-Herzegovina in 2008, I interviewed a business leader from Brčko District, the only officially multi-ethnic district in the country following the 1992-1995 war. I was interested in how citizens in Brčko District experienced life in a political community which national and international observers alike had designated as successfully reconciled. I asked my interviewee a series of questions which highlighted my concerns over the lack of public space for dissent and conflict, for alternative narratives to the one of success. My interviewee told me that while it may be intellectually interesting to wonder at the value of disagreement, if I had lived the generations of violence that his family had lived then I would feel thankful for the peace despite its supposed costs.[1] I have since then often reflected on this conversation, feeling the responsibility to ask the critical questions while at the same time recognizing that they are posed from a position of privilege; I have less to fear from conflict and dissent for I have not personally experienced their violent consequences. I also return to this conversation for an intellectual purpose, to understand the role that seeking order and consensus plays in addressing violent conflict and its consequences for diverse, inclusive, or radical alternatives.

During the intellectual journey that I have travelled since that conversation in Brčko District I have continued to work at the intersection between citizenship and justice-seeking following violent conflict. The concept of citizenship has offered me a fruitful entry point into important debates about the agency of people who are too often cast as disempowered victims, about the longer-term political struggles of individuals and communities, and about the limits of the justice which is on offer when societies seek to address the past – a process referred to as transitional justice. Such a process may include truth-seeking, prosecutions, institutional reform, or reparation, and each individual instance is now inseparable from a global project: 'The question today is not whether something should be done after atrocity but how it should be done. And a professional body of international donors, practitioners and researchers assists or directs in figuring this out and implementing it' (Nagy 2008: 276). As I elaborate in the chapters which follow, this global project and its dominant script (Sharp 2018) too easily narrow our understanding of justice and push context, contestation, and citizenship into second place behind a particular pursuit of justice.

In this book I bring together these threads of my work and thinking to propose a new concept of the 'transitional justice citizen'. This is a term that I have coined[2] to refer to a two-fold understanding of the citizen in a society undergoing a transitional justice process, bringing together scholarship on transitional justice with scholarship on citizenship. On the one hand there is *the citizen who is imagined* by a transitional justice process through its policies, mandates, aims, and statements made by transitional justice advocates. Such imagining contains certain assumptions about the citizen, namely that they accept and participate in a democratic peace contract. Through certain virtues and behaviours, the citizen can 'roll out' transitional justice aims and ensure a sustainable and just peace for the future. On the other hand, there is *the citizen who acts*, who pre-exists, and engages with, a transitional justice process. This is a citizen who does not merely *receive* justice but who actively *seeks* justice. Importantly, this seeking of justice may overlap with the kind of justice on offer from a transitional justice process, but it may also go beyond, challenge, or seek to redefine it.

When societies begin a process of transitional justice it is because they have suffered large-scale violations of human rights. These violations have been referred to as unspeakable (Palmer, Jones et al. 2015: 177), as art, science, and conversation fail to capture the full horror of these experiences. The solutions for redress are thus often defined by a desire to separate the past from the future, to generate order from violence, and to identify, label and address specific crimes. This has the effect of removing the violations and experiences of them from their contexts, and thus limits our ability to understand why we need a transitional justice process in the first place. I contend that in our desire to make whole those societies which have been divided by violence, we must first engage with the origins, unfolding and dynamics of those divisions over time. More concretely, in order to understand, analyse and redress human rights violations, the historical, cultural, economic and political contexts which have given rise to them must also be understood (Duthie and Seils 2017). Transitional justice, by which is meant the sum of processes and mechanisms designed to address large-scale human rights violations of the past, has unfortunately developed limitations and blind spots with regard to this subject of context. Too often the tribunals, truth commissions, reparation programmes and institutional reforms which constitute the primary tools of a transitional justice process are designed and implemented in an ahistorical and decontextualised manner (Fletcher, Weinstein et al. 2009).

These blind spots are a problem for the field of transitional justice both as a normative endeavour, which believes in the moral good of seeking justice, and as a practical endeavour, which seeks to achieve its aims within the boundaries of what is possible. As this book explores, the injustices on which a specific transitional justice process focuses are not the only injustices of relevance to the people living in the societies in which the process takes place. If we wish to understand in greater depth these important nuances of context it is imperative that we not only listen more carefully to those actors who are the supposed beneficiaries of transitional justice, but that we fully realise their agency and its relevance. In recent years there has been a significant increase in interest in local transitional justice (Shaw and Waldorf 2010), in transitional justice from below (McEvoy and McGregor 2008), and in ensuring that transitional justice is more sensitive to the cultures and histories of the communities in which it is embedded (Arthur 2011). However, while this work has significantly shaped the field and makes an important contribution to the necessary de-centring of transitional justice, it does not move far enough away from a tendency to begin with the transitional justice intervention itself. Too often such work starts from a position of there being a need to *re*-claim agency, to *re*-discover the local, to *give back* power to those who have been marginalised through violence and continue to be so through attempts to redress it.

By contrast, this book begins with the assumption that agency of local actors already exists, and that power is already being contested and used by local actors before the transitional justice process takes place. This approach broadens our analyses and has the potential to capture what exists in context beyond that which interacts directly with a transitional justice process. As I have written previously, there is a problematic tendency for scholarship on transitional justice to start with the transitional justice process and look outwards to its reactions and effects (Jones and Bernath 2017). If we start with transitional justice then our analyses accept transitional justice as the norm, in relation to which other phenomena such as political will, population buy-in, and perpetrator deterrence are judged. However, if we shift our vision and start with the actors, the society in which transitional justice intervenes, we become alert to the possibility that what we observe is more than a phenomenon which can be understood only with reference to the transitional justice process. As such, this book is part of the body of critical studies which seeks to 'stimulate new thinking by attempting to deconstruct aspects of transitional justice, and thereby *strip it of its sense of naturalness and inevitability*' (Sharp 2018: 14, emphasis in original). We can see the power of such an approach in recent work by transformative justice scholars who focus on transformations of socio-economic relations and structures of injustice. McAuliffe argues that:

> [t]ransitional justice theorizing is so busy imagining where justice should go that it neglects to consider where it begins – an inside–out view means starting from the point of transition within the state, and not with our own conceptions of justice from outside it. As such, it requires the state to be considered as a site of social and political conflict. (McAuliffe 2017: 22)

Hoddy and Gready follow such a method in their work on the root causes of injustice and violence in Tunisia where they asked participants 'about their experiences, needs and priorities in the context of political transition rather than in relation to transitional justice' in order to 'develop an account of the societal roots of unmet need and to allow perspectives to emerge that are not necessarily framed around transitional justice and its mechanisms' (Hoddy and Gready 2020: 565–566). By taking an inside–out approach as these other scholars have done, I argue that we can only understand transitional justice by focusing on what is not transitional justice, by shifting our gaze to start with the society itself.

This book takes as a starting point the belief that those living in societies experiencing a transitional justice process have always been agents and express their agency in contexts with varying degrees of freedom and restrictions. The figure of the transitional justice citizen both pre-exists transitional justice and is created by transitional justice. Starting from this point, with the actors themselves in context, may appear to be only a small variation on literature which focuses on local empowerment and locally informed transitional justice, but it makes a substantial difference to the way in which the discussion in this book is framed. This book focuses on the context and the political struggles which cut across, pre-date and shape how transitional justice empirically unfolds. This allows us to understand transitional justice in its own context, as a set of interventions implemented within a period of time and situated within a longer-term trajectory of deciding, contesting and re-defining the boundaries of the political community. Indeed, many of the current debates in the field of transitional justice, as we shall explore in this chapter, pivot on an apparent disjuncture between the contexts of long-term struggle and short-term calls for justice. I argue that my concept of the transitional justice citizen offers an entry point to, and analytical framework for, reconciling this disjuncture. In the rest of this chapter, I will provide a framework for the theoretical task which this book undertakes in elaborating the concept of the transitional justice citizen. Each of the debates presented here is a building block for how I will argue we can understand the transitional justice citizen.

1.2   CITIZENSHIP AND TRANSITIONAL JUSTICE

The way in which transitional justice has developed as a field has led to a failure to take into account the articulation (and its impact) of varied political projects. Transitional justice is concerned primarily with certain crimes, and individual experiences of these crimes, and is deeply embedded in the discourses and practices of contemporary neoliberalism and globalization (Sharp 2018). There is a lack of work which engages substantially with the figure of the citizen in transitional justice efforts beyond a concern with how citizen participation and the virtues of the 'good' citizen can be leveraged for the objectives of a given transitional justice process or intervention. To move beyond this, and to contribute to the field, this book connects the longer-term historical struggle over the boundaries and content of citizenship with contemporary claims for justice made as part of a transitional justice process. It does so by conceptualizing the figure of the 'transitional justice citizen' in a way which takes account of the role of dissent and disorder and of the non-linearity of political struggle. It rejects an approach which confines the politics of the past to the time of the past and is underpinned by an approach which acknowledges and foregrounds the agency of the supposed beneficiaries of a transitional justice process.

When tracing the development of transitional justice as a field of scientific enquiry, Arthur (2009) describes its distinct character as deriving from its dual focus on human rights within contexts of political transition and on the normative aim of facilitating a transition towards democracy. The combination of human rights frameworks with literature on democratic transition by the transitional justice field 'made the question of justice central to democratic transitions, but also made the question of political transformation central to the idea of justice' (Hansen 2014: 106). While transitional justice has expanded and now includes transitions in societies negotiating settlements in protracted social conflicts in addition to post-conflict and post-authoritarian states (Bell 2009: 8), transitional justice is still inherently concerned with the transformation of political communities and the political subjects operating within them. The label of transitional justice can be used for 'the common enterprise of finding a mechanism for 'dealing with the past' that will sustain political settlement' (Bell 2009: 14) i.e., that transitional justice is concerned with justice (the law) and democratic transition (political science) (Bell 2009: 22). Thus 'transitional justice is not only about human rights violations; it is a process to shape citizens' understanding of justice and a re-foundation of democracy' (Arenhövel 2008: 580). However, the transitional justice field lacks a conceptualization of citizenship which can help us to clarify these elements, including the nature of citizens' understandings of justice, the nature of a common enterprise, and how the figure of the citizen may be connected to a sustainable political settlement. Indeed, very little has been written about what we might term the actually existing citizen who holds these understandings and plays these roles, as opposed to the citizen as a normative idea – that being the citizen who plays their role to support a transitional justice process in specific ways.

According to Henderson, at the core of the idea of the democratic peace, for which transitional justice strives, the citizen is party to a contract in which they are responsible for desiring, achieving and maintaining peace (2006: 199). In countries such as Rwanda (Buckley-Zistel 2011: 101–113), South Africa (Amstutz 2006) and Bosnia-Herzegovina (Kostić 2008), we have seen this in calls for national unity based on a joint, rather than a particularistic citizenship, which is deemed to be integral to processes of transition. Pearce has suggested that civic participation can act as a peacebuilding tool in contexts of transition (2007: 27) and an emphasis on participation by citizens in a 'new' political community is common in transitional justice discourse. This idea of the citizen makes an explicit distinction between the citizen and other roles such as the subject or the 'native'. The citizen is 'civilized', able to play a role in the political community, in a way which non-citizens cannot. However, as Andrieu points out, '[b]ecause peacebuilding and transitional justice still rest on a high-politics vision of the state, both focus more on the consolidation of democratic institutions than on the nurturing of democratic politics' (2010: 545). This means that the figure of the citizen remains instrumentalized as a tool for achieving democratic transition, rather than being understood as an agent in their own right. We can see this clearly if we look at work on civil society and transitional justice, which has a primary interest in what citizen participation can do for transitional justice, namely that 'civil society organizations (CSOs), play a critical role in deconstructing authoritarianism, rebuilding the state and establishing a firm foundation for strong democracies' (Okello and Hovil 2011: 333). This has led to a distinction between 'good' and 'bad' civil society (Chambers and Kopstein 2001); and its gentrification through transitional justice interventions (Jeffrey 2008) reflects a narrowing of the concept of civil society 'to a contingent, ideologically preferential sub set' which assumes that civil society is by definition, and indeed *should be*, composed of groups working for the public good – in this case peace and justice – and that there is a unified concept of the good towards which they strive (Waters 2015: 165–166).

The instrumentalised citizen is also an idealised one. Assumptions (and demands) of civility run like a thread through transitional justice literature, which asserts the importance of civil society to the operationalization and success of a given process or intervention. Porter elaborates with regard to Northern Ireland that: 'Despite our differences there is no good reason why commitment to a common citizen dignity should not translate into a common civic identity. And if we care about the society in which we live, there are compelling reasons why it should' (2003: 172). In this understanding of the citizen, they are able to offer a potential for a new type of political community through their civic virtues, in which divisions associated with violence are overcome. This is not only hoped for, but expected, and proponents of transitional justice stress the importance of consensus among citizens for building a common identity which unites them as part of the same political community (Arenhövel 2008: 570). However, in this literature the hoped-for citizen is not elaborated or understood to be embedded in a context, or indeed to be an agent in their own right. The 'we' to which transitional justice processes allude remains concerningly vague, while its inherently contingent nature (Schaap 2007: 9) demands that we look more closely at the transitional justice citizen. The valuable, yet limited, work on this has shown us how post-war models of citizenship become fixed to war narratives (Theidon 2003), and how attempts to mould post-war citizens through civic education can oblige citizens to behave in particular ways (Oglesby 2007). Importantly, although such frames can work in favour of certain objectives of transition, they can also exclude a multitude of narratives and practices of citizenship which are informed by historical struggles, and demands for state accountability, and which may challenge the terms of the transitional social contract.

The exclusion of certain narratives and practices can be attributed to what has been termed the 'dominant script' of transitional justice, meaning the 'liberal-legalist' paradigm which determines what is emphasised and what is marginalised (Sharp 2018: ix). This paradigm has been a potent rallying cry for activists, non-governmental organisations, and international organizations in acknowledging and addressing large-scale violations of human rights, but it has also led to a narrow policy focus. Transitional justice as a field of policy and practice has directed its efforts towards certain types of (physical) political and civil violence; has a tendency to implement processes through a top-down, template-driven tool-box approach; and has been accused of drawing too heavily on Western and liberal modalities of justice (Sharp 2018: ix-x). Structural forms of violence, non-state-led forms of change and non-liberal modalities of justice, often referred to as 'traditional', have therefore been relegated to the background or even considered as a threat to transitional justice with their calls to look beyond frames of individualised guilt/victimhood:

[T]ransitional justice aims to] bring societies together in the construction of shared truths about the past, which are not founded in any form of communitarian identification that conceptualises the past in collectivised or socio-economic terms. Rather, underpinned as it is by the lexicon of human rights law, transitional justice simultaneously individualises the past by producing members of transitional societies as the individual victims of human rights abuses [...] transitional justice aims to create the same kind of 'empty solidarity' that defines the neoliberal project as a whole. (Bowsher 2018: 85)

We have seen elements of this tendency to obscure collective histories and solidarities in cases such as Rwanda, where a government policy of constructing a Rwandan citizenship through denial of ethnic forms of political belonging renders invisible the country's colonial past, regional dynamics, and the complex identities of perpetrators, victims, and bystanders. Such a policy also has the effect of reducing the public space for discussion and dissent regarding the post-genocide terms of political association (see for example Buckley-Zistel 2006, O'Connor 2013). In Bosnia-Herzegovina,

> [t]oo much focus on ethnic identity, or any line of division during conflict, and not on the other capacities in which people act and interact has eclipsed a recognition of affinities and common interests along other lines, common in any complex society. (Eastmond and Selimovic 2012: 523)

But there is also pushback in many contexts. In Australia, contradictions of citizenship continue for Aboriginal people (Howell and Schaap 2014). In this case, the ideal of citizenship is associated with a discourse of colonization which posits that the 'natives' lack the qualities of agency and industriousness which distinguish citizens. However, through actions such as erecting a Tent Embassy,[3] Aboriginal people also use citizenship as the basis for contesting settler ideology and for demanding a re-negotiation of the terms of political association between Aboriginal and non-Aboriginal people. In Bosnia-Herzegovina a series of 'people's protests' in 2014 evolved into the establishment of plenums[4] as direct democratic assemblies in which citizens could voice concerns with the political elite, with economic mismanagement, and with lack of opportunities for young people (Jones 2015). A key underpinning narrative of these plenums was that it is 'not ethnic nationalism that divides Bosnia [but] social inequality and political dissatisfaction [that] unite the people of Bosnia' (Keil 2014). We begin to see in these examples a phenomenon which should not surprise us at all: that people living in societies undergoing a transitional justice process continually strive to re-define the lines which separate individuals, and which underpin commonality and common endeavour. This is a political project which intersects but does not necessarily coincide with the political project of transitional justice processes. It is also too easily ignored when calls for social order and political closure are voiced loudly by transitional justice advocates.

1.3   TRANSITIONAL JUSTICE, THE ORDERING OF POLITICAL COMMUNITY, AND THE DESIRE FOR CLOSURE

One important way in which transitional justice seeks to create order is through creating a clear temporal break with the past and thus the violations which are associated with it:

> In transitional societies the basic importance of human rights and their efficacy in governing conduct often need to be established. The new political order that commits to such rights protections needs to be legitimized, and the previous political order that officially and publicly sanctioned violence rejected. There is thus a need to draw a line between what communities sanctioned in the past and what will be sanctioned in the future. (Murphy 2017: 18)

The necessity to do this – both looking backwards to the past and forwards to a new and bright future – leads to a teleology according to which the past is violent, but is behind us, while the future is peaceful, and is ahead of us, if we 'do the right thing'. In between is a window of opportunity which the transitional justice process utilises to acknowledge and redress harm while initiating reforms aimed at reparation and non-recurrence. The very term 'transition' implies a beginning, middle and end of a process, as one state (violence, war, authoritarianism) turns into another (peace, justice, democracy). As such, scholars have identified a 'common trope that transitional justice allows countries to "start over" by settling accounts with the past' (Fletcher, Weinstein et al. 2009: 207). It is this framing which implies that transition is a temporary moment of exception following a rupture in a pre-democratic state which can be repaired and, in so doing, leads to a set of pre-identified outcomes.

However, recent scholarship on transitional justice is uneasy with this teleology. For Meister, 'the cost of achieving a moral consensus that the past was evil is to reach a political consensus that the evil is past. In practice, this political consensus operates to constrain debate in societies that regard themselves as "recovering" from horrible histories' (2002: 96). Indeed, through seeking order, transitional justice has often been used to consolidate the authority of the new individuals and governments in power (Ilif 2012), which has been shown to be just as likely to consolidate the power base of illiberal regimes as to support a move towards democracy (Sharp 2018: x). In this context, a desire to separate the past temporally and morally from the present ensures that the holders of power during a transitional justice process can distance themselves from past injustices. This can draw attention away from ongoing human rights violations, as we have seen in Cambodia, and from ongoing political violence, as we have seen in Côte d'Ivoire. It can also take our attention away from the instrumentalization of transitional justice for political ends, as we have seen in Uganda, where President Museveni has called on the International Criminal Court (ICC) to investigate crimes committed by his opponents while denying crimes committed by his own forces. As I have argued previously, the moral battleground of transitional justice inevitably leads to the marginalization of certain voices and to the consolidation of others' power. This does not always occur in predictable ways and is often connected to political jostling (Jones and Bernath 2017). A danger of the impulse to ensure democratic order is that these ongoing dynamics are denied in the grand quest to seek a clean break from the past.

The impulse to order also risks placing limits on the possibility of justice. This may be because of the need to compromise to reach a solution in the immediate present with a promise for a protected future (Turner 2013). Christodoulidis and Veitch argue that the political discourse of our time calls on us 'not just to put the traumas of the past behind us but also, in a sense, to put behind us the very politics of the past' (2007: 1). Such a demand is made on the basis that today's order can lead to the future's peace and stability. The implementation of order in the present is driven by the fear of a return to violence. This is of course useful for those in power, as elaborated above, but we should also remind ourselves of the words of my Bosnian interviewee who expressed a perfectly legitimate desire to exchange some form of agency and expression of conflict for the guarantee of no future violence. It prompts us to continue to reflect on whether the price of the desire for political order is worth paying.

I would suggest that this is, however, a question posed on false premises. To suggest that disorder and violence is the opposite of order and peace makes two assumptions: firstly, that disorder is not constitutive of peace; and secondly, that order will provide the prize of peace. Too often the political order which accompanies a transitional justice process, as I highlight above, distracts us from focusing on ongoing violence, human rights violations, and restrictions of freedoms. It also does not acknowledge that disorder and dissent can be vital constituents of democratic life, and that an active democratic politics may be more important than the institutions and procedures which so often occupy transitional justice advocacy (Andrieu 2010). We would do well to remind ourselves that:

> [w]hile disorder can undermine the process of democratization by making participation in public life and governing impossible, the erasure or suppression of disorder is an equal threat to democratization. This is because disruption is often a strategy in expanding the field of public address and an important element in broader struggles to expand and reorder the democratic public. (Staeheli 2010: 68)

The terms of political association which are negotiated and contested as part of a transitional justice process have also been negotiated and contested long before transitional justice was an option. A process of transitional justice will no doubt alter the negotiating ground but debates about how to live together in a peaceful future must always be informed by how such debates have played out in the past and must not be confined to the terms set by transitional justice.

When the past is framed as the target of a transition designed to (re)turn to a future, transitional justice processes risk being dislocated from longer-term historical contexts of struggle. When this happens, we erroneously forget the struggles which placed dealing with the past on the political agenda in the first place (McEvoy and McGregor 2008: 4–6). This is a significant gap, because the violence which renders transition 'necessary' is part of longer-term contestations over the meaning of, and who belongs to, a given political community. Such contestations will remain relevant throughout the transition and beyond, shaping responses to transitional justice as well as affecting what such initiatives will be able to achieve. As Fletcher et al. explain, 'the past seeps into transitional justice – whether by design or as an unintended unwelcome intruder' (2009: 207–208). This book builds on and contributes to these critiques of the transitional justice field. While the transitional justice project may have internal logics and purposes, the targeted beneficiaries of the interventions are not passive recipients of these constructions. They are agents who act through silence, stillness, movement, participation, resistance, contestation, and many other manners of actualizing themselves as those who *seek* justice rather than those who merely *receive* it.

1.4   THE NON-LINEARITY OF STRUGGLE

As the field of transitional justice was consolidated, a certain conceptualization of transition, and therefore theory of change, developed. With its origins in transitology, the transitional justice approach to transition unsurprisingly emphasises teleology, stability and order (Mac Ginty 2018). This has led to a paradigmatic transition exemplified by early cases of transitional justice, such as that of Argentina and its transition from military junta rule to democracy following the violence of the 1970s and 1980s (Arthur 2009). The paradigmatic transition has been widely discussed and debated in the literature and is broadly characterised by three components: firstly, that the previous regime is understood to be illegitimate; secondly, that the changes brought about by the transition are relatively uniform throughout the state; and, thirdly, that it is a process of closure (Ní Aoláin and Campbell 2005: 173, 181–182). The challenge in these early paradigmatic cases was to identify the appropriate legal tool to address past human rights violations without threatening a transition towards democracy in the present (Murphy 2017: 29), specifically a transition to a liberal democracy understood in relatively procedural terms (Ní Aoláin and Campbell 2005: 176). The ideal vision of such a liberal democracy is that it operates with the consent of the governed, thereby generating legitimacy both in the sense of meeting normative standards and in the sense of acceptance by the citizenry (Ní Aoláin and Campbell 2005: 183). However, this paradigmatic transition makes a series of assumptions about the nature of democracy, the nature of change, and the linearity of struggle, which are not borne out by empirics or indeed continued conceptual development of the field.

As critical studies of transitional justice have grown in number, and our empirical knowledge of how transitional justice processes play out in practice has increased, the features of the paradigmatic transition have been called into question (Murphy 2017: 29). The founding scholars of the field connected a clear beginning and end to the process of transition, making it possible to understand transitional justice as an imperative to act during a specific window of opportunity, the transitional 'moment'. The idea of change which accompanied this was short-term and disruptive – a break with the past – rather than long-term and incremental (Sharp 2018: 76). However, we have seen both a vertical and horizontal expansion of the field (Hansen 2014), and

> [i]n terms of time and process, it is now clear that transitional justice efforts can be initiated prior to a political transition and often extended for decades after the process of democratization has begun, calling into question earlier ideas about the field being limited to short-term, corrective measures during a brief window of transitional opportunity. (Ní Aoláin and Campbell 2005: 77)

This has informed a key debate of the field about whether a different kind of justice, or rules of justice, can or should be applied in contexts of massive human rights violations, which are far from the ordinary domestic contexts of national law. Ohlin describes this tension, arguing that justice is meant to evoke a universal, normative goal, whereas transitional defines an exceptional and limited moment (Ohlin 2007). The challenge is that

> [c]riminal justice systems are designed to maintain order in societies where violation of law is the exception. These systems simply cannot cope when, either as a result of state-sanctioned human rights abuses or internal conflict or war, violations become the rule. (Paul van Zyl cited in Murphy 2017: 9)

One way of managing this tension has been to fall back on a discourse of exceptionality and pragmatism. If transitional justice is exceptional, then 'consolidating a democracy cannot be subject to the same moral standards we would use to evaluate the regime it hopes to produce' (Eisikovits 2013: 236). However, this requires a greater discussion about the extent to which moral complacency can be allowed and for how long a state can be considered to be transitional (Eisikovits 2013). In addition, we often hear calls to pragmatism in the literature, asking critics to acknowledge the imperfect world in which transitional justice principles are applied (De Greiff cited in Murphy 2017: 28), to think through what is actually possible in a given context (Waldorf 2012), and implicitly requesting the acceptance of a 'good enough' justice. In reality, the envisaged beneficiaries of transitional justice often refuse to adopt the proclaimed reading of exceptionality. In doing so, they invoke an alternative logic of the ordinary, seeing neo-colonial and/or other perfectly mundane political and economic interests at work behind the transitional justice rhetoric of exception (Anders and Zenker 2014: 407). This is true from the protests of the grandmothers of the Plaza de Mayo in Argentina to the legal cases brought against big business by the Khulumani Support Group of South Africa. Across the world we can see cases where 'beneficiaries' demand more of the justice process.

Such a rejection of the exceptionality of transitional justice moments urges actors to take seriously the non-linearity and contested nature of the changes inherent to democratic transitions which occur alongside and in interaction with transitional justice. By non-linearity I mean that power relationships and contexts are continually changing and that societies are not always progressing towards an agreed end point. The liberal-legal dominant script of transitional justice cannot easily accommodate this sense of struggle. The idea that change (progress) occurs through individual rights and the advancement of liberalism stands at odds with the histories of many countries where transitional justice processes are implemented. These include the many African countries that were subject to structural, violent and revolutionary change as they experienced decolonization and independence movements (Anders and Zenker 2014).

Indeed, the desire for order, and for teleological forms of change, means that certain types of politics are considered to be less legitimate or desirable as part of the new democratic peace contract. In reference to Northern Ireland, Little has commented that the supposedly 'dysfunctional' political wrangling before and following the Good Friday Agreement may in fact be more normal than the practice of politics imagined by the liberal ideal type (2009). For Little, 'normal' politics is that which can be reasonably expected in such contexts where conflict has turned violent and where a transitional justice process intervenes with a particular discourse about politics and political change. I would argue that political contestation, blockage, or disagreement is necessary to work out the new terms of association in a context of insecurity and change. Diaz illustrates this argument well in her analysis of actors 'from below' and their contestation of the transitional justice process in Colombia. The activities of ex-combatants, civil society organizations and victims' groups reflect a desire to ask more of the process and a refusal to compromise in light of contemporary transitional justice 'progressively abandoning goals of real political transformation and rather serv[ing] as an instrumental variant of "conflict resolution" which favours the interests of the powerful' (Diaz 2008: 197). In reference to the case of Burundi, Rubli (2016) argues that what is often identified as a lack of political will to implement transitional justice is in fact a comprehensible working out of the alliances and shifting positions within the political elite. This is partly in response to views on transitional justice but is more understandable when seen through the lens of the complicated state building which accompanies a transitional justice process.

The idea of 'normal' politics is thus not only what can be reasonably expected to occur in transitional contexts, but also a commentary of what should occur in the politics of such processes and what kind of political community societies should be aiming for. Balibar's observation that 'the presumption that violence can be eliminated is a constitutive element of our idea of politics' (2015: 2) can be extended here to claim that a constitutive element of the idea of transitional justice is that conflict can be eliminated. This occurs through an ability to know and name acts of conflict – in the form of certain crimes, practices of truth seeking and acknowledgement – and our ability to control conflict through institutional reform. Transitional justice disciplines and seeks order through the hegemony of the law and the lexicon of human rights (Ojara 2012: 180), which names violence in particular ways and prescribes forms of change. Because violence is situated in the 'past', it becomes difficult to hold those responsible for ongoing violence to account. Because violence is political and civil, it becomes difficult to seek justice for social and economic crimes or discuss ongoing structural violence. Because justice is 'good', it becomes difficult to make claims which contest or reject the justice on offer. Because transition is temporary, it becomes difficult to contextualise it as part of an ongoing series of struggles and injustices of which it may even be a part.

1.5   A CITIZEN-SHAPED PIECE OF THE PUZZLE?

In Mamdani's seminal work on citizenship in Africa, he writes that political identities 'shape our relationship to the state and to one another through the state. In doing so, they also form the starting point of our struggles' (2001: 22). We know from the transitional justice field that these struggles are an important part of the context in which transitional justice processes play out. We also know that there are a series of debates which define the current critical literature on the subject: whether and how the past/present/future should be separated; the ramifications of seeking order and closure as counterpoints to disruption and dissent; and the need to (re)define the boundaries and content of political community. We also know that the conflict, violence and justice claims which are the focus of a given transitional justice process are not the entire story. There are divisions, struggles and conflicts which pre-exist and intersect with transitional justice processes. By taking an inside–out approach, this book focuses on these struggles to understand how transitional justice processes unfold, rather than focusing on transitional justice as a way of illuminating the struggles that surround and shape it.

The entry point to this approach is the transitional justice citizen. The citizen is at the heart of these struggles, as well as at the heart of many assumptions underpinning transitional justice. The citizen is, however, under-theorized in the field despite what this can offer as an entry point and analytical framework to address key debates. Robust and in-depth theoretical work can provide deeper context and substance to help us respond to critiques of transitional justice (Fletcher, Weinstein et al. 2009; Sharp 2018: 13). This book proposes a two-fold conceptualization of the transitional justice citizen: the citizen as imagined by a transitional justice process; and the citizen who acts to make claims and seek justice in ways which may coincide or stand in tension with the justice being offered by a transitional justice process. In doing so, I draw on not only the critical studies within the transitional justice field but also pertinent work from citizenship studies.

Citizenship has commonly been defined as a 'status that carries rights, entitlements and responsibilities' (Saward 2013: 50). Early definitions of a more passive status which is 'bestowed on those who are full members of a community' (T.H. Marshall cited in Lister 2003: 14) have informed much of the modern liberal political tradition in which a limited state guarantees the freedom and formal equality of the citizen who is sovereign (Lister 2003: 13). However, citizenship in practice is necessarily more complicated and its definition has been altered, reconstructed, expanded and reclaimed in the face of citizenship struggles (Hoffman 2004: 1). Feminist scholars have highlighted the importance of gender intersecting with citizenship in the lived experience (Lister 2003) and the importance of recognizing different identities encapsulated in any one citizen (Deiana 2016), political geographers have shown how citizenship emerges and gains meaning in space and place (Darling 2017), while development studies scholars have focused on how 'the history of citizenship in both North and South has been a history of struggle over how it is to be defined and who it is to include' (Kabeer 2005: 1). Insights from a wide range of different disciplinary studies of citizenship have come to underscore that citizenship can (and should) be understood in many ways which go beyond legal status. Examples include: as a 'momentum concept' in a constant process of contestation (Hoffman 2004: 12); as an 'enabling condition' predicated on socio-economic status, social ties, political mobilization and access to resources (Sassen 2006: 190); as 'insurgent' efforts of the marginalized to claim rights and space (Olivius 2019); and as an active practice (Jones and Gaventa 2002: 5), among many others.

Recognizing the varied terms used to describe and define citizenship, Staeheli refers to the citizen as a Waldo-esque 'elusive' figure and citizenship as a 'multifaceted' and 'slippery concept and category' which defies easy definition in the midst of intellectual debate over its universality versus particularity (Staeheli 2011: 393–394). However, she also suggests that emerging from debates over where to find and recognize the citizen is a recognition that '"actually existing citizenship" cannot be detached from broader currents and processes shaping society' (Staeheli 2011: 394). I take from this body of work a concern with struggle, and with the need to pay attention to actually existing citizenship. In particular, I find the concept of 'acts of citizenship' offered by Isin and Nielsen (2008) to be helpful both as an analytical lens and as a constitutive idea of the transitional justice citizen. Isin's theorization of acts of citizenship in particular (2008) has gained considerable attention in recent years from scholars interested in citizenship exclusions and marginalization (Darling 2017: 729). However, this interest has not extended to the transitional justice field, which, perhaps unsurprisingly given that the field in under-theorised in general (Buckley-Zistel, Beck et al. 2014; Davidovic 2020; Hoddy and Gready 2020: 562), has not drawn on the rich literature around citizenship to inform discussions of either the conceptualization of transitional justice or its policy and practice (for one exception see Fullard and Rousseau 2011).

Isin and Nielsen, like much of the literature cited above, argue that the focus should not be on the individual citizen and their status and responsibilities, but on their acts of citizenship, which are not reducible to either the individual or their status (2008: 2). This is an approach which clearly separates status and acts (Pykett, Saward et al. 2010: 526). In doing so, they emphasize how citizens may be constituted through acts rather than determined by rights and membership within an identifiable political or territorial community (Fullard and Rousseau 2011: 56). Acts of citizenship are further defined by Isin and Nielsen as 'collective or individual deeds that rupture social-historical patterns': '[they] disrupt habitus, create new possibilities, claim rights and impose obligations in emotionally charged tones; pose their claims in enduring and creative expressions; and, most of all, are the actual moments that shift established practices, status and order' (2008: 2 and 10). This break with habitus is significant in distinguishing between everyday practices of citizens and the acts of citizenship as defined by Isin and Nielsen (Pykett, Saward et al. 2010: 526–527). Their acts of citizenship are about disruption, new possibilities, and shifts in established order. We can therefore recognize an act as occurring when 'established scripts and subjectivities are disrupted, thus creating a new script and bringing into being political subjects that did not exist previously' (Squire 2016: 265).

Importantly for this book, acts of citizenship have the potential to link longer-term struggles, current justice claim-making, and visions of future peace and stability. As described by Isin and Nielsen, an act of citizenship 'implicitly asks questions about a future responsibility towards others', and contains within itself the 'question of how to act, exposing the need to develop new, creative responses to those occasions where we no longer recognise the context of action' and explore 'active and reactive ways of being with others' (2008: 2–7). Transitional justice processes are implemented in contexts in which prior expectations or understandings of how to act have been disturbed, and where an exploration of how to be with others is foremost in the minds of the political elite and society at large. We could describe a time of transitional justice as ripe for, and indeed in need of, the questions and explorations which acts of citizenship evoke. Importantly, Isin and Nielsen's theorization of acts understands them as not necessarily purposive, but recognizable through their political implications or effects (Squire 2016: 266). An individual actor does not need to wilfully 'act'; rather we can see them as having 'acted' through the disruption, the new scripts, and the political implications generated. In her work mobilizing acts of citizenship as an analytical lens, Squire finds that 'an analytics of acts remains attuned to the dynamics of power-resistance across concrete sites and pays attention to how far interventions by bodies in action effect a transformation in being through producing new subjects and scripts' (Squire 2016: 267). My use of the acts of citizenship lens helps me to demonstrate that while the transitional justice citizen may be framed in particular ways by transitional justice discourse, policy and practice, the transitional justice citizen also comes into being as a political subject capable of disrupting old scripts and evoking new ones. In the context of this book, the new scripts evoked relate to pushing the boundaries around who can make claims, what claims can be made, and how claims should be made.

Employing 'acts of citizenship' as a lens to both describe and construct the idea of the transitional justice citizen is thus useful in several ways. As explored in this introductory chapter, during transitional justice processes there is an interplay between rupture and change and a desire to establish order and consolidate new authority. There is also a need to keep the connection with the struggles in which both violence and justice are rooted, as well as the contexts in which transitional justice unfolds. My contention is that the figure of the transitional justice citizen responds to these needs – which are both conceptual and pragmatic – and that such a figure can be understood as imagined through discourse and policy and as coming into being though acts of citizenship.

1.6   APPROACH AND OUTLINE OF THE BOOK

1.6.1   Structure

The proposal of a citizen-shaped piece for the puzzle will take place in two distinct and interlinked stages: (1) an analysis of the citizen as imagined through specific transitional justice processes; and (2) an analysis of the actually existing citizen who makes claims to justice. Both stages respond to the questions: how is the citizen constructed through transitional justice? How does the citizen connect historical struggle with contemporary calls for justice as part of a transitional justice process? What do these citizenship acts tell us about the empirical unfolding of transitional justice? What struggles are most important at times of transitional justice and what happens to them as a transitional justice process unfolds? The concept of the transitional justice citizen covers many different types of citizens as individuals actualise themselves as citizens in varied ways. The concept of the transitional justice citizen aims to capture the monolithic approach to citizenship, which is part of the imaginings of a transitional justice process, and to contrast this with the varied and multiple actually existing citizens who seek justice on their own terms.

The first phase of the conceptualization of the transitional justice citizen occurs in Part 1 of the book. Here the chapters build on work which has already begun to explore assumptions about citizenship in transitional justice scholarship, policy, and practice. Throughout Part 1 we see the transitional justice citizen framed and understood as a relatively passive figure constructed as a receiver of the justice that is provided through mechanisms and processes supported by international norms. Chapters 2 to 4 take as their framework the common articulation of the citizen as described above – through rights, duties, and virtues. Chapter 2 focuses on the transitional justice citizen as a bearer of rights, who must be protected through international norms as well as duties undertaken by the state and fellow citizens. This citizen is imagined through the international bureaucratization of transitional justice and is sustained by a dominant discourse which normalizes and justifies intervention at the same time as constructing victimhood. Chapter 3 explores the transitional justice citizen as a bearer of duties through a discussion of transitional justice participation and outreach programmes, which are designed to generate 'buy-in' from beneficiaries, rather than to provide a structure for the articulation of claims or visions of justice. This citizen has duties towards the functioning and outcomes of a transitional justice process without a matching empowerment to shape and determine that same process. In Chapter 4 the focus is on the virtuous nature of the transitional justice citizen. Implicit and explicit expectations of virtuous behaviour by citizens align with the legal-liberal dominant script of transitional justice and preclude more radical understandings of who a citizen is or can be or how change can occur outside of a managed transitional justice process.

In this part of the book, I thus align myself in my analysis with critics who point out that the individual-human rights-violation approach seeks to install a liberal-democratic citizen as the subject of a political order that has only been transformed in limited ways (Fullard and Rousseau 2011: 55). It is this central problematic which connects Part 1 of the book to Part 2, where we see the actually existing citizen, through their acts, bringing struggle and marginalized claim-making back in. Acts of citizenship are particularly pertinent to a conceptualization of the transitional justice citizen and allow the analysis to move from the *imagined citizen*, framed through and by transitional justice, to the *actually existing citizen*, who is in a process of becoming, of demanding, and of disrupting.

In Part 2, Chapters 5 to 7, acts of citizenship are described and analysed in three categories of acts: acts of inclusion; acts of expansion; and acts of disruption. These categories directly emerge from Part 1. Acts of inclusion contest *who* can make claims in response to the framing of rights in Chapter 2. Acts of expansion contest *what* claims can be made in response to the framing of duties in Chapter 3. Acts of disruption contest *how* claims can be made in response to the framing of virtues in Chapter 4. Each of the chapters in Part 2 also focus on a particular case study: Côte d'Ivoire in Chapter 5; Tunisia in Chapter 6; and Bosnia-Herzegovina in Chapter 7. The analysis is then narrowed further with a focus on particular actors: supporters of the former president in Côte d'Ivoire; Black activists in Tunisia; and secondary school students in Bosnia-Herzegovina. And finally, each chapter focuses on particular acts: resistance to the transitional justice process in Côte d'Ivoire; submission of a dossier to the truth commission and lobbying for legal reform in Tunisia; and street demonstrations in Bosnia-Herzegovina.

1.6.2 Methodology

This book draws on the last decade of my work which has focused on the intersection between citizenship and transitional justice. This includes significant desk-based work analysing transitional justice policy documents, NGOs' programmes of action and research, and an overview of the academic state of the art. It also includes my own qualitative fieldwork in Bosnia-Herzegovina, Côte d'Ivoire, and Tunisia, as well as insights I have drawn from qualitative empirical work during other projects on the cases of Burundi, Cambodia, Colombia, El Salvador, and South Sudan. This work brings together a series of conceptual threads which have provided coherence to my sustained interest in the politics of societies following large-scale violations of human rights.

My previous work published on reconciliation, civil society, resistance, and politics of knowledge is all brought to bear and used to inform the claims on which I construct the concept of the transitional justice citizen.

Part 1 draws on analysis of transitional justice policy documents and secondary literature within the field. These include reports of United Nations Special Rapporteurs for Truth, Justice, Reparation, and Guarantees of Non-Recurrence, policy documents from other key multilateral organizations such as the Office of the High Commissioner for Human Rights (OHCHR), the European Union, and the African Union (AU), as well as policy and programme reports from key NGOs in the field such as Human Rights Watch. The selection of these reports was made both through purposive sampling based on my knowledge of the field and on snowball sampling following leads from the texts themselves which refer to other reports or studies. Other texts were identified through citations in academic work that formed the literature review part of my research.

The analysis in Part 2 is informed by both desk-based research and qualitative empirical research. As this book draws together the conceptual threads of the last decade of my research on transitional justice, so too does it draw together the different empirical research that I have done at different points in time. The empirical data used for Chapter 5 comes from fieldwork conducted in 2014 in Côte d'Ivoire in collaboration with Dr Adou Djané Dit Fatogoma. I have since continued to work on the Ivorian context, visiting the country again in 2018 and working closely with colleagues in Côte d'Ivoire on varied projects and outputs. The empirical data used for Chapter 6 comes from fieldwork conducted by me in 2007 and 2008 in Bosnia-Herzegovina. I have also continued to work on the Bosnian case since then, visiting the country again in 2012 and 2013. The empirical data used for Chapter 7 comes from more recent interviews I conducted at a distance in 2021. I had visited Tunisia as part of a transitional justice project in 2018, but unfortunately the COVID-19 pandemic made it impossible to travel back to the country for fieldwork in 2021. Instead, interviews were conducted on MS Teams or Zoom. The fieldwork conducted in each case study was qualitative and consisted primarily of semi-structured interviews. The analytical approach taken was also the same for each case, with a close reading of interview transcripts followed by thematic coding and re-reading. This was an interpretive approach which 'rejects the idea that causes can be identified in the social world and which focuses instead on understanding meanings, symbols, identities' (Hoddy and Gready 2020: 564).

My desire to explain, build theory, and analyse in-depth different instances of citizenship acts suggests a case study approach (Yin 2009: 4), but this is not a comparative case study design. Rather, each case was purposefully selected from the different countries where I have conducted transitional justice fieldwork. This intentional logic (Leuffen 2011: 145) led to the selection of cases because of their ability to speak to the themes of the book and because of the presence of acts of citizenship which could be analysed for the purposes of developing the concept of the transitional justice citizen. The three different case studies I have chosen are different in their geography, history, economics, and culture, but they are all instances of transitional justice processes and are all instances of citizenship acts. They sit side by side not in direct comparison but with the aim of drawing out cross-case conclusions about how citizenship acts demonstrate that the transitional justice citizen is a justice *seeker* as well as a justice *receiver*.

The implications of this work for the field of transitional justice are elaborated in greater detail in the concluding chapter. However, the key aspects are worth outlining here as they run as threads through all the subsequent chapters. While transitional justice frames citizens as justice receivers, they are in many instances justice seekers both through and beyond a given transitional justice intervention. A concept of the transitional justice citizen which takes us from the justice receiver to the justice seeker enables us to better understand the contradictions and difficulties of the empirical unfolding of transitional justice, a challenge which attracts the attention of many scholars, not least because the field is largely invested in the normative project of responding to past large-scale violations of human rights in the most ethical and effective way possible. Importantly, it also challenges the tendency of transitional justice to demarcate the boundaries of acceptable demands by citizens (Miller 2008: 291) by beginning with the struggles themselves, by foregrounding citizenship acts and by assuming that the contexts which have placed transitional justice on the agenda in the first place will not be fully addressed by it. To go beyond the boundaries set by a transitional justice intervention may well enable us to imagine a more just justice.

1.6.3   A Note on Ethics and Positionality

No need to hear your voice when I can talk about you better than you can speak about yourself. No need to hear your voice. Only tell me about your pain. I want to know your story. And then I will tell it back to you in a new way. Tell it back to you in such a way that it has become mine, my own. Re-writing you I write myself anew. I am still author, authority. I am still colonizer the speaking subject and you are now at the center of my talk. (hooks 1990: 24)

I have struggled since I first began working on transitional justice to reconcile my positionality with the content of my research and claims to knowledge. On the one hand I want to write about agency, disempowerment, injustice, and the politics of knowing. On the other hand, I write the stories and voices of others from the relative comfort of my home or office. I have no personal experience of the violence and harm about which I write and despite my inclusive approach to research, my co-authorship with scholars from the case study countries, and my engagement with policy makers and practitioners, my work does not directly benefit those about whom I write. But I continue to write about them and their experiences because I see value in doing so, in bearing witness, and in acknowledging what has been suffered.

I hope that my own research will contribute to nuance and complexity in thinking about transitional justice, and that it will help to unsettle problematic assumptions and power relations that imbue the field. Because of this I consider it to be of vital importance that I conduct ethical research in addition to employing methods that shift the power further away from me and towards the subjects of my research. Ethical research includes but also goes beyond that which is required to receive approval from university ethics committees. It is certainly about informed consent, anonymity, secure data storage, and doing no harm. It is also about writing in a way which does justice to others' voices, which is empathetic and humble, and which recognises their contribution to my work. I will surely not have reached perfection in this ambition, but I do hope that my awareness of this requirement and of the struggle between representation and re-presentation is a step in the right direction. As Simić has pointed out, transitional justice researchers

> do not easily turn their analytical lenses inwards and talk about their ethical and methodological journeys and interactions in a personal way. Those who do disclose in a reflective way are rare since they are willing to expose themselves to the possibility of being "accused" of limiting their findings. (Simić 2016: 102)

It is also perhaps because of the dominance of the law in the evolution of the transitional justice field, that much of the personal, social, and political character of research on transitional justice is often rendered invisible (Nouwen 2014: 233).

In each of my case study countries from Part 2 of the book – Bosnia-Herzegovina, Côte d'Ivoire, and Tunisia – I was a clear 'outsider'. I am White-British, a woman, a European, educated, and middle-class (among many other things). I spent more time in Bosnia-Herzegovina than the other countries but never learned the language to a good level. I could speak the (colonial) language in Côte d'Ivoire and Tunisia but was unable to spend any significant length of time in Tunisia and only visited Côte d'Ivoire in a series of shorter fieldtrips. My legitimacy in laying claim to knowledge about these places and the people I interviewed sometimes felt shaky at best. While I could complement my primary data collection with extensive desk-based research, conversations with colleagues, and peer-review, the ethics of speaking for the people I interviewed, and by extension wider society, was and is complex and challenging. As Mazzei and Jackson caution,

> Letting readers "hear" participant voices and presenting their "exact words" as if they are transparent is a move that fails to consider how as researchers we are always already shaping those "exact words" through the unequal power relationships present and by our own exploitative research agendas and timelines. (2009: 2)

I am particularly aware of this problem as it pertains to this book. In the chapters that follow I re-package others' voices to fit my own intellectual agenda to explore and create the concept of the transitional justice citizen.

Speaking for, as well as speaking about, others elicits unease, among other reasons, because where one speaks from affects the meaning of what is said (Alcoff 2009: 117–120). I am speaking from a position of privilege and using others' voices to fit my own desire to make an intellectual contribution to the field of transitional justice. The interviews quoted in Part 2 of this book are mediated by my position and agenda as a researcher. This certainly includes a normative aim to improve the study of transitional justice and to indirectly influence the policy and practice of it. As a scholar of transitional justice, I care deeply about the realities of injustice in the world and engage in an emotional labour (Simić 2016) through my research which acknowledges, describes, and responds to human rights violations. But it also includes the promotion of my own ideas, my own interpretations, and my own voice. Finding a balance between the multiple visible and invisible voices in this book is an impossible task. I hope it helps to acknowledge it as such and to aim to write with empathy, humility, and openness.

NOTES

1. Field Diary, July 2018, Brčko District, Bosnia-Herzegovina.
2. Although the term was coined by the author, it was developed through previous work with Alex Jeffrey and Michaela Jakala: Jones, B, Jeffrey, A and Jakala, M (2013). The 'Transitional Citizen': Civil Society, Political Agency and Hopes for Transitional Justice in Bosnia-Herzegovina' in Simic, O and Volcic, Z eds *Civil Society and Transitional Justice in the Balkans*. Springer.
3. The Aboriginal Tent Embassy was established in 1972 in from of Parliament House in Canberra, protesting the government's approach to land rights. In 1992 it was permanently established in the same location as a focal point for protests related to land and other issues such as sovereignty and self-determination.
4. These 'popular assemblies' were established by civil society activists who encouraged all citizens to attend meetings where grievances could be discussed and solutions proposed.

PART I

THE CITIZEN AS JUSTICE RECEIVER

The decision to structure this book in two parts – 'The Citizen as Justice Receiver' and 'The Citizen as Justice Seeker' – is not intended to imply that the two aspects are neatly distinct and do not interact. In fact, the way in which the citizen is framed and imagined through transitional justice policy, discourse, and practice is intimately connected to the way in which the citizen acts: the way a citizen is imagined shapes the way a citizen acts, and the way a citizen acts shapes the way the citizen is imagined. It is, however, useful to take an analytical approach which addresses the imagining and acts of the citizen separately. This is partly to distinguish between the words and deeds of the transitional justice advocates and actors and the supposed beneficiaries of transitional justice. These two categories are again not simply divided but are necessary for any analysis which wishes to take seriously the role of longer-term historical struggles as distinct from a particular transitional justice process. Distinguishing between the imagined citizen and acts of citizenship also allows us to see where the two meet and the transitional justice citizen as a figure emerges. The dynamic interplay between the citizen as imagined through policy and discourse and the citizen as a series of acts in contexts of time and place allows us to see how the transitional justice citizen is never fixed, but rather always in a process of becoming. This is important because it avoids the limitations identified in the introduction to this book, namely of decontextualised and dehistoricised approaches to transitional justice.

In her work on a positive theory of transitional justice, Murphy underlines the importance of the normative character of justice: '[w]e theorize about justice so as to understand what we should do as individuals and communities' (2017: 19). The purpose of transitional justice, in Murphy's view, is to transform relationships among citizens into relationships premised on reciprocal respect for agency (2017: 34). This relational transformation, which is at the heart of her theory of transitional justice, alters the terms of political interaction among citizens and between citizens and officials so that they are no longer structurally unequal (2017: 121). She holds that it is possible for transitional justice to have a direct effect on such transformation 'by strengthening the rule of law, increasing trust among citizens and officials and among citizens, and/ or enhancing the relational capabilities and capability to avoid poverty of citizens' (2017: 140). Murphy's work is part of a broader move in the transitional justice field which recognises the importance of the beneficiary population in shaping citizen participation and justice. However, beyond Murphy's contribution, this broader move in the transitional justice field has not yet adequately grappled with how to conceptualise the transitional justice citizen.

As outlined in the introductory chapter, the citizen in the field of transitional justice is currently understood in three main ways, as a threat to the process, as responsible for actively participating in the process, and as a virtuous product of the process. These current understandings of citizenship have been presented as summaries which distil the key elements and, in this way, are necessarily simplistic. The intention is not to construct 'straw' arguments but rather to set the stage for the discussions in the chapters of Part 1. As we shall see in more detail, these current understandings are limited by a lack of context, an individualization of the political subject, and an over-emphasis on the linearity of political change. This should be understood in the context of what has been discussed earlier, with regard to the 'dominant script' of transitional justice, meaning the 'liberal-legalist' paradigm which determines what is emphasised and what is marginalised (Sharp 2018: ix); more specifically, the individualization of guilt, the dominance of the lexicon of human rights, and the marginalization of communitarian identification which may lead to an 'empty solidarity' (Bowsher 2018: 85). This individualization goes hand-in-hand with the instrumentalization of political agency: the citizen *receives* justice and in return holds up their end of the democratic peace pact. The possibilities offered by more agency-centred approaches to the citizen have not been taken up by the transitional justice field, as discussed in the introduction to this book. This is a problem because it does not reflect the reality of how citizens make sense of, engage with, and make claims from a transitional justice process. With this in mind, we now turn to three chapters which focus on the transitional justice citizen as a receiver of justice, and in particular a citizen who is imagined and produced through transitional justice policy and discourse. The chapters focus on the rights (Chapter 2), duties (Chapter 3), and virtues (Chapter 4) of the citizen. This aligns with the three main understandings of citizenship in the transitional justice field as discussed in Chapter 1, as well as the liberal paradigm approach to the citizen. The red thread which connects these chapters is the intersection or disjuncture between longer-term struggle and shorter-term justice processes.

2. The citizen as rights bearer: victims, norms and transitional justice entrepreneurs

In his book, *Saviors and Survivors: Darfur, Politics and the War on Terror*, Mamdani critiques contemporary humanitarianism with reference to a distinction between the rights of the human and the rights of the citizen:

> To the extent that the global humanitarian order claims to stand for rights, these are the residual rights of the human and not the full range of rights of the citizen. If the rights of the citizen are pointedly political, the rights of the human pertain to sheer survival; they are summed up in one word: *protection*. The new language refers to its subjects not as bearers of rights – and thus active agents in their own emancipation – but as passive beneficiaries of an external responsibility to protect. (2009: 274–275)

There is a tension between the implied agency which comes with being a bearer of rights and the disempowerment which comes with having those rights protected, especially in the humanitarian regime. In the United Nations 2004 report *The Rule of Law and Transitional Justice in Conflict and Post-Conflict Societies*, a key text in the emergence of transitional justice as a global norm, a contradictory emphasis is placed on both the vulnerability of victims and the importance of their agency. The summary boldly declares that: 'We must learn […] to eschew one-size-fits-all formulas and the importation of foreign models, and, instead, base our support on national assessments, national participation and national needs and aspirations' (UN 2004: 1). The report then lists the vulnerabilities and deficits in the target populations:

> the heightened vulnerability of minorities, women, children, prisoners and detainees, displaced persons, refugees and others, which is evident in all conflict and post-conflict situations, brings an element of urgency' […] [a]nd yet, helping war-torn societies re-establish the rule of law and come to terms with large-scale past abuses, all within a context marked by devastated institutions, exhausted resources, diminished security and a traumatized and divided population, is a daunting, often overwhelming, task. It requires attention to myriad deficits. (UN 2004: 3)

This document illustrates the tension inherent in the way that the citizen as rights bearer is constructed: as an agent with rights whose participation is necessary, but who at the same time must be framed as in need of protection through narratives of disempowerment and vulnerability.

This chapter begins with a discussion of the way in which transitional justice as a global norm has emerged and gained strength. This includes the close relationship between transitional justice and liberal peacebuilding and how the citizen-victim is constructed through key texts of organizations that produce and reinforce this norm. Having discussed the international community as a 'protector' of the citizen-victim, the chapter looks at transitional justice entrepreneurs and advocates and how their work frames a particular kind of passive victim, even when we take into account a strengthening interest in the politics and power of victimhood. The chapter finally reflects on how transitional justice policy and practice imagine the citizen-victim, the paradoxes inherent within this, and the role (or not) of the struggle for justice.

2.1   THE CITIZEN'S PLACE IN A GLOBAL NORM

2.1.1   Transitional Justice and Liberal Peacebuilding

Transitional justice is widely accepted to be a global norm which 'entails an insistence against unwilling governments that it is necessary to respond to egregious violence and atrocity' (Nagy 2008: 275). Indeed '[t]he question today is not whether something should be done after atrocity but how it should be done. And a professional body of international donors, practitioners and researchers assists or directs in figuring this out and implementing it' (Nagy 2008: 276). We begin to see here the playing out of the tension highlighted above; there is an imperative for action which requires a body of 'experts' in the form of donors, practitioners, and researchers. If the aim of transitional justice as articulated in the United Nations (UN) report of 2004 is indeed to base that support on 'national assessments, national participation and national needs and aspiration' (UN 2004: 1), then there is a delicate balancing act between those whose agency is to be enabled and protected, and the power of those who enable and protect others. I will return to this in more detail in 2.2, when I discuss the transitional justice entrepreneur. However, it is helpful to highlight here the existence of a bureaucracy which supports and reinforces a global norm of transitional justice, one which has been increasingly strengthened through the professionalization of the field in think tanks, consultants and a burgeoning of university and executive education courses on the subject (Rubli 2012).

According to Nagy, the global project of transitional justice consists of a body of customary international law, normative standards, and local, national and global dimensions embedded in the broader process of globalization (Nagy 2008: 276). This sets it squarely in the liberal peacebuilding field and infrastructures (Sriram 2007), leading to the consolidation of the paradigmatic transition as outlined in the introduction to this book. This paradigmatic transition has a liberal democracy as its endpoint (Sriram 2009) and emphasises procedure and institutions (Ní Aoláin and Campbell 2005: 176). Ideally, a liberal democracy operates with the consent of the individuals it governs, thereby generating legitimacy both in the sense of meeting normative standards and in the sense of acceptance by the citizenry (Ní Aoláin and Campbell 2005: 183). This operates, however, with a series of assumptions about how change in such a transition works. The convergence of peacebuilding, development, and transitional justice has crystalised transitional justice as a global norm, meaning that transitional justice 'form[s] an integrated part of good governance, human rights and peacebuilding programmes in the developing countries in which these agencies work' (Hansen 2014: 107–108). This convergence is underpinned by an assumption that political change is transformation through individual rights and liberalism (Anders and Zenker 2014), which marginalises and even delegitimises collective interests and struggle (Bowsher 2018). As Pospisil writes, 'Contemporary peacebuilding discourse approaches peace processes and post-conflict transitions as a predominantly governed and sequenced affair' (Pospisil 2020: 329). Liberal, incremental forms of change through institution building and reform disregard more radical forms of change; and within the transitional justice-liberal peacebuilding nexus there is a citizen-victim with associated individual rights and interests.

2.1.2   The Citizen-Victim

At the state level, Zaum has written of a sovereignty paradox. According to this paradox, state sovereignty comprises rights and duties; and when these duties are not fulfilled multilateral organizations such as the UN can intervene, thereby removing state sovereignty as part of a process which claims to support it (2007: 7). This is a paradox because, for the state to prove that it has the attributes necessary to be considered sovereign (such as the protection of citizens), sovereignty must be compromised through interventions such as peacekeeping missions, international justice, or military action on the right to protect agenda. This paradox can be helpfully scaled down to think of the citizen-victim in transitional justice – an individual whose rights are primarily recognised through their absence, protection, and restoration by others. Mamdani's human here stands in stark contrast to the full possibilities of citizenship. This can be explained further by exploring in more detail the events and sources which frame and justify transitional justice policy and practice.

The human rights movement is a foundation of the contemporary field of transitional justice, exemplified in the post-Nuremberg human rights declarations of the UN. There is a wide and nuanced literature on human rights as a distinct field, and one element which is pertinent for the discussion here refers to the 'grand narrative of human rights' which 'contains a sub-text that depicts an epochal contest pitting savages, on the one hand, against victims and saviors, on the other' (Mutua 2001: 201). This runs as a thread from the early text of the Universal Declaration of Human Rights (Mutua 2001) to the contemporary right to protect agenda (Mamdani 2009). Core to this savage-victim-saviour trope is the figure of the victim, 'the giant engine that drives the human rights movement. Without the victim there is no savage or savior, and the entire human rights enterprise collapses' (Mutua 2001: 227). This is indeed the case for the transitional justice field where victims are the *raison d'être* of any given transitional justice process. Since the early years of the field, when prosecutions of perpetrators pushed forward the advances of transitions in Latin America (1980s) and Eastern Europe (1990s), there has been a notable shift towards a focus on the victim:

> the idea of victim participation has become a mantra in the field of transitional justice. However, the rhetorical commitment to these ideas is not matched consistently by actual practice, and even less by systematic analysis of relevant experiences or by sustained efforts to establish comprehensive means of making them effective. (UN 2016: 3)

These words, written by the former UN Special Rapporteur on the promotion of truth, justice, reparation and guarantees of non-recurrence (hereinafter 'Special Rapporteur'), come from his report on victim participation. The first person to hold this post, Pablo De Greiff, presented three annual reports to the UN Human Rights Council with a specific focus on victims: on reparations (de Greiff 2014), national consultations (de Greiff 2016) and victim participation (de Greiff 2017). He also presented others which can be considered victim-minded: on sustainable development (de Greiff 2013a), truth commissions (de Greiff 2013b), and guarantees of non-recurrence with a special section on truth commission archives (de Greiff 2015). From the beginning of the Special Rapporteur mandate, the figure of the victim has played an important role in motivating and legitimising transitional justice policy. Within the mandate of the Special Rapporteur, the UN includes the need '[t]o integrate a victim-centred approach throughout the work of the mandate'[1] and De Greiff certainly took this on board during his mandate, and there is every sign that the current Special Rapporteur, Fabian Salvioli, will do so too. Salvioli's first report outlined seven areas of interest: the fight against impunity and establishment of trust; national and regional experiences; guarantees of non-recurrence; gender; non-state actors; participation of victims and the question of ownership; the sustainable development goals; and corruption (Salvioli 2018a). His second report then finalised a list of four main lines of engagement: transitional justice, prevention and sustaining peace; harnessing youth's creative agency for transitional justice; accentuating the gender perspective in transitional justice efforts; and the intersection of human rights (with a focus on economic, social and cultural rights) and the Sustainable Development Goals in the context of transitional justice (Salvioli 2018b).

While the UN is not the only important actor in setting the policy and practice tone for transitional justice, it is key in 'mark[ing] the further institutionalization of TJ at the international level and the beginning of a shift toward more direct engagement of TJ advocacy in international policy making' (Subotić 2012: 110). The role of the UN Special Rapporteur has been significant, not least because Pablo de Greiff continued his work with the International Centre for Transitional Justice (ICTJ) during his mandate. The ICTJ is dominant in the field of transitional justice, consulting and advising on numerous transitional justice interventions in varied geographical contexts. It is referred to as a 'gatekeeper organization' with comparatively high levels of funds, a large staff body, and a high level of international visibility (Subotić 2012: 108). De Greiff's work cannot be made synonymous with that of the ICTJ, but the overlap in personnel indicates that the Special Rapporteur role was undertaken by someone of standing in the field, so that his reports and views could be disseminated widely within the transitional justice field.

Other agenda-setting texts include the European Union Policy Framework on Support to Transitional Justice, which was adopted in November 2015 and is the first dedicated strategy towards transitional justice by a regional organization[2], and the African Union Transitional Justice Policy which was adopted in February 2019 after a decade of discussions and debate. The European Union (EU) policy states that any transitional justice process

> must be locally and nationally owned, inclusive, gender sensitive and respect states' obligations under international law... Transitional justice is seen today as an integral part of state- and peace-building and therefore should also be embedded in the wider crisis response, conflict prevention, security and development efforts of the EU. (EU 2015: 1; emphasis in original)

Despite this bold statement there remains a lack of detail on what local and national ownership means in the context of a process which is also embedded in EU agendas and activities, leading to the same tensions we see in other multilateral statements and policies on transitional justice. This is visible in the way in which victims are included in the policy framework:

> The EU therefore supports reforms of national criminal legislation in order to ensure that it complies with international law [...] the EU also supports alternative ways of establishing justice (mediation practices or tradition-based mechanisms which are in line with international standards);

The EU supports close cooperation between truth commissions, victims' groups and civil society';

The EU encourages a participatory, victim-focused approach to reparations policies with the aim of restoring justice and the full reintegration and rehabilitation of victims';

The EU encourages states to engage in meaningful consultation with civil society throughout the reform process and beyond. The EU, recognising the power of education to transform societies, supports education programmes as well as comprehensive training programmes on human rights and international criminal and humanitarian law standards, drawing lessons from a country's own experience of violations and abuses. (EU 2015: 5–7)

According to this text, victims are primarily actors with whom the mechanisms of transitional justice – namely the four UN pillars of justice (courts), truth (truth commissions), reparation (reparation programmes) and guarantees of non-recurrence (institutional reform) – must work closely, and whose capacity to take part in the justice process must be built to achieve international standards. They are *ideally* consulted but this is by no means a prerequisite for a successful or indeed legitimate transitional justice policy. The partnerships which are described through consultation and collaboration are not equal. International norms and standards take precedence over the preferences of local and national actors who have been consulted (I will return to this in Chapter 3).

The role of the victim which is implied in this EU document contrasts the stated aims of both the UN and EU to prioritise victim needs and preferences. The UN, as mentioned above, lists a victim-centred approach as important for the mandate of the Special Rapporteur, while the EU lists as its first principle that 'the process of transitional justice must be nationally-owned, participative, consultative and include outreach' (EU 2015: 8). As we will see in Chapter 3, there are, however, limits to the participation of victims. Victim participation can reach the threshold of international norms and policy but can go no further. The AU transitional justice policy marks a shift in how the victim and the target population are framed. As part of a broader debate in both scholarship and policy about an African transitional justice (Bennet, Brems et al. 2012), the AU explicitly seeks a transitional justice policy 'as part of the drive towards the "Africa-We-Want"' (AU 2019: iv) setting up the document less as a technical discussion of how transitional justice can be implemented in a way which fits with international standards and more as a statement of a set of values which should underscore an African approach: transitional justice in Africa should be 'home-grown, unique to Africa, rich in its progressive methodologies and approaches, and rooted in African shared-values, traditional justice

systems and experiences' (AU 2019: iv). This stated aim stands in contrast
to the UN and EU policy documents, which encourage an engagement with
traditional forms of justice and context-specific approaches only insofar as this
engagement does not conflict with international standards.

The AU defines 'victims' in its document as 'persons who individually or
collectively suffered harm, including physical or mental injury, emotional
suffering, economic loss or substantial impairment of their fundamental rights,
through acts or omissions that constitute gross violations of international
human rights law, or serious violations of international humanitarian law' (AU
2019: 4) and go on to refer to 'partnerships' and 'national ownership' (AU
2019: 5) in a similar way to the other key documents. They go a step further
in defining national ownership to include 'primacy of national resources and
capacities' (AU 2019: 5), indicating a subtle but important shift from capacity
building by international bodies – which we see in the EU and UN documents
– to recognising and working within the capacities which already exist. The
reference to a collective form of suffering, and therefore collective victimhood
in the definition of victim, differs again from other key texts and the prevailing
norm of the individualization of the victim (Bowsher 2018). Another shift can
be seen in the declaration that: 'a society in transition may choose, through
inclusive consultative processes, to put more or less emphasis on the reconciliation, healing or justice dimension of the combination of TJ measures required
for its realities' (AU 2019: 6). In this statement, the AU does not significantly
diverge from the UN's four pillars, but it does suggest that choice beyond
mere consultation is important to have a real sense of national ownership.
The document refers to special support measures and the active participation
of women and youth victims (AU 2019: 7) but does not detail on what terms
this participation takes place and where the balance of power lies between the
victims and the transitional justice decision-makers. Again, the 'full participation of victims' occurs when implementation of mechanisms is discussed with
victims themselves (e.g. AU 2019: 16) but this does not include details about
what this discussion entails and where the limits of such participation may lie
(I return to this problem in Chapter 3).

The key texts of transitional justice policy from the UN, EU and AU are
illustrative and constitutive of the global norm of transitional justice as well
as the bureaucracy which sustains it. They each highlight the importance of
the victim, not only as the focus of a transitional justice intervention through
victim-centred justice, but also as a bearer of rights which must be upheld.
The AU refers to 'a culture of human and people's rights' to be promoted
and institutionalised (AU 2019: 20), and each organization refers frequently
to protection of victims and victims' needs and expectations, as well as to
a broader prioritization of context-specific interventions and national ownership. However, we must also read this 'turn to the victim' with other aspects

in mind: the discipline of the norm which demands and expects states to implement transitional justice policies; the burgeoning of think tanks and consultancies ready to advise on policies; and the dominance of the liberal peacebuilding structure with individuals, institutions, and procedures at its heart. The individualization of the victim as well as their vulnerability sustains the transitional justice norm and, as we shall see in the section which follows, requires a transitional justice advocate.

2.2 SPEAKING FOR VICTIMS: THE ROLE OF THE TRANSITIONAL JUSTICE EXPERT AND ENTREPRENEUR

The global norm of transitional justice imagines a citizen as an agent with needs, expectations, and rights; but at the same time as a vulnerable figure in need of protection. It assumes that if victims are protected they will be empowered, and if they are empowered civic trust will increase, and transitional justice will be more successful (de Greiff 2009). This assumption requires enablers and entrepreneurs who are able to protect, to empower and to implement transitional justice interventions; points of liaison between the citizen-victim and the transitional justice architecture. Literature which critiques transitional justice policy and practice has started to look more closely at these roles, referring most often to the transitional justice 'expert' and the transitional justice 'entrepreneur'. A turn towards victim-centred approaches within transitional justice has been important for highlighting the agency of victims and reminding transitional justice advocates about the purpose of their work. It has also been important as a self-legitimation tool for such experts and entrepreneurs, as McEvoy and McConnachie point out: 'Justice or support for victims are often *the* reasons advanced by lawyers, judges, psychologists, human rights activists and others for their involvement in transitional justice' (McEvoy and McConnachie 2013: 490).

In this section of the chapter, I return to key transitional justice policy texts, as well as critical scholarship on the subject, to reflect on what the existence of experts and entrepreneurs means for the concept of the transitional justice citizen. As Subotić has observed, 'TJ processes […] do not occur by themselves. They are designed, guided and executed by a network of domestic and international actors, states, NGOs and local activists' (2012: 111). These roles have, however, been under-researched and there is limited work which focuses on transitional justice promoters (Subotić 2012: 111) despite their importance for both the discursive and material practices of transitional justice, as well as their relevance for any discussion of agency of the victim. As highlighted by McEvoy and McConnachie, there is an acute sensitivity required in transitional justice processes where lawyers, activists and other such actors 'manage' the voices of victims (McEvoy and McConnachie 2013: 495) – a sensitivity which should also translate into humility and awareness that power and choice are exercised in the construction of victim voices by others (McEvoy and McConnachie 2013: 497).

Any discussion of the transitional justice expert and entrepreneur should avoid the danger of setting up a straw man. It is, of course, necessary to critique those in positions of privilege and power, especially in the transitional justice field. In these contexts, claims by transitional justice promoters to be working for the public and moral goods of justice, peace, and reconciliation mean it is more challenging to speak against them and/or their actions. We will address this critique as the discussion progresses, but it is important to highlight here that transitional justice experts and entrepreneurs enable connections to be made between victim constituencies and processes of transitional justice, with the aim of fulfilling the promises of the transitional justice norm and international standards. Key transitional justice policy texts emphasise, in addition to victim rights, the duties of states and multilateral organizations towards victims. In his report on victim participation, the former Special Rapporteur, Pablo de Greiff, makes recommendations which place expectations and demands on 'the United Nations system', 'those responsible for the design of transitional justice measures', and 'all Member States' (de Greiff 2017), highlighting both the responsibility of those actors, and the means they possess to act as enablers of victims' agency. Likewise, the EU outlines five key objectives for its transitional justice support work: ending impunity; providing recognition and redress to victims; fostering trust; strengthening the rule of law; and contributing to reconciliation (EU 2015: 2). It is not surprising that policy texts from such organizations focus on, and make an argument for, their role in transitional justice processes and in enabling victims to articulate their needs and have their rights fulfilled. The promotion and protection of their role are intimately connected with the development of human rights duties. These duty-bearing responsibilities, which follow from the recognition of the rights of victims, include the respect, protection and fulfilment of rights (Besson 2015: 251). Although these duties are important, the way in which policy texts present them demonstrates a lack of detail on how victims can make demands as subjects rather than objects of protection, and on what happens when victims' needs conflict with international norms and standards.

2.2.1   Transitional Justice Entrepreneurs

While policy and practice increasingly reference a victim focus, scholarship on human rights has highlighted a sense of distance between the constituencies of justice (including victims and the society in transition) and justice 'entrepreneurs'. This can include researchers as well as information missions by courts, truth commissions, or reparation commissions: 'There are various intermediaries bearing witness to distant conflicts and atrocities. They travel to distant parts of the world to collect different kinds of evidence and stories' (Bake and Zöhrer 2017: 81). What is significant in the development of the transitional justice field is the role of technical and mobile experts who advise on a supposedly universal transitional justice in varied geographical, social, political, and economic contexts:

> In sum, the technical assistance approach to transitional justice encourages de-politicized and de-contextualized engagements. It defines expertise as profes-sionalized and internationally mobile knowledge rather than knowledge that is situated in activist commitments and knowledge of local context; it favours models that are already legible to the field and its 'best practices', rather than innovations that may extend or challenge the field as we know it. (Nesiah 2016:34 cited in McAuliffe 2017: 180)

This can partly be explained by the dominance of the UN four pillars, the associated bureaucratization of transitional justice, and the significant over-laps between the epistemic communities of research, policy, and practice. Transitional justice began as a field dominated by lawyers and human rights advocates and activists grappling with the legacies of authoritarian regimes and the practical concern of how to address past violations to ensure successful transitions towards democracy (Arthur 2009). The academic field has tried to catch up, reflecting a creative tension surrounding the prominence of the policy and practice communities in defining the agendas of the transitional justice field of scholarship. Miller is worth quoting at length here:

> Transitional justice operates through the actions of a series of groups: policy makers who plan and implement the institutions; victims groups defined by commissions or courts; the larger citizenry implicated, but not named, by a final report or court decision; scholars who write the literature about specific country contexts or the phenomenon in general; and practitioners who work for nongovernmental organiza-tions (NGOs) that consult on the possible manner of transition [...] The consistency of language and terminology employed in a wide diversity of postconflict contexts reveals a global phenomenon and its seemingly successful export/import from one country or region to another over the course of the past several decades. The quest to reveal a blindness in the field springs from the global nature of the enterprise itself; the movement of ideas about and modes for transition bespeaks not only a series of 'lessons learned' but also potentially the transfer of ideological preoccupations that underpin the seemingly neutral discourse of the project. (2008: 271)

This 'vertical expansion' of the field of transitional justice has meant that 'actors both above and below the State level are increasingly perceived as being relevant for shaping and implementing transitional justice solutions' (Hansen 2014: 105). However, as Miller illustrates, there is still a hierarchy of actors within transitional justice processes, with those who conform to 'certain ideological preoccupations' (Miller 2008: 271) able to occupy more influential positions. These are often more likely to be actors who are not from the transitioning society, but are instead a group of transnational advocates who 'have made rules, set standards and defined principles of action[…]They have formulated global issues, promoted ways in which these issues should be resolved and lobbied states to enact policies consistent with their principles' (Subotić 2012: 112). There has been an important shift 'from do-gooder volunteerism to professionalization, specialization and bureaucratization, all of which have brought great visibility and international credibility to these efforts' (Subotić 2012: 118). This shift has also generated greater distance between the 'expert' and 'entrepreneur' on the one side and the victim and the society in transition on the other.

This expansion and professionalization of transitional justice advocacy and promotion is further characterised by an overlap between research, policy, and practice. Miller has pointed out that:

> [t]he role of international actors in the process of spreading the ideas and ideals of the 'movement' of transitional justice has not yet been fully explored in the literature, perhaps because of (at least in part) the tendency of scholars or ex-commissioners to become consultants to, rather than fully external critics of, the enterprise. (2008: 290)

This intertwining of critical scholars, consultants, policy makers and practitioners is significant for what it does to the 'expert' and the 'entrepreneur'. In the case of transitional justice, the 'vulnerability' of victims, which is presupposed by the key policy texts and the human rights 'saviour' trope (see 2.1.2), places particular ethical demands on those who represent and work for them. Reflecting on this dilemma, Madlingozi has observed that:

> The transitional justice entrepreneur gets to be the speaker or representative on behalf of victims, not because the latter invited and gave her a mandate but because the entrepreneur sought the victim out, categorized her, defined her, theorized her, packaged her, and disseminated her on the world stage [...] Despite writing critically and passionately about the situation of the victim, the victim is not only left in the same position but this encounter could be an act of further violence and dispossession. (2010: 210–211)

Madlingozi raises the issue of legitimacy in evaluating the relationship between transitional justice promoters and victims. It is true that there is an instrumental value in transitional justice moving towards a victim-centred justice (Findlay 2009: 189). However, the legitimacy which emerges from victim satisfaction, as Findlay puts it, is crucial given transitional justice's promotion of liberal democracy as well as its position within the liberal peacebuilding architecture

(2009: 193). A demand for democratic forms of engagement with the victim constituency will be addressed further in Chapter 3. This demand determines the type of relationship between transitional justice promoters and victims, a relationship which emerges and is promoted through transitional justice processes.

2.2.2 Transitional Justice Experts and Legal Ways of Knowing

Transitional justice entrepreneurs often rely on claims to expertise which allow them to speak on behalf of others. The idea of expertise and the role of experts are thus connected to the themes discussed above. The claiming of expertise, and the assumption of expertise being located within specific actors, have implications for the way in which the victim is denied agency, and the way in which the transitional justice citizen is imagined as a passive actor. There is a tension inherent in the way in which experts lend their expertise to the cause of the victim, while at the same time re-producing the victim's disempowerment (McEvoy and McConnachie 2013: 498). Rarely is the victim framed as an expert of their own experiences, instead they are mediated through the acts and words of the experts who mobilise their own expertise in the cause of transitional justice.

It is useful for this discussion to look towards recent work in the field of international relations which focuses on the role of experts, looking at them as distinct actors in world politics, their language, rationalities, and meanings of expertise, as well as the practices of expertise and how they are historically and materially situated (Bliesemann de Guevara and Kostić 2018). Kennedy's *A World of Struggle*, which focuses on experts in global political and economic life, is particularly useful when he highlights that:

> Expert rule mobilizes knowledge as power. The knowledge part combines common sense assumptions about the world that may be neither conscious nor open to debate with technical and more broadly ideological material that is often disputed. But expertise is not just knowledge learned in professional study or downloaded from the culture at large. It is also a mode of work. Expert work provides the interpretive link between decisions about what to do and the context within which those decisions are made. (Kennedy 2018: 7)

Transitional justice combines Kennedy's idea of common-sense assumptions about the world – that justice and peace are 'good' things – with technical material produced by only a small and well-defined epistemic community to the exclusion of others. In previous work I have defined expertise in this context as

> a relationship between knowledge and power: we can think of expertise as that knowledge which has been accorded greater legitimacy, partly because of its ability to "speak the truth", but also partly because of the relationships of power that determine whose voices are heard and whose voices should be heard. (Jones 2015: 294)

Because of the importance of lawyers in the development of transitional justice, it is important to reflect here on the effect of the dominance of legal 'ways of knowing' and the figure of the legal 'expert' for how the victim is constructed in transitional justice and how their agency is framed.

Wilson's work on the use of expert witnesses in international courts is particularly illuminating, claiming that it 'lays bare the tacit assumptions about the construction of knowledge in a legal process' (2016: 730). More specifically, Wilson finds that the kind of evidence which is most accepted by lawyers and judges during international trials is determined by what kind of evidence does not 'undermine the entire legal enterprise of an international trial that is primarily based on the (shaky) premise that a foreign cultural setting is intelligible to them and requires no further specialized scientific knowledge' (Ibid: 742). This is partly due to the structural fragility of international law which directly impacts the knowledge-making process 'insofar as it generates uncertainty in evidentiary matters and compels judges to exclude evidence that threatens their precarious authority' (Ibid: 243). This has been described elsewhere as a kind of 'theft' where the lawyers pick out, appropriate and re-present victims' voices to suit the aims of the prosecution (McEvoy and McConnachie 2013: 495). The basis on which this is done is an explicit and implicit claim to expertise; but in the course of helping amplify victims' voices in court, lawyers may also disempower them as their voices are instrumentalised for a legal purpose which defines in narrow ways what counts as evidence, and what counts as relevant experience.

Wilson's work on the structural fragility of international law and its effect on the knowledge-generating process can be complemented by the work of other scholars on the 'clash of knowledge' between different ways of knowing violations of the past and establishing the truth. In previous work, I have explored the importance of tensions between the way in which lawyers, scholars, and local populations 'make sense of both the experience of violence, or more broadly construed harm, and the response to these harms…[of] different ways of knowing' (Palmer, Jones et al. 2015: 174). To apply this to human rights work, 'the abuse occurs in a physical sense, but the way or the form in which it is accounted, represented, and interpreted influences how it is known' (Ibid: 176). This work recognises that the knowledge generated and used in transitional justice processes is always incomplete (Ibid: 174–175). This is partly because of the requirements of the law itself. According to Wilson, within international criminal courts the history of a conflict is shaped by the legal actors' strategies and motivations, as they emphasise the most useful accounts of the past, and construct categories such as genocide (2011: 70). Kelsall makes a similar point in his political anthropology of the Special Court for Sierra Leone, observing that the 'prosecution team applies linguistic techniques to excavate a particular version of the truth from a contested history' (2006: 587). This chimes well with Campbell and Turner's warnings over the 'hegemonic quality of the law', which 'risks being complicit in a renewed disenfranchisement' (2008: 378, 381).

However, while such scholarship points to the incomplete knowledge of transitional justice experts, and the hegemony of legal ways of knowing, the 'local turn' in transitional justice has not yet strongly challenged the role of the transitional justice expert who is embedded in the transitional justice bureaucracy. There are calls from scholars and practitioners for justice to come from 'below' (McEvoy and McGregor 2008); for justice to take into account different positionalities and standpoints in a 'localized' transitional justice (Shaw and Waldorf 2010), to contest foreign knowledge in its search for an African transitional justice (Bennet, Brems et al. 2012), and to acknowledge increased struggles over who owns a particular transitional justice process (Vinck and Pham 2010). These movements to localise transitional justice suggest the possibility of a more 'ethical relationship to the other', a relationship which for Colvin has 'failed' in transitional justice (2008: 424). According to Kennedy, 'Expertise dictates in the name of the universal, the public good, the general will, the practical necessities of reason, or the objective truths of scientific knowledge' (2018: 3). Transitional justice expertise certainly does this, and in so doing often belies its inherently contested and political nature. It sets up an expert and an entrepreneur predicated on the vulnerability and disempowerment of victims who are to be protected, rather than understood as citizens who are 'active agents in their own emancipation' (Mamdani 2009: 275). While it would be disingenuous to deny that many victims may need help with access to relevant skills and resources, the mode of engagement must recognise the power relations and discursive effects involved (McEvoy and McConnachie 2013: 499).

2.3   THE STRUGGLE FOR JUSTICE AS A BEARER OF RIGHTS

The foreword to the AU Transitional Justice Policy begins with the following statement:

> The history of Africa is characterized by different political upheavals, struggles for liberation and socio-economic transformations. These political struggles and transformations include, for instance, the fight against colonialism and apartheid; the war against military authoritarian regimes; and the struggle for and entrenchment of democratic and participatory governance, human rights, constitutionalism, and the rule of law. These experiences undoubtedly have brought with them different transitional justice (TJ) initiatives, like national dialogues, national truth and reconciliation commissions and national reparation funds, among others. The concept of TJ is therefore a necessary step in moving from a divided and painful past to a commonly shared and developed future. (AU 2019: vi)

It is important not to forget those struggles which put transitional justice on the agenda in the first place (McEvoy and McGregor 2008). However, the way that transitional justice policy has developed through international norms and standards has increasingly eclipsed that indebtedness to struggle. The technical assistance approach now dominates (McAuliffe 2017), sustaining a transitional justice bureaucracy which is as focused on the infrastructures of the liberal peace as it is on the needs and expectations of the victims, who are supposedly at the centre of transitional justice. The way in which the victim has been constructed through international norms and standards of transitional justice comprises a recognition of (individual) victim rights and of associated duties:

> a right gives a person (a right-holder) a claim to the respect of a duty by another person (the duty-bearer) whose duty is directed to the right-holder. As such, a right is a normative relation between a right-holder and a duty-bearer, pertaining to a protected object. (Besson 2015: 248)

The human rights movement which underpins transitional justice has, however, focused on the supply side of human rights, resulting in an overemphasis on protection (Besson 2015: 246) and, as we have seen in the key transitional justice policy texts cited in this chapter, the vulnerable victim is key to the logic of protection and intervention.

There has also been an overemphasis on certain kinds of rights (Besson 2015: 246), namely civil and political rights, at the expense of socio-economic rights. This is directly related to the 'liberal imprint' of transitional justice in which 'civil and political rights provide individuals with their protected sphere of autonomy' (Zunino 2019: 49). This has meant that 'the discourse of transitional justice concentrates on violations of civil and political rights and instances of physical violence to the detriment of violations of socio-economic rights and structural violence' (Zunino 2019). The expansion of transitional justice to include a concern with socio-economic crimes and rights is much debated in the scholarship. McAuliffe, along with others associated with a more transformative turn in transitional justice, recently argued:

> The justifications for including issues of structural violence and inequality as integral components of transitional justice are pragmatic (peace can only be sustainable with attention to root causes), philosophical (an ethical preference for distributive justice and equity) and sociological (polls of survivor populations overwhelmingly demonstrate that socio-economic concerns trump the desire for criminal justice or truth in transitions). (McAuliffe 2017: 2)

Waldorf cites a survivor of the Rwandan genocide who stated, 'We've got used to the genocide; it's daily life that's the problem' (2012: 175). This reflects what many authors argue: that the focus on civil and political rights does not adequately represent the needs and expectations of victims, despite the rhetoric contained in international norms and standards. The focus on civil and political rights is another instance where the individualization of the victim precludes more collective forms of experience and solidarity (Bowsher 2018). Socio-economic crimes and socio-economic rights often have a collective dimension and consider historical injustices and long-term experiences of marginalization and inequality. Evans explores this with reference to the subject of land redistribution in South Africa, highlighting the limitations of transitional justice to meet historical injustice and inequality and the importance of social movement praxis for a more collective and transformative justice agenda (2016: 13).

However, the victim in transitional justice discourse remains an individual whose civil and political rights are to be protected through the interventions of transitional justice experts and entrepreneurs. The victim is thus a bearer of certain kinds of rights to be expressed through individual harm and individual redress. As the discussion in this chapter has shown, this is often at odds with the stated needs and expectations of consulted victims. This will be discussed further in Chapter 3, but it is relevant here because it raises a problem for the legitimacy of the transitional justice norm. As Besson points out:

> [T]o be democratically legitimate, such rights must be recognized legally through inclusive and deliberative processes. Transitional justice traditionally focuses on victims of specific human rights violations but beneficiaries often wish to make claims as citizens who have the right to claim certain goods, standards of living and protection from the state. We might ask when should these claims be made? Through which channels? And how might associated duties be articulated and enacted? The difficulty is that there is no universal political community where indi-

viduals may grant each other equal rights and where those rights could constitute an equal political status. (2015: 249–250)

In his critique of victim constituencies in international criminal law, Findlay finds that '[c]itizenship is protected through globalization where it accords with the constructs of the global community and its market economies, liberal democracies, democratic styles of government and allegiance to the modernization project' (Findlay 2009: 196). We are left wondering what discursive and material space there is for the citizen-victim to make claims which go beyond, or even contest, this set idea of the individual transitional justice victim with certain rights to be protected. The struggles which are alluded to in the AU policy framework, and which appear in scholarship which seeks to contextualise and historicise transitional justice, should be investigated through the collective harm and collective agency of the citizen-victim. If we know that longer-term struggles have underpinned the violence which rendered transitional justice necessary, then it should follow that they form part of the global norm 'solution' which protects rights and articulated duties. But the struggle is absent. This is significant and will run as a red thread through the chapters which follow. While this chapter has outlined the transitional justice norm, the place of the victim, and the nature of the rights to be protected and the duties to be fulfilled, Chapter 3 investigates concrete practices of engaging the citizen-victim as an agent and a participant in transitional justice. While this could bring us closer to the rights of the citizen rather than the rights of the human, we will see the limits of this victim participation and victim consultation in the discussion which follows.Notes

NOTES

1.   See www.ohchr.org/EN/Issues/TruthJusticeReparation/Pages/Mandate.aspx(last accessed 1 July 2019).
2.   See https://eeas.europa.eu/headquarters/headquarters-homepage_el/2158/%20EU%20adopts%20its%20policy%20framework%20on%20support%20to%20transitional%20justice (last accessed 10 July 2019).

3. The citizen as duties bearer: participation, outreach and consultation

In the previous chapter we saw how transitional justice discourse and policy frames a particular victim with the civil and political rights of a human, which need to be protected, rather than as a citizen with agency and the ability to make a wide range of claims to justice. This understanding of the victim has emerged as a function of the human rights movement savage/saviour trope, the bureaucratization of the field of transitional justice, and the liberal imprint of transitional justice discourse and practice. This liberal imprint, which favours liberal democracy as an outcome of transitional justice processes, frames not only the rights-bearing transitional justice citizen but also the duties-bearing transitional justice citizen. The democratic peace model of transitional justice requires a citizen who is party to a contract in which they are responsible for desiring, achieving and maintaining peace (Henderson 2006: 199). As the Head of the Kenya National Commission on Human Rights is cited as saying:

> [P]ublic participation improves lawmaking while giving citizens a stake in it. By inviting participation, lawmakers not only gather important information on which to make better laws, they also express their respect for the citizens whom they consult. In turn, those consulted become more engaged and responsible in public life. (cited in Triponel and Pearson 2010: 142–143)

For transitional justice interventions this responsibility, or duty, to participate plays out in two key areas: outreach programmes which aim to generate 'buy-in' from the transitioning society; and consultation processes which seek to gather information on the needs and expectations of victims and the society at large. Indeed, the concern for participation, which we started to discuss in Chapter 1, is important because it 'embraces not only the victims and survivors, but the broader community of citizens and other stakeholders in the transitional justice process' (Lambourne 2012: 236). While it is thus capable of constructing a space in which citizens can make claims to justice, we will see in this chapter what happens when the rights of participation come face to face with the duty to desire, achieve and maintain democratic peace through transitional justice.

The previous chapter reflected on the tension between the rights of a human, which are defensive rights of survival, and the rights of a citizen, which concern political agency. The passivity of the subject who is to be protected creates a problem for transitional justice policies and programming, which have been criticized for disempowering victims. De Greiff attempts to reconcile this in his discussion of the links between transitional justice and development, which envisions transitional justice as a conduit for inclusive forms of citizenship:

> The argument is that citizens can enjoy as rights – and not merely as dispensations from those who hold power – the protections that are meant to be provided by the traditional liberal civil rights enshrined in laws that satisfy the formal conditions of the ideal of the rule of law only if, at the same time, they can enjoy rights to political participation [...] The core idea, then, is that transitional justice measures can be thought of as efforts to enable the activity and participation of citizens who were previously excluded and marginalized [...] This process not just of turning victims into citizens but thereby of strengthening inclusive citizenship – something that I hasten to reiterate cannot be achieved by transitional justice on its own – may, in the end, be the most significant contribution transitional justice can make to development. (de Greiff 2009: 62)

The ambition of an inclusive citizenship is undermined, however, by the way in which inclusion is framed during transitional justice processes. Tension arises between participation and power, an issue which has been substantially debated in other connected fields such as international development. Mirroring the transitional justice 'turn to the local', some years earlier, Kothari and Cooke edited a book titled *Participation: The New Tyranny* in which they challenged the mainstream approach to participation in development. This approach intended to 'make "people" central to development by encouraging beneficiary involvement in interventions that affect them and over which they previously had limited control or influence' (Kothari and Cooke 2001: 5). The book deconstructs this aim, highlighting debate over whether participation is a means or an end, whether it masks the continued centralization of control over development, and whether it in fact furthers the interests of the most powerful. In doing so, Kothari and Cooke identify three tyrannies of participation: the tyranny of decision-making and control, where participatory facilitators override existing legitimate decision-making processes; the tyranny of the group, where group dynamics lead to participatory decisions that reinforce the interests of the already powerful; and the tyranny of method, where participatory methods drive out other advantageous methods (Kothari and Cooke 2001: 7–8). The first two tyrannies are most pertinent for our discussion of transitional justice, and we can see their dangers clearly in the following sections of this chapter.

3.1 PARTICIPATION, OUTREACH, AND THE SEARCH FOR AGENCY

It is generally accepted in scholarship on transitional justice that '[f]or post-conflict and postauthoritarian outcomes to address the needs of affected communities, it is necessary for them to be involved in the process of shaping these outcomes' (Evans 2016: 8). There is a general move to conceptualise and even advocate for transitional justice from below (McEvoy and McGregor 2008), or a localised transitional justice (Shaw and Waldorf 2010), acknowledging that there are both instrumental and normative reasons for doing so. Vinck and Pham distinguish between arguments of pragmatism and transformation in the literature on participation in transitional justice (Vinck and Pham 2010). This mirrors the debate in development studies, where participation as a means or end is central to the critique of mainstream approaches to instrumentalizing participation. Whether or not participation should be valued in and of itself is not always clear from transitional justice research or policy statements, with arguments moving between these two positions often without delineating where one is to be favoured over another.

Former Special Rapporteur Pablo de Greiff's 2017 report to the UN Human Rights Council makes a distinction between 'epistemic' and 'legitimacy' arguments in favour of victim participation. By this he means that participation can increase knowledge (with positive consequences for transitional justice practice), and that participation itself can empower victims and increase the legitimacy of a transitional justice process. Importantly, de Greiff adds that this makes victims visible, 'helping them achieve a place in the public sphere that may have been denied to them before' (de Greiff 2017: 5–6). However, this fails to consider the quality of participation. What kind of participation is required in order to empower victims? The EU begins to address this in its transitional justice support policy: 'Active, free and meaningful participation empowers all rights-holders to articulate their needs and expectations. Identifying the relevant stakeholders at the outset of a transitional justice strategy is essential in order to understand and consider their specific needs and demands' (EU 2015: 7). We should note here the use of the word 'consider', which is small but important. The language chosen makes it clear that 'meaningful' participation is in fact limited to an opportunity to express preferences which may or may not change policy. This contradiction underlies the EU position and prompts us to ask who really holds the power, and to be reminded of Kothari and Cooke's tyranny of decision-making and control: if the act of participation merely functions to legitimate a decision-making process controlled by others, can we really describe it as '[a]ctive free and meaningful' (EU 2015: 7)?

The AU offers a framework for participation which is a little different, referring to 'religious or cultural legal sources' as well as international standards to
determine and ensure participation (AU 2019: 16). This goes beyond a consid-
eration of the needs and demands of stakeholders, which is the EU position. It
is possible, as part of the AU's articulation of its approach to participation, to
imagine a scenario where participation gains its legitimacy from a process or
set of standards which do not conform to those of the UN and the global transitional justice norm. In this case, however, it is important to know more about
where the balance of power lies between the participant, the religious and
cultural legal sources and the international standards. It should also be noted
that there is no detail on the legitimacy of religious and cultural legal sources
for participation, their inclusivity and thus implications for the nature of the
participation and its ability to provide a space and set of engagements which
are empowering for victims. These absences in the way that participation in
transitional justice is framed by the UN, EU and AU hint at some key issues
which are relevant for a concept of the transitional justice citizen, and which
will be explored as we move through the chapter: who participates? Who and
what do participants represent? What are the limits of participation? On whose
terms does participation take place?

3.1.1   The 'Dark Side' of Participation? Its Possibilities and
Limitations in Transitional Justice Discourse and Practice

An Impunity Watch report, which analyses six cases of victim participation in
transitional justice mechanisms, refers to the 'the darker side of participation'
in which '[s]ecurity problems, political pressures, and continued discrimination faced by victims prevent participation from becoming an empowering,
dignifying and healing experience' (Sprenkels 2017: 4). The reasons highlighted for this are: a tendency to see participation as a technical rather than
a political process; failures to guarantee inclusiveness; a lack of follow-up;
and damaged trust. Significantly, the report finds that 'when victims take
action themselves outside of formal TJ mechanisms, they operate like real
political forces that have the capacity to significantly influence the process',
calling for additional research on this (Sprenkels 2017: 5). But the research,
policy and practice on victim participation remain dominated by concerns
over how and with what effect participation in transitional justice mechanisms
can be understood. Taking transitional justice as the independent variable, as
it were, participation is often discussed in terms of how it can be designed to
maximise the desired effects: increased knowledge and increased legitimacy.
Transitional justice is taken for granted and operates as the norm. While the
existence of a given transitional justice process or mechanism is rarely questioned, the extent to which victims and others participate is. In reality, victims

are most often participating in a fixed version of transitional justice which they have limited power to change, and are not able to act like 'real political forces' (Sprenkels 2017: 5) outside of the formal transitional justice mechanisms.

This can be seen in the increase in public outreach programmes as transitional justice has evolved and established itself as a field of practice (Triponel and Pearson 2010: 116). According to Lambourne, these programmes are intended to educate and inform local populations about the transitional justice process; and to engage local populations in the process through methods such as victim participation in trials and truth hearings (2012: 238). Lambourne nuances the discussion of outreach with the concept of 'inreach', which she uses to 'describe the process of obtaining ideas, opinions and feedback from local populations about their expectations and responses to the transitional justice process'. The voices of local populations are not just used in a tokenistic fashion or 'considered', as the EU policy states (2015: 7), but are 'communicated to, and taken into account by, the transitional justice institution' (Lambourne 2012: 238). In her analysis of outreach in Rwanda, Timor-Leste, Sierra Leone and Cambodia, Lambourne interrogates the stated versus actual aim of transitional justice outreach and participation:

> If transitional justice is intended to promote justice and reconciliation for victims and survivors, and peacebuilding for local communities, then a critical goal of transitional justice would be not only to provide information but also to solicit input as part of a truly engaging outreach/inreach programme involving all relevant stakeholders in a transformative peacebuilding process. (Lambourne 2012: 261)

This is not to say that there is a conscious attempt by transitional justice promoters to only provide information and not to solicit input from victims. However, it is important to highlight the contradictions between the stated aims in policy and practice – to engage and empower victims and the transitional society through participation – and the ways in which the discourse and practice of outreach and participation activities work to limit victims' participation and claims for justice.

Much of the literature on participation has focused on forms of victim participation and outreach programmes used by the courts. It should be remembered that the legal forms of transitional justice have traditionally been seen as less victim focused. This is for numerous reasons: firstly, because they aim to identify and punish perpetrators; secondly, because they are selective in what they are willing and able to address in terms of past violations by focusing primarily on punitive justice for political and civil rights violations; and thirdly, because they narrate experiences of violence through legal categories. There was some attempt to engage local populations with the earlier international tribunals, such as the International Criminal Tribunal for Rwanda (ICTR) which

operated from 1994–2015 in Arusha, Tanzania and was established by the UN
in order to 'prosecute persons responsible for genocide and other serious violations of international humanitarian law committed in the territory of Rwanda
and neighbouring States, between 1 January 1994 and 31 December 1994'.[1]
The ICTR faced a series of legitimacy challenges which made it important to
have greater visibility in Rwanda, including: the court's significant geographical distance from the location of the genocide; conflicting conceptions of
justice among a polarised Rwandan population; the slow pace of prosecutions;
and perceptions of anti-Hutu bias and fear of interference from the Tutsi-led
government, meaning that 'from the start, some officials at the Tribunal envi-
sioned an outreach programme not only to keep Rwandan citizens abreast of
the court's goals and accomplishments, but as a strategy to repair the institution's deteriorating image' (Peskin 2005: 950–951). The outreach programme
began late in the operation of both the ICTR and the other *ad hoc* tribunal, the
International Criminal Tribunal for the Former Yugoslavia (ICTY); something
for which both tribunals were heavily criticized (Pentelovitch 2008: 451).

Hybrid tribunals, such as the Special Court for Sierra Leone (SCSL) and
the Extraordinary Chambers in the Courts of Cambodia (ECCC), provide, in
theory, greater opportunity to engage the local population in more frequent and
substantive dialogue over justice due to their location in the situation countries
(Pentelovitch 2008: 447–448). The idea that outreach programmes for these
tribunals could perform a communicative function, where justice is 'seen to
be done' (Pentelovitch 2008: 449), responds to the legitimacy concerns of
the more geographically distant *ad hoc* tribunals. Learning from the delayed
start of outreach processes at the ICTR and ICTY, the SCSL 'instituted an
ambitious outreach programme[…]less than six months after the Court was
established and well before the first trials began' (Lambourne 2012: 244). This
programme included frequent town hall meetings, the publication of booklets
and posters, group-targeted training and outreach activities, making court proceedings accessible, and establishing a grassroots network of district officers
to consistently undertake outreach activities across the country (Pentelovitch
2008: 455). Such practices represent a shift from the outreach of ICTR and
ICTY which was focused on ensuring that the local populations understood
what was happening in the courtroom. In addition, the hybrid tribunals also
sought to communicate with the local population, to reassure them that justice
was happening and to use their geographical proximity to the local population
for the benefit of trial preparations and conduct.

The establishment of the ICC, which began functioning on 1 July 2002, built
on the participation activities of the *ad hoc* and hybrid tribunals, holding some
promise for the position of victims in a new era of justice. The ICC's website
presents its key features, three out of six of which explicitly focus on participation: the need to ensure that victims' voices are heard; the need to ensure

that participating victims and witnesses are protected; and the need to ensure that outreach creates a two-way dialogue.[2] This is reminiscent of Lambourne's outreach/inreach approach (2012). However, the notion of a two-way dialogue is watered down by the description of aims in the ICC's outreach strategy:

> (1) provide accurate and comprehensive information to affected communities regarding the Court's role and activities; (2) promote greater understanding of the Court's role during the various stages of proceedings with a view to increasing support for them among the population; (3) foster greater participation of local communities in the activities of the Court; (4) respond to the general concerns and expectations expressed by affected communities and by particular groups within these communities; (5) counter misinformation; and (6) promote access to, and understanding of, judicial proceedings among affected communities. (Vinck and Pham 2010: 423)

There is no explicit outreach aim to gain information from the population which will enable a redesign of the ICC's way of working or activity priorities. It is a one-way dialogue, evidenced by the lack of examination of lessons learned by outreach practitioners (Vinck and Pham 2010: 424). This is not, therefore, much of an improvement on the practices of the *ad hoc* tribunals of the ICTR and ICTY, where outreach programmes were 'late additions', partly forgotten in the 'haste to create international criminal tribunals' and partly resisted by Tribunal officials who 'did not regard community outreach or public relations as the responsibility of a court' (Peskin 2005: 953).

Despite good intentions regarding early inclusion of outreach programmes made (at least discursively) central to the work of the ICC, there has been significant criticism of the court for its 'lack of outreach to general populations in the situation countries and to victims in particular' (Glasius 2009: 409), as well as its ineffective work when populations are reached:

> The people living in the Court's areas of involvement are generally unfamiliar with the Court, traumatized by conflicts with the civilian population as their main target, and acquainted only with their own largely dysfunctional legal system. They cannot be expected to comprehend the ICC's intentions, procedures, and limitations without an extensive effort to have these explained to them. (Glasius 2009: 511)

This is a reasonable and yet also liberal critique of the court: it fails to educate and inform people, who, if provided with the correct information, would then support or engage with the ICC activities. Vinck and Pham observe that 'the assumption appears to be that developing a proactive public information and outreach effort is sufficient to improve public awareness and knowledge, and ultimately spur a transformative process that will reduce violence and promote reconciliation' (2010: 424). The leap from outreach programme to empowerment of participant to wider societal transformation is significant, but is not explained by policy texts or programme materials themselves (Lambourne 2012). This is because the assumption that outreach leads to increased information transfer and societal transformation relies on a notion of transformation which is dependent on, and almost synonymous with, the transitional justice process itself. Anders and Zenkers' work discussed in Chapter 1 (see 1.1.1) is useful here, as it distinguishes between two types of societal transformation: firstly, transformation through individual rights and liberalism; and secondly, structural, violent and revolutionary transformation, which occurred throughout decolonization and independence movements (Anders and Zenker 2014). Because transitional justice takes transformation through individual liberal subjects as a given, the linear process whereby information about a transitional justice process is conveyed to an individual, providing them with the knowledge needed to participate in the process of societal transformation, does not need further explanation or interrogation by transitional justice entrepreneurs.

3.1.2   How Far Does Outreach Reach?

The tendency to design outreach rather than to seek 'inreach' (Lambourne 2012) is further exacerbated by the limited reach of outreach programmes. Even the ICC, with its early inclusion of outreach, has failed to be as inclusive as it could be:

> Use of mass media is the primary communication strategy for the ICC to reach out to the general public...[which] is an effective strategy for increasing awareness and knowledge about the Court. However, information is most likely, on average, to reach a male, educated and wealthy elite, leaving out the information poor. (Vinck and Pham 2010: 437)

Not enough participation programmes acknowledge that 'individuals in affected communities differ in how they gather information, as well as in their needs and expectations about transitional justice' (Vinck and Pham 2010: 440). This can lead to certain victims having opportunities for participation from which others are excluded. Individuals and groups who already occupy marginalised positions vis-à-vis transitional justice processes – women or displaced persons, for example – are further marginalised by exclusionary participation processes. This limits the emancipatory potential of the current methods of participation used in transitional justice.

There is a potential fear among transitional justice promoters that increasing victims' participation in transitional justice could lead to more radical forms of engagement and claim-making. As highlighted in Chapter 1 (see 1.2), the forms of expertise and technical knowledge which constitute the identity of the transitional justice entrepreneur are disconnected from activist, local knowledge and construct an image of the passive victim-citizen. In order for the transitional justice promoter to retain relevance and power, the necessity of their role needs to be protected. This works against a recognition of other forms of expertise, knowledge and agency and is exemplified by the way that participation is constructed and limited through policy and practice. Forms of outreach which encourage engagement – as frequent interaction and dialogue – have been said to entail 'both risk and opportunity' (Peskin 2005: 954). For Peskin, more substantive forms of participation in the ICTR may have led 'Rwandans to raise critical questions in public forums about the Tribunal's performance. One danger is that dialogue will turn into a political chance for the government and closely aligned survivor groups to attack the Tribunal for betraying its mandate to provide justice for genocide survivors' (Peskin 2005: 954). In relation to the ECCC, Lambourne writes that:

> the ongoing accusations of corruption of both the government and ECCC could provide a partial explanation of the decision to focus on public affairs as a means to bolster donor support, while at the same time avoiding transparency and engagement through outreach. (Lambourne 2012: 248)

Concerns over the risks involved when critical questions are raised in public forums, or that greater transparency will lead to greater corruption, do not distinguish between a general concern around spoilerism and more complex questions about the role and importance of alternative voices in the larger social debate over what justice is, and who it is for. This is one of the key themes which continues as a thread throughout this book and constitutes a primary building block of the transitional justice citizen, who is engaged in claims to justice which are more varied and radical than those permitted by and through mainstream transitional justice. Transitional justice policy and programming on the question of participation, both in the narrower sense of knowledge provision and in the wider sense of dialogue, end up describing participation and outreach in primarily instrumental terms. They serve a purpose, whether to generate visibility for a transitional justice intervention, to generate legitimacy, or to create a sense of 'buy-in' from a more informed population. Each of these purposes aims to help the transitional justice entrepreneur in their work. As with the previous discussion about the transitional justice entrepreneur (see Chapter 1, 1.2), the intention is not to make a blanket statement about all transitional justice entrepreneurs as engineering outreach to serve their own aims. Many individuals working on outreach programmes, in courts or in truth commissions believe passionately in what they are doing and the right of the population at large to have more knowledge about and access to the transitional justice process. However, the fear of too much participation, of too much oversight, and of too many voices making different claims is apparent throughout the scholarship on participation and outreach, as well as in the way that policies and programmes are set up.

A key finding of the Impunity Watch report on victim participation in different transitional justice mechanisms in Burundi, Cambodia, Guatemala, Honduras, Kenya, and Tunisia was that:

> the lack of consideration for victim participation in the set-up and implementation of TJ also sometimes responds to a political logic. This means that key decision makers and political stakeholders are reluctant to share control over key aspects of the transitional justice process with subaltern groups. (Sprenkels 2017: 45)

When victims are invited – for it is an invitation into a space rather than a claiming of a space – some are able to participate more effectively than others. The report goes on to observe that:

> Indeed, the case studies show that participation in TJ mechanisms has been beneficial for most of the victims who have been able to participate; being recognised and heard gave them a sense of purpose. However, formal participation opportunities include only a fraction of the total number of victims…This leads to a rather unequal distribution of possible benefits among victims. (Sprenkels 2017: 23)

Examples are given in the report of benefits accruing to victims in Cambodia who participated as civil parties in the ECCC; and in Burundi where gender dynamics have marginalised militarised masculinities, determining who comes forward to participate (Sprenkels 2017: 44–7). These dynamics also lead to an unequal visibility of voice. The design of specific programmes affects the reach of outreach and the kind of participation possible. In Guatemala, for example, the Historical Clarification Commission found that 83 per cent of the victims of violence were Mayans, but most of the outreach programmes of the truth commission were in Spanish rather than indigenous Mayan languages (Triponel and Pearson 2010: 119–120).

We are prompted to ask whether calls for 'justice from below' by critical scholars (McEvoy and McGregor 2008) are being mainstreamed to create buy-in to an agenda developed in the corridors of the UN, among transitional justice entrepreneurs, or through the toolkits and trainings offered by transitional justice NGOs. It is not clear whether the transitional justice bureaucracy (see Chapter 1, 1.1) is interested in, or capable of, incorporating alternative perspectives and agendas. If participation is intended, or enacted, in a limited way, this can have damaging effects: 'a lack of meaningful participation by affected communities can lead to the institutionalization of unequal, corrupt, socially exclusionary, or otherwise negative processes, undermining positive outcomes in the long term' (Evans 2016: 8). If outreach can be problematised for its limited reach, uneven distribution of benefits, and marginalization of those who do not participate, it is also important to reflect on a complementary yet distinct policy change introducing consultation as part of the design and implementation of transitional justice.

3.2   CONSULTING THE CITIZEN-VICTIM

3.2.1   The Framing of National Consultations for Transitional Justice in Policy Documents

Participation is an integral to how transitional justice is framed and enacted, for reasons both of legitimacy and instrumental outcomes. This can include outreach, but we have also seen in the last ten years an increase in national consultations prior to the design of specific transitional justice interventions. Consultations have been understood to operate in ways more akin to the 'inreach' (Lambourne 2012) discussed above: 'Meaningful participation involves integrating feedback received from the public into the transitional justice mechanism, as opposed to outreach which focuses on educating the public' (Triponel and Pearson 2010: 107). During the 2000s, there was a shift in thinking by transitional justice policy makers and practitioners, and processes led by the UN started to include consultations with the public in situation countries before the details of a transitional justice response were finalised (Triponel and Pearson 2010: 121). Such consultations have increasingly been used by national governments, who ask the population for input on a variety of issues: whether the particular transitional justice mechanisms proposed should be adopted; how implementing legislation for a transitional justice mechanism should be drafted; and request that NGOs raise awareness and generate support among the public for the transitional justice process (Triponel and Pearson 2010: 132). This shift was strengthened by two UN documents: the 2009 *Rule-of-Law Tools for Post-Conflict States: National Consultations on Transitional Justice* by the OHCHR and the 2016 report to the UN Human Rights Council by the former Special Rapporteur Pablo De Greiff on the subject of national consultations and transitional justice. These remain the primary policy documents which frame approaches to national consultations in a context of limited research and academic literature on the subject.

The Special Rapporteur, as with his report on victim participation discussed in 2.1.2, identifies both epistemic and legitimacy arguments for national consultations. Epistemic arguments for national consultations refer to 'the type of knowledge or insight the people who are consulted may produce and the positive consequences that improvements in understanding may have'. According to legitimacy arguments: 'The process of consulting is in itself a measure of recognition of, and empowerment of, victims and helps them to gain a place in the public sphere, which may have been denied them before'; and they 'may widen the circle of stakeholders in justice processes' as well as 'facilitate the identification of commonalities of experiences, values and principles among different groups' (de Greiff 2016: 4–5). What is interesting is that even the legitimacy arguments are framed in instrumental terms. For example, the report specifies that the 'consent and participation' of justice stakeholders help to determine the 'success and sustainability of transitional justice measures'. Likewise, it explains that the identification of commonalities of experience 'is important for forming coalitions and consensus and is crucial in the adoption of policies on contentious issues' (de Greiff 2016: 5). It would be naive to suggest that the UN Special Rapporteur report would be framed without reference to implementation and policy design, but we see in the examples of consultations in practice discussed below that the legitimacy arguments for empowerment, inclusivity and recognition are often required to play second fiddle to the instrumental arguments for consultations.

The rule-of-law tool *National Consultations on Transitional Justice,* published by the OHCHR, focuses less on the instrumental argument for consultations and more on their importance in terms of both obligations under international law and the positive effects they can have on victims and communities at large. The first section of this document defines national consultations by virtue of the element of dialogue:

> National consultations need to be distinguished from outreach activities. They are not intended as mere one-way information channels to keep the community informed of work that may be under way. Nor can they be mere public relations exercises. Instead, national consultations are a form of vigorous and respectful dialogue whereby the consulted parties are given the space to express themselves freely, in a secure environment, with a view to shaping or enhancing the design of transitional justice programmes. (OHCHR 2009: 3)

But there is a tension between consultation as an exercise in 'communication between the state and society and among different parts of society' as the former Special Rapporteur puts it (de Greiff 2016: 5), and the aim of generating buy-in to ensure that a transitional justice agenda set outside of the situation country can be implemented effectively. We see this in policy discussions on capacity-building, with the Special Rapporteur highlighting that 'The level of participants' prior knowledge with respect to human rights and transitional justice concepts has an impact on the outcome of consultative processes' (de Greiff 2016: 12).

His report goes on to list examples of training designed to prepare officials and the population before consultations take place, such as sharing copies of relevant documents and legislation, information dissemination via local radio and television, and outreach (de Greiff 2016: 13). Referring to the example of Yemen, the Special Rapporteur identifies the difficulty of carrying out consultations in contexts where there is limited prior knowledge of key human rights concepts but notes that 'Training sessions brought the discussions closer to international standards' (de Greiff 2016: 13). This is echoed in the OHCHR document, which asserts that 'Regardless of the form or precise objective of the consultations, they need to be accompanied by a tailor-made sensitization programme' because 'The extent to which the language and the concept of transitional justice may be alien to a population cannot be overstressed' (OHCHR 2009: 12). Like the former Special Rapporteur's report, the justification for national consultations is framed with reference to international standards and norms. The OHCHR document includes a section dedicated to articulating why national consultations are a human rights legal requirement established by the 'International Convention on Civil and Political Rights, [which] in article 25, guarantees the right of every citizen to take part in the conduct of public affairs' (OHCHR 2009: 4).

3.2.2 National Consultations in Practice

There is significant variety in the type, nature, and inclusivity of transitional justice consultations. In their review of different processes, Triponel and Pearson find that in Timor-Leste a steering committee responsible for determining the nature of a truth commission was able to conduct consultations in all districts of the country in 2000 and 2001 and consulted with a wide variety of actors, including political parties, jurists, human rights organizations, and victims' groups (Triponel and Pearson 2010: 127). However, much narrower consultations took place in Sierra Leone and Cambodia, led by the UN. In Sierra Leone, between the signing of the peace agreement on 7 July 1999 and the signing of an agreement for the SCSL on 16 January 2002, a UN planning mission held consultations. However, these mainly involved government actors and not Sierra Leonean legal professionals. In Cambodia, the UN consultations with civil society groups took place at the same time as the negotiations with the Cambodian government on the structure of the court to be established; participants complained that the sessions were more about providing information than soliciting feedback (Triponel and Pearson 2010: 121–122). The inclusivity of consultations is affected by political constraints around live negotiations, which are compounded by practical constraints around budgets and timing. In Kenya, the National Commission on Human Rights was consulted before the Truth Justice and Reconciliation Commission was set up, but the short timeline meant that the National Commission was not able to consult properly with its constituencies (Triponel and Pearson 2010: 142).

A decade later the national consultations in Tunisia in 2012 were seen by some as a 'novel consultative initiative to transmit transitional justice demands into transitional justice legislation' (Lamont and Boujneh 2012: 32).

In January 2012 the Ministry of Human Rights and Transitional Justice was created to 'launch a national consultation on transitional justice in order to have a common vision that would incorporate input from victims and human rights activists and reflect their needs'. This led to the submission of a first draft of the Transitional Justice Law on 28 October 2012 (ICTJ 2013). The ICTJ had, however, already held a conference in April 2011 to 'introduce the concept of transitional justice' (ICTJ 2013) along with the OHCHR, the Arab Institute for Human Rights, and the Tunisian League of the Defense of Human Rights. Describing themselves as 'providing guidance and expertise' (ICTJ 2013), this exemplifies the kind of capacity building referred to in the Special Rapporteur and OHCHR reports discussed above. Despite this claim to novelty, transitional justice debates had already been initiated by the soon to be ousted President of Tunisia Ben Ali 'to quell growing public unrest through concessionary measures announced in his last official address to the nation on 13 January 2011, which included proposals to establish commissions to examine rights abuses, corruption and political reform' (Lamont and Boujneh 2012: 33). We might then think of the ICJT not as introducing the concept of transitional justice but as introducing a particular version of the concept in line with the international standards so often referred to in policy documentation.

Such sensitization activities prior to, and during, consultations are common. Sensitization activities inform a population about the purpose of national consultations and how the population will be involved. In Burundi, UN-supported national consultations were held in 2009–2010 following lobbying by the ICTJ from 2006 onwards. Rubli found in her research that the presentations which opened the consultation sessions were mainly based on the conception of transitional justice promoted by the ICTJ (Rubli 2012: 7), a conception which aligns with the international norm discussed in Chapter 2. In Zimbabwe, research on the EU-funded 'Taking Transitional Justice to the People Programme' of the Zimbabwe Human Rights NGO Forum finds similar problems related to the nature and content of sensitization. Njeru and Masiya found that, prior to consultations regarding which transitional justice mechanisms would be the preferred options of the population, the Forum had a 'Northern' template of non-negotiable principles, reflecting the international norm of transitional justice and thereby narrowing the scope of the consultation (Njeru and Masiya 2021). Critical of this, Njeru and Masiya state that:

> In the Taking Transitional Justice to the People Programme the Forum postured as part of the international human rights movement, and took the trajectory of substituting emancipatory politics based on active citizenship and went on to prop up the politics of demobilization and passivity. Their approach to the communities resulted in an encounter between the expert and victim. (Njeru and Masiya 2021)

This is evidenced by the use of training materials based on the work of Global North scholars such as Ruti Teitel and Priscilla B. Hayner, references to European events and trajectories of transitional justice such as the Nuremberg Trials, and the holding of dialogues in colonial rather than indigenous languages (Njeru and Masiya 2021). This tension between the two stated aims of consultations – to open dialogue between the state and society and to educate society about transitional justice – runs the risk of generating an echo chamber of consultations. If organizations tell the population what transitional justice is, and then the population is consulted about what they think justice should be, there is a danger that they will merely repeat what they have already been told by the very same actors who are asking them for their views.

Aside from this echo chamber concern, consultation processes often take place in a politicised context in which there is an additional danger that they will be instrumentalised (Lamont and Boujneh 2012). Jostling to make claims regarding the justice preference of populations is not uncommon. Although the 2003 Kenyan Government report claimed that over 90 per cent of the Kenyan population supported a truth commission process, this 'seems to have been based on a figure picked almost at random', while the process of determining the character of the truth commission was in fact dominated by and 'highly personalized around a small group of civil society activists' (Bosire and Lynch 2014: 262). The Kenyan Task Force for the Truth, Justice and Reconciliation Commission had a mandate to consult with the Kenyan population on '*whether* they wanted a truth commission, the form it should take and the scope it should have' (Bosire and Lynch 2014: 263, emphasis in original). Question marks were raised over the number of Kenyans actually consulted, with Bosire and Lynch finding that the process of public consultation obscured a prior decision that the Task Force had already decided to recommend a truth, justice and reconciliation commission and use the narrative of public consultation to legitimise its establishment (Bosire and Lynch 2014: 262–263). The truth commission was not established until October 2008, relatively quickly after the post-election violence of December 2007–February 2008. However, no additional consultations took place in response to this violence. The search for truth became a state-led process, supported and led by politicians who were often implicated themselves in the post-election violence (Bosire and Lynch 2014: 266).

Such instrumentalization of consultation processes has also been found by Rubli in her in-depth analysis of the national consultations in Burundi. She describes them as a 'negotiating arena', meaning that 'the national consultations were a negotiated political process in which various actors attempted to construct and form the social world and the state rather than a simple technical exercise' (Rubli 2016: 149). Indeed, the implicated actors – the UN, the Burundian government, civil society – attempted to shape the design and methodology of the consultations so that the results would reflect their preferred transitional justice outcome (Rubli 2016: 172). For example, in line with the discussions around international norms in this and the previous chapter, the UN requested that the questionnaire exclude amnesty for international crimes as an option (Rubli 2016: 173–174). The national consultations in Burundi did not include questions concerning amnesty, as this had already been negotiated and decided upon by the UN and the Burundian government. The decision to exclude amnesty was also supported by civil society organizations, which feared that the political elite could instrumentalise popular opinion against a tribunal to avoid being held to account (Rubli 2016: 174). The final report was delayed due to the political wrangling over upcoming elections (Rubli 2016: 153) and the national consultations only took place after the institutional design of the transitional justice process had been negotiated and decided upon by the UN and the Burundian Government, and so was focused on the mandates, composition and procedures rather than decisions over which mechanisms of transitional justice should be chosen (Rubli 2016: 149). This limitation on the substance of participation was further exacerbated by the ultimate legacy of the consultations:

> While the non-binding character of the recommendations left certain flexibility to the actors regarding taking into account and use of the results of the consultations, this also means that actors cannot enforce their implementation and the final report remains a toothless document, only serving as a basis for advocacy work. (Rubli 2016: 176)

These examples of different national consultations beg the question: are consultations able to make a difference to transitional justice policy design? The challenges outlined thus far suggest that there is a gap between theory and practice. Given the contexts of sensitization and political instrumentalization, it is difficult to fully unpick what a given individual or population group wants to see as part of a transitional justice intervention. Even when there is a majority view expressed through the consultations, it is not necessarily the case that transitional justice policy will be changed as a direct result, as seen in the case of Burundi. The OHCHR does, however, cite a series of positive cases. In Timor-Leste, 'the consultation process prior to the establishment of the Commission for Reception, Truth and Reconciliation delivered findings that led to a significant expansion in the Commission's mandate…[including] local community-based procedures for justice and reconciliation' (OHCHR 2009: 6). In Sierra Leone, consultations with NGOs 'led to the non-governmental groups forming a common position on the need for a truth and reconciliation commission and successfully arguing for its inclusion in the peace agreement adopted later that year (the Lomé Agreement)' (OHCHR 2009: 14), with the same report citing praise of the national consultations in Afganistan (OHCHR 2009: 1–2).

However, while the consultations which took place in Afghanistan in 2002 were particularly inclusive – comprising 4,151 survey responses, 200 focus groups, and 2,000 participants across 32 of the country's 34 provinces, as well as refugee populations in Iran and Pakistan – research has found that expressed preferences for lustration, vetting and criminal accountability have not been implemented (Nader Nadery 2007). In Burundi, where the 2010 report on the national consultations stated that the population favoured truth telling through a truth and reconciliation commission and (with reservations) criminal prosecution for those most responsible, 'political decision making in the field of transitional justice has not been strongly affected by popular expectations' (Vandeginste 2012: 362). We also see this in the former Yugoslavia, where public opinion surveys conducted between 2000–2002 found that there was a lack of demand for international prosecutions (OHCHR 2009: 7). However, the ICTY's mandate, which lasted from 1993–2017, implicated 4,650 witnesses over 10,800 trial days and generated 2.5 million pages of transcripts[3] at a cost of €762 million (Skilbeck 2008: 1). Limitations on the ability of views expressed to directly shape policy may occur for numerous reasons, including the instrumentalization of the process by those in power (as discussed above). The failure to take into account the views expressed in national consultations also occurs because the transitional justice process is already underway, such as in Colombia, where consultations occurred after the adoption of legislation determining the type of transitional justice mechanism to be implemented (OHCHR 2009: 12); and in Uganda, where the principal elements of the transitional justice intervention had already been decided before national consultations took place (OHCHR 2009: 14).

3.3 THE STRUGGLE FOR JUSTICE AS A DUTIES BEARER

In his report on national consultations, the former Special Rapporteur Pablo de Greiff makes the following statement:

> The interactions that are part and parcel of a well-designed consultation process also offer the potential for stakeholders to identify common grounds; they can come to an understanding of shared experiences (including shared experiences of pain and harm), shared needs (for various forms of support, security and responsive institutions) and shared basic values and principles. (2016: 19)

Other than its ambitious framing, this normative statement is worth dwelling on as it provides a link to Chapter 4 which follows – a link between the rights, duties and virtues of the transitional justice citizen. In contrast to critiques discussed in the previous chapters, those that identify transitional justice as a neoliberal project which individualises harm and delegitimises collective struggle (Bowsher 2018), the statement by the Special Rapporteur emphasises shared experiences and collective values and principles. This tension between the individualism of liberalism and the shared experiences of large-scale violations of human rights and their repair is a key characteristic of the framing of the transitional justice citizen.

In this chapter we have seen how participation in transitional justice, not only by the beneficiaries but also by society as a whole, is a key part of the dominant norm of transitional justice and how it is framed in policy and practice. There are a series of underpinning assumptions that are implicit in key policy texts and examples of practice. The first is that there is a linear and causal relationship between participation and transitional justice outcomes. The belief is that access to information and education about transitional justice – whether through outreach programmes or consultations and sensitization activities – will translate into 'buy-in' to transitional justice as a project and then support for the transformation at which it aims. If the population knows more about transitional justice, then the transitional justice will be more effective, and if transitional justice is more effective then society will transform. This leads us to the second assumption: that participation should be based on knowledge about a specific kind of transitional justice. Outreach programmes are focused on knowledge about mechanisms of transitional justice which are already in place, not those which could be alternatives. Sensitization activities, as well as the consultations themselves, limit the range of options available to those which meet international standards. Examples include conducting dialogue in colonial rather than local languages, or only teaching populations about concepts of transitional justice from the Global North, such as the UN pillars of transitional justice. There is an implicit fear that action taken outside of this framework will challenge both the transitional justice norm and the current power structures. It is interesting that the Impunity Watch report cited in this chapter found that 'when victims take action themselves outside of formal TJ mechanisms, they operate like real political forces that have the capacity to significantly influence the process' (Sprenkels 2017: 5). The same report finds that very little is known about the potential of this action and the possibility of a causal relationship between acting outside of a process and the efficacy of political action. Instead, policy and practice ensure that the possibilities of action remain within the framework of the international standard that has crystallised around the transitional justice global norm.

The third assumption is that once the population at large knows about the transitional justice norm, and once the possibilities for action have been articulated within this framework, that transformation will lead to a peaceful, liberal democracy. This is a teleological idea of change precluding more radical, structural, or collective models of change. As such, it stands in tension with the stated ambition of participation policy and practice to engage a broad community of citizens beyond those directly implicated in a specific mechanism or process. This tension continues into the fourth assumption, which is that international standards will always trump the preferences of this community of citizens. The limit of participation is found at the door of the international institutions and NGOs which have shaped, lobbied for, and promoted the transitional justice global norm. The tyranny of decision-making, much discussed in development studies (Kothari and Cooke 2001), holds true for transitional justice where participation goes only so far. As such, the limits to participation are limits to the kinds of claims to justice which can be made and to the ability of citizens to act.

This chapter is, therefore, broader than a discussion about official participation policies and practices. It refers to a disconnect between the population in a situation country and official transitional justice policies, and the mechanisms by which this disconnect could be contested. It refers to a delicate balancing act between the individual victim/perpetrator and the collective power of claim-making and change. It also refers to the impulse to delimit and order the possibilities of political action through transitional justice – not only in terms of who participates, how one participates, and in what one participates, but also in terms of the normative demands for certain values and behaviours. The OHCHR report on consultation states:

> In Uganda, it is widely considered that the decision of the parties to the 2007 Agreement on Accountability and Reconciliation to consult across the country, even in areas untouched by the violence, generated useful findings that also served to impress upon people that the responsibility for reconciliation lay with the entire nation. (OHCHR 2009: 16)

It is to this responsibility that we turn in Chapter 4, for there is not only a duty to participate for the transitional justice citizen, but also a duty to practice the virtues promoted by the transitional justice global norm.

NOTES

1.   See http://unictr.irmct.org/en/tribunal (last accessed 22 July 2019.
2.   See https://www.icc-cpi.int/about (last accessed 18 July 2019.
3.   See http://www.icty.org/node/9590 (last accessed 12 September 2019).

4.   The citizen as a holder of virtues

I have argued in Chapters 2 and 3 that transitional justice discourse and policy imagine a particular citizen – an individual victim in need of protection who is also expected to participate in and generate support for transitional justice as part of a democratic peace pact. This citizen is implicit in the ways in which transitional justice is designed; they are evoked as a necessary actor instrumentalized for particular ends but often denied any agency. Opportunities to debate and define justice, or to make claims beyond that which is on offer, are foreclosed, even in outreach and victim participation programmes. Because of this historical struggle, ongoing injustice, and the political ideology of transitional justice remain unchallenged. The question of whether transitional justice and the type of justice which it offers are themselves part of the problem has not received adequate attention; and 'more robust theoretical constructs and paradigms that might help to provide deeper context and substance to these specific critiques has been largely lacking' (Sharp 2018: 13–14). In this chapter I continue my response to this gap and address a third element of the transitional justice citizen as imagined through transitional justice: the citizen as a holder of virtues.

Transitional justice has been described as 'unabashedly offering itself as a moral project, a ritual cleanse such that a community of interested actors—advocates, funders, policy makers, practitioners, scholars, and victims—is invested in its success' (Fletcher and Weinstein 2018: 191). Hand-in-hand with this moral project is the moral transitional justice citizen who lives the virtues associated with, and required by, the vision of the 'good society' which we see in transitional justice. In addition to the rights and duties discussed in Chapters 2 and 3 there are expectations of behaviour which accompany the imagining and framing of the transitional justice citizen. For it is not just a question of which claims to justice can and should be made, but also the manner of this claim-making which is important. This chapter explores this idea through reference to the virtue of civility, an idea which is understandably often central to work on violence and its resolution. Balibar famously addresses this in his work *Violence and Civility: On The Limits of Political Philosophy*, in which he states that 'there must be a moment of civility in politics, over and above citizenship, in order to introduce the demand for anti-violence or resistance to violence' (2015: 144).

For Balibar, civility is positioned 'over and above' citizenship, but the reference to non-violence as civility, and violence as incivility, is a trope which is important to work on citizenship and peacebuilding and to transitional justice. This comes from ideas that citizenship is founded on mutual respect, equality and the capacity to empathize (Hoffman 2004). These foundational aspects of citizenship demand forms of civility which work well with the demands of transitional justice. Porter writes of Northern Ireland that reconciliation requires strong civil virtues from its citizens, in particular forgiveness, magnanimity and reasonableness (2003: 67). He acknowledges that this is particularly complicated in post-conflict contexts but argues that it is crucial given the requirements for fair interaction between members of opposing groups, the overcoming of agonistic divisions by occupying common ground, and the need for a society in which all citizens have a sense of belonging (Ibid 2003: 94–100). While civility itself may seem to be an obvious 'good' intertwined with the transitional justice project, its framing and operationalization within transitional justice discourse and practice risk narrowing the terms of claim-making and legitimizing certain forms of justice and injustice. In particular, as this chapter explores, narratives of civility too often discipline, control and prescribe behaviours and, by extension, the manner of claim-making. This means that transitional justice is less able to acknowledge or incorporate historical struggle, alternative claims, or more inclusive justice.

There is an informative tension between the 'good' that is evoked through transitional justice and the ability of others to contest and redefine this 'good'. The normative ideals which are the 'driving force behind any transition' (Venema 2012: 74) are not exclusive to the transitional justice entrepreneurs and experts discussed in Chapter 2; they are also present in the population and part of longer-term struggles for justice. These longer-term struggles are not adequately captured by transitional justice framing of the 'good' (and 'bad'). This is important because the exact nature of the 'good' which is promised in transitional justice discourse remains open in terms of its meaning (Zunino 2019: 33). For Zunino, this has the effect of ensuring that transitional justice is 'an open textured discourse' which can be contested and reconceptualised (2019: 34); but others have found that such openness has a disciplining effect, marginalizing alternative voices. Too often, the 'empty universals' of transitional justice mean that concepts such as 'peace', 'justice' and 'reconciliation' can be mobilised to suit contemporary ideological projects, 'rigging discursive options' (Pensky 2012: 97). Renner applies such an analysis to the concept of reconciliation, showing how it is stabilised in relation to existing and non-universal meaning (2012: 60), thus performing a series of functions: 'political practices, subjects, or objects become re-defined in relation to reconciliation and thus constructed as conciliatory practices or as parts of reconciliation or in opposition to reconciliation'; 'only those practices that are articulated into the reconciliation discourse will seem legitimate and will be put in a positive semantic relation to reconciliation'; and 'various political parties can relate it to their particular political goals, accept it as a universal ideal and eventually act collectively for this common goal' (2012: 61).

Renner's approach can be generalised beyond a specific focus on reconciliation to the transitional justice field, where we see values, acts, and behaviours judged in terms of their legitimacy vis-à-vis the specific project of transitional justice in use. The virtuous transitional justice citizen is not universally defined; they are defined in history, in context, and in reference to the needs and expectations of transitional justice. The transitional justice citizen as a bearer of virtues is part of the continuing obfuscation of the politics and ideology of the dominant script of transitional justice. This dominant script has been increasingly tackled by critical work which aims

> at destabilizing traditional conceptions of transitional justice and challenging its existing modi operandi. It reveals concealed interests, ideological limitations and repetition of historical patterns of class domination obscured by its rhetoric. It is sensitive to the exclusions, oppression and suppression transitional justice might entail' (McAuliffe 2017: 175).

If we understand transitional justice discourse as operating through a series of key concepts – concepts which can be appropriated for a wide variety of meanings – then we can clearly see a continual movement between the possibility of contestation and the redefinition of claim-making and the actual foreclosure of options. This is a tension at the heart of transitional justice with implications for the transitional justice citizen as a bearer of virtues.

This chapter will tackle the transitional justice citizen as a bearer of virtues through two interconnected strands. Firstly, the impulse to order and discipline, which is inherent in transitional justice discourse, extends into ideas of individuals' obedience in the countries under transition. The desire for stability, linear transformation and the establishment of liberal democracy combines ideas discussed in previous chapters with a focus on order and thus the behaviour of citizens. Secondly, a distinction between 'good' and 'bad' victims tells us about the expected virtues of the transitional justice citizen vis-à-vis the way justice claims should be made and the expected endpoint of justice claims. Through this we see that claim-making is not part of an ongoing process of struggle and continual debate over what justice is and could be, but rather confined to a series of specific engagements with transitional justice interventions designed to satisfy certain current claims and foreclose the possibility of future ones.

4.1 TRANSITIONAL JUSTICE AND THE IMPULSE TO ORDER

In Chapter 1 of this book the discussion highlighted the way in which transitional justice as a project of intervention and transformation is embedded in the broader liberal peacebuilding framework and infrastructure. This has had a particular effect on the way in which transitional justice has focused on the individual rather than the collective in terms of justice, and the way in which change is assumed to be linear and incremental. It has also influenced the way in which disorder and disruption are understood, meaning that the kind of disruptive struggle which accompanies claims for justice is often delegitimised. In the previous two chapters we saw how the boundaries around who can make claims to justice, and what these can entail, are formed through discourses and practices of transitional justice. In this chapter we will see that there are also boundaries around *how* claims to justice can be made. Order and consensus are given value in ways which risk marginalizing certain forms of struggle and contestation.

Barma's work on post-conflict political order highlights how liberal peacebuilding reflects the international community's vision of political order, which 'rests upon the notion that an engineered process of simultaneous state building and democratization can bring modern political order to post-conflict states' (2017: 1). While Barma argues that the priorities of domestic political elites, political survival and power require a neopatrimonal political order (Ibid), for the purpose of this book I will assume/argue that there is a particular version of political order which accompanies the liberal imprint of transitional justice and that disruptions of such order are considered to be de facto illegitimate. This is related to assertions that 'Liberal peacebuilding may contain conflict, but it rarely transforms it' (McAuliffe 2017: 171), meaning that the focus of transitional justice is often on interventions of containment or order, rather than the messier process of grappling with the root causes of the conflict itself. Indeed,

> Transitional justice, no less than peacebuilding, represents the increasingly internationally accepted practice of solving problems through institutional legal settings … Transitional justice is oriented more towards strengthening or legitimizing the state peacebuilders attempt to reconstruct rather than towards challenging it. (2017: 172)

State building processes involve the transformation of individuals into obedient citizens (2017: 203) and this is as true for transitional justice as it is for other aspects of liberal peacebuilding interventions. The impulse to order in transitional justice's liberal imprint emanates from the importance which teleology plays in framing the kind of political and social change advocated for, and legitimised, by transitional justice entrepreneurs. Zunino attributes transitional justice teleology to the focus in discourse and practice on the attainment of goals. These goals are associated with the time 'before' transitional justice, when there was conflict and violence, and the time 'after' transitional justice, when there will be peace and stability (2019: 46–47). The lens of 'transition' is used to label change from one state to another and structure the attainment of goals. This was not an 'inevitable' outcome of the early developments of the field but it has 'heavy implications for the shared mental maps that transitional justice experts use to structure their thinking, debates, and practice' (Sharp 2018: 75). The emphasis placed on the movement towards liberal democracy has been useful for the justification and promotion of the liberal peacebuilding architecture but has also distracted from the practice of the application of transitional justice in non-transition contexts or by illiberal yet peaceful regimes (Ibid 2018: 78–79). This 'messy' reality, which exists between the input of transitional justice and the outcome of the goals of justice and peace, is neither acknowledged by mainstream discourse, nor easily captured or understood in the burgeoning work which evaluates the impacts of particular transitional justice mechanisms (Payne, Olsen et al. 2010). The birth of the field of transitional justice was motivated by a post-Enlightenment and then post-Cold War faith in reason, progress and improvement (Colvin 2008: 416), rendering a successful transition which conforms to a managed and linear progression towards peace, justice and democracy (Jones and Bernath 2017). In this conceptual framing transitional justice discourse and practice is 'invested in an idea that with the proper tools and systems in place, their goals can be accomplished effectively and efficiently. A notion of the need for careful planning and proper technique is at the heart of their efforts to remake the world' (Colvin 2008: 413). In this approach evaluating transitional justice becomes an exercise in measuring the attainment of narrow goals following specific interventions.

The character of transitional justice as a technical enterprise of ordering and managing transition has led some to suggest that it is linked to a colonial civilizing mission. Critiques of liberal peacebuilding for seeking to bring order are well developed, identifying the ways in which places of conflict are seen as possessing barbarity, excess and irrationality (Duffield 2002), and the need for external interventions to 'democratise the unruly' (Pugh 2009: 85). This work draws red threads between colonial bureaucracies and imaginaries and present-day liberal peacebuilding, illustrating how the Orient of the minds of the first explorers and colonisers has become the dangerous and disorderly Global South war zone. These same critiques have emerged in recent scholarship in reference to transitional justice. Firstly, transitional justice has a blind spot when it comes to colonial violence and crimes, focusing instead on the violence which occurred after the colonisers left (Zunino 2019: 206–207). This is part of a founding 'myth' of transitional justice. Maddison and Shepherd

(2014: 262) have summarised this point eloquently and it is worth quoting them at length:

> The exceptionalism that defines the context of transitional justice is in itself a colonial practice of power. The imagined history of transitional justice that locates its inception at the Nuremberg Trials effectively posits that transitional justice mechanisms [were] literally brought forth into existence by the horror of the Holocaust. This discursive move allows the 'international community' to reset the standard of justice and, by association, delineate a new boundary around crimes that were so severe as to require new ways of dealing with them. These crimes were considered exceptional, and thus in need of new mechanisms and new conceptual frameworks. Except such crimes were not exceptional. Such crimes were part of the everyday lexicon of colonial power. Empires such as those founded by the same powers that organised post-World War II to ensure that Nazi war criminals were brought to justice, were founded on violence, often genocidal violence.

Secondly, transitional justice is associated with colonial civilizing missions. In Chapters 2 and 3 it was clear in transitional justice policy documents that the principles of local ownership and approaches to justice were 'allowable' only up to the point where they conformed with international standards. This is reminiscent of colonial 'repugnancy clauses' where 'principles of civilization' trumped all local laws and traditions (Sharp 2018: 71). Mutua (2009) has argued that international human rights law is closely associated with colonial conquest, and such law has too often been seen as the highest form of civilization (Pillay 2016). The application of this law through transitional justice, when married with the impulse to order the violent and irrational place of conflict, continues the colonial mindset of control and order associated closely with a mission to civilise. The idea of civility is important for the framing of transitional justice beneficiaries as well as the mission of transitional justice entrepreneurs. The desire to use transitional justice interventions to create 'islands of civility' among the population, which have 'civilizing effects on actors, encouraging new understandings, values and attitudes' (Andrieu 2010: 245–7), has led to a distinct focus on civil society as a key partner in achieving transitional justice goals (Hovil and Okello 2011, Jeffrey and Jakala 2015: 44). Civil society is seen as important 'not only to enhance the effectiveness of any particular intervention – such as a TJ measure – but also in order to contribute to the broader social change goals of civic engagement and democratization' (Arthur and Yakinthou 2018: 3). This contribution is seen to come from the building of trust, both between citizens and between citizens and institutions (Arthur and Yakinthou 2018: 9–11).

In multiple reports the former Special Rapporteur Pablo de Greiff makes reference to the shared values and principles which must be fostered to support transitional justice processes and outcomes. In 2017 he wrote that victim participation 'facilitates the identification of commonalities of experiences, values and principles among different types of victims as well as between victims and non-victims, which is important for the sake of coalition- and consensus-formation regarding transitional justice policies' and in 2016 that:

> the interactions that are part and parcel of a well-designed consultation process also offer the potential for stakeholders to identify common grounds; they can come to an understanding of shared experiences (including shared experiences of pain and harm), shared needs (for various forms of support, security and responsive institutions) and shared basic values and principles. (de Greiff 2016: 19)

This approach tracks with his other statements as Special Rapporteur as well as academic publications on the importance of civic trust, assumed to lead to reconciliation, peace and democratization (Arthur and Yakinthou 2018: 10–11), and papers by NGOs such as the ICTJ which connect civil society with civic trust building in transitional justice contexts (Duthie 2009).

This is, however, a reductionist version of 'good' civil society which is 'a contingent, ideologically preferential sub-set' working towards a unified concept of the public good (Waters 2015: 165–166). This 'gentrification' of civil society relies on a concept of civility which 'draws our attention to the idea of a set of principles and assumptions relating to social behaviour set out by elite arbiters that serve as key elements of social and political ordering' (Jeffrey 2008: 741). It is also a liberal approach to civil society and citizenship, based on the idea that the relationship between state and citizen and between citizens themselves is regulated by the rule of law, the recognition of rights, and the legitimate monopoly of violence by the state; all relationships which are under strain in contexts of violence (Pearce 2007: 8).

The mobilization of this particular idea of civility also designates actors and acts which align with transitional justice goals as working for the public 'good', while those who have alternative perspectives or work through other modes of resistance are designated as 'bad' civil society (Jones and Fatogoma 2018). A specific understanding of civility as ordered and controlled thus underpins the broader civilizing mission of transitional justice, preventing different forms of injustice and violence from being acknowledged, as well as the potential value of difference, disagreement, and dispute. Political geographers have long acknowledged how disorder and disruption may expand 'the field of public address [as] an important element in struggles to expand and reorder the democratic public' (Staeheli 2010: 68), and warned against charges of incivility for 'masking and managing disruptive demands to inclusion in the public realm' (Zerrilli cited in Edyvane 2017: 350). This is problematic because it erroneously assumes that social conflict is reconcilable (Schaap 2006) and that order is more aligned with justice and peace than disorder. In contexts of violence rooted in historical injustices, contexts of complex identity formation, and contexts of ongoing contestation and violations, this approach not only fails to capture the realities of people's lives, but also reduces access to claim-making and narrows what counts as acceptable justice-seeking behaviour. In the section which follows this is discussed in more detail with reference to 'good' and 'bad' victims and the possibility of accounting for and accommodating resistance in transitional justice discourse and practice.

4.2 THE 'GOOD' AND THE 'BAD' VICTIM IN TRANSITIONAL JUSTICE

This chapter is concerned with the construction of the transitional justice citizen as an individual with specific virtues, and the effect that this has on the perceived legitimacy of different manners of claim-making. In Chapter 3 the discussion of outreach and participation highlighted how the transitional justice citizen is expected to participate in transitional justice and, in so doing, to support the type of justice on offer and the goals of the transitional justice process. Non-participation is interpreted as a rejection of transitional justice, and as a form of deviancy from the values and goals articulated by transitional justice experts and entrepreneurs. The foundation of the transitional justice global norm and the evolution of the transitional justice field, discussed in Chapter 2, has created the following binary: one is either *for* transitional justice or *against* transitional justice. The legitimacy of actions, views, and behaviours is determined in relation to transitional justice itself, continuing the theme of 'naturalizing', of rendering 'normal', transitional justice which has appeared in each of the chapters thus far. The division of acts into those which are for and those which are against transitional justice further divides the population into 'good' and 'bad' in terms of their virtues. Building on the civility discussion in the previous section, this part of the chapter addresses narratives of the 'good' and 'bad' victim, how transitional justice acknowledges and responds to resistance and how actor-centred approaches might shape an understanding of the transitional justice citizen.

Although the character of transitional justice as a series of trade-offs and compromises (Newman 2002: 32) is well recognised, the transitional justice field has, to date, not effectively grappled with the question of what to do when people disagree. Van de Merwe et al. point out that actors will hold different perspectives on transitional justice, including a 'deep satisfaction with, and alienation from, the process' (2009: 3). The answer to this question of what to do when people disagree is implied in the policy documents discussed in the preceding chapters – alternative practices are allowed insofar as they do not contradict international norms and standards (Sharp 2018: 71). This does not, then, take us far from the triumphalism associated with liberal peacebuilding and leaves transitional justice squarely in the dilemma of liberal internationalism: imposing justice through unjust means. Theorists of agonism point towards the 'liberal proclivity to only grant respect to those in whom it recognises the self-same moral attributes and liberal commitments', 'coupled with a penchant for violence as a means to secure peace as a disciplinary order' (Shinko 2008: 482). While in liberal theory 'a choice with neither substance nor alternatives is no choice at all' (Hughes 2009) there has always been this tension, from Rousseau's social contract which forces men to be free (Rousseau 1968) to the former UN Secretary General Kofi Annan's *The Rule of Law and Transitional Justice in Conflict and Post-Conflict Societies* which demands conformity with international standards (UN 2004). This is the basis on which the transitional justice citizen is judged to be 'good' or 'bad', based on the liberal lens of peaceful and democratic virtues.

This dynamic is exemplified by the discourse around 'good' and 'bad' victims. In Chapter 2, I elaborated one part of the transitional justice citizen, that of the citizen-victim – an individual with human rights which need to be protected rather than a citizen with claims and agency. This victim with rights is also a victim who is expected to hold certain virtues, to accept the justice on offer and to conform with the requirements and aims of transitional justice. Such a construction of the 'good' victim flows directly from the preoccupation with order and consensus that was discussed in the previous section of this chapter. To put it simply, the victim who asks too much of transitional justice and who does not *receive* the justice on offer is disruptive, deviant and lacking in the virtues necessary to be a valued member of the new political community. The democratic peace pact makes demands, even of those who have survived oppression, violence, and marginalization. Criminal justice literature has challenged the instrumentalization of victims for institutional ends, as well as their exclusion from decision-making about justice; and in this way, human rights and post-conflict justice work has been advanced by, at least rhetorically, placing victims at the centre (Holder 2018: 5–6). However, there is a growing body of work by transitional justice scholars which deconstructs implicit and explicit narratives of the 'good' and 'bad' victim, and which illustrates how the 'victim' remains framed as a passive *receiver* of justice rather than an individual who has an interest in the way justice works for all and is an active *seeker* of justice (Holder 2018: 12).

Victim-centred approaches in transitional justice are important for ensuring that those who have been victimised are not further marginalised, and justice *for victims* has been at the centre of the normative evolution of the field of transitional justice, enshrining in norms and laws the duties of states to protect victims, as well as the rights which victims hold, including participation in justice (Mendez 2016), as discussed in the previous chapter. Despite this being the case, scholars of victimology and transitional justice have offered counterpoints by demonstrating how victimhood is socially constructed (Jankowitz

2018: 217); how in reality complex political victims go beyond the dichotomy of 'innocence' and 'guilt' on which transitional justice relies (McEvoy and McConnachie 2013, Bernath 2016); how individuals may be reluctant to accept others' definitions of victimhood or indeed to self-identify as a victim at all (Lacerda 2010); and how politically charged and controversial it is for a transitional justice process to identify who is a victim (Moffett 2016). In such societies 'victimhood is inevitably mapped onto competing narratives of community, nation and the contested past all the more starkly' (McEvoy and McConnachie 2013: 504).

This work draws our attention to the interplay of victimhood, virtue, and citizenship. In her analysis of complex political victims and the ECCC, Bernath identifies the prevalence of terms such as 'victims victims', 'real victims' and 'pure victims', which explicitly connects ideas of innocence and purity with victimhood (2016: 60). This is not unusual for discourses and practices of transitional justice. In Peru, legal and political documents attempting to redress the violence of 20 years of armed conflict emphasise the innocence of victims, as if leading to a reluctance of victim-survivors to self-identify as victims, for if they

> are expected to be innocent, they are implicitly assumed to have no responsibility for what occurred during the internal conflict [...] This inextricable connection between innocence and passivity as inherent traits of victims further intensifies the negative connotations ascribed to the term. (de Waardt 2010: 448)

This can generate hierarchies between victims. Importantly, the status of 'victim' given by a transitional justice process is not an innate category, rather it is as 'reliant on subjective assumptions about the contexts and correlates of harm as it is on the experience of harm itself' (Jankowitz 2018: 217). In a conflict or post-authoritarian context these subjectivities are intertwined with the long-term historical struggle over who belongs, who can access resources, the link between identities and power, and potentially ongoing violence and repression.

The body of work in transitional justice which deconstructs discourses of 'good' and 'bad' victims identifies hierarchies of victims which 'compete' for victim status as well as unreasonable expectations of victim virtues. The denial of complex identities – where victim-survivors are implicated in violence or struggle – writes out their agency as rights-bearing citizens, as members of a political community, and as justice *seekers* with a stake in defining justice *for what* and justice *for whom*. This intersects with the impulse to order discussed in the previous section and can be seen clearly when we look at what happens when victims disagree with transitional justice process and outcomes. In my previous work on resistance to transitional justice I found that acts of disruption and disagreement, coming from arguments about what justice should be, are too often dismissed as acts of deviance from the global norm (Jones and Bernath 2017). We see this in the narrowness of the work on resistance to transitional justice, focused primarily on former regime loyalists (Subotic 2014), or social elites who have benefitted from previous systems and injustices (Hansen 2014: 119), whose views are delegitimised by association with the violent past which is to be overcome. 'Bad' victims are also those who resist the terms of justice on offer, the 'unreconciled or recalcitrant' members of the victim groups (Meister 2002: 96). These 'bad' victims who do not accept the past as past and 'move on' to the future are problematic for the transitional justice teleology. Hamber and Wilson illustrate this point using the case of the *Madres de la Plaza de Mayo*:

> [O]ver the years, they have changed from being the "Mothers of the Nation" to *"Las Locas"* or the "Crazy Little Old Ladies" [...] The recalcitrant *Madres* were demonized as they no longer embodied the state's vision of a reconciled nation. (Hamber and Wilson 2002: 45)

Their lack of acceptance of the closure which was expected of them can be seen as a continuation of revolutionary struggles (Lefranc 2002: 114–115) but is most often portrayed as resentment. As 'recalcitrant victims' they are portrayed as 'traumatised, self-preoccupied, resentful, and vindictive' (Brudholm 2008: 2)

The pressures placed on individual citizens to accept the justice processes on offer and to play their role in the democratic peace pact can be seen, on the one hand, as important calls for unity in the face of divided pasts and presents. This might be the civic virtues Porter calls for in Northern Ireland, the 'forgiveness, magnanimity and reasonableness' (2003: 67) crucial for reconciliation and peace and for creating a society in which all citizens have a sense of belonging (2003: 94–100). But such calls are also intertwined with the problematic dismissal of disagreement as disorder, and with political projects of control. In her work on Kenya, Lynch writes of the projects of peacebuilding and justice which placed 'an emphasis on the contribution that ordinary citizens could make to peace in a context where deeper structural changes seemed unlikely' (Lynch 2018: 43) In this context, the good citizen was one who lived in harmony with neighbours, voted in peace, waited and accepted election results and actively participated in a culture of non-violence (2018: 32). This peace narrative determined which activities were deemed politically legitimate, leading to a ban on public demonstrations during the 2013 elections and a high level of self-censorship in the media (2018: 55).

4.3 THE STRUGGLE FOR JUSTICE AS A BEARER OF DUTIES

This chapter has focused on the figure of the citizen as virtuous. One of the challenges of transitional justice discourse and literature has been a problematic assumption that because the aims of transitional justice processes are 'good' (peace, justice, stability, prosperity), the associated practices and relationships of power cannot be substantively questioned and criticized. Likewise, the citizen must hold certain virtues of civility associated with the neoliberal dominant script of transitional justice to play their role. The key message of this chapter is that a focus on social and political order and on individuality of responsibility precludes more radical formulations of the citizen, denies realities of citizen action, and assumes that social change and transformation can be managed.

This chapter, along with the rest of Part 1, has explored the discourse of an international norm of transitional justice and the implications of this for how the citizen is framed, indeed imagined, through and for transitional justice. We have seen how the conditions of the emergence of transitional justice as a field have imbued it with a sense of purpose and a set of values, its 'lasting normative imprint' (Zunino 2019: 231) which determines which claims to justice are considered relevant, or even, I would argue, legitimate. As Zunino describes:

> Spontaneous expressions of popular justice, unofficial tribunals, land reform programmes and popular tribunals were non-legalistic, non-liberal or non-state-centric initiatives that did not fit the normative frame of reference that transitional justice inherited from its process of emergence. (2019: 231)

The keywords 'spontaneous' and 'popular' stand out here. A negative binary has developed whereby the state-sanctioned, formal acts of claim-making which align with the international norm are on one side and the spontaneous, popular, decentred acts are on the other. It is no surprise that the discourse of transitional justice can appear so monolithic and can, whether individual actors have that intention or not, discipline so effectively the types of claims and the manner of claim-making which are considered to be legitimate. In the introduction to Isin and Nielsen's *Acts of Citizenship* we learn that acts of citizenship are acts of disruption:

> By theorizing acts or attempting to constitute acts as an object of analysis, we must focus not only on rupture rather than order, but also on a rupture that enables the actor (that the act creates) to remain at the scene rather than fleeing it. (Isin 2008: 27)

As we move from Part 1 to Part 2 of this book we take with us a series of tensions within the 'order' or rather 'ordering' of transitional justice discourse, policy and practice: that despite the rhetoric of victim-centred justice, of participation and outreach, and of seeking redress for harms, only certain people can make justice claims, only certain justice claims can be made, and justice claims can only be made in certain ways.

These tensions require a deeper look at the empirical unfolding of transitional justice, a turn towards *acts* rather than *imaginations* of the citizen, if not to resolve them then to render them creative and analytically useful. For if we are to move beyond the albeit important critiques of transitional justice which have been discussed in Part 1, then we need to be able to do more than merely list the tensions identified above. We need to find a way of articulating a concept which can render legible these tensions while offering a response to them. The transitional justice citizen is one such concept and in Part 2 of the book which follows I explore the second, interconnected, aspect of this figure: the citizen who acts, and in doing so actualises themselves through engagement with or against a transitional justice process. This is a citizen who disrupts and who also refuses to flee the scene. A citizen who has something to say about what kind of justice should be part of transitional justice and which claims to justice should not be forgotten.

PART II

THE CITIZEN AS JUSTICE SEEKER

Part 1 elaborated three significant ways in which the transitional justice citizen has been imagined through transitional justice discourse, policy, and practice. Each places a boundary around the transitional justice citizen, defining who they are and how they can behave. Firstly, there are limits to *who* can make claims. The global norm of transitional justice is reproduced by transitional justice entrepreneurs and experts who speak on behalf of victims with human rights who need to be protected. This renders the transitional justice citizen relatively marginalised and disempowered, even in a process which is supposed to directly benefit them. Secondly, there are limits to *what* claims can be made. Transitional justice outreach and consultations reinforce ideas of what justice should look like and limit them within the liberal-legalist paradigm. This renders the transitional justice citizen less able to make claims which go beyond the justice on offer through a transitional justice process. Thirdly, there are limits to *how* claims can be made. Expectations of certain virtues to be demonstrated by 'good' victims in an impulse to order delegitimise alternative ways of expressing and demanding justice. The transitional justice citizen is thus not expected to demand too much or to disrupt the transitional justice process.

It is clear in these ways that the transitional justice citizen is imagined as a justice *receiver* and not as a justice *seeker*. The transitional justice process bestows upon the citizens of the target society forms of justice which they are told are adequate redress for harms suffered. Possibilities to contest the justice on offer or to have more agency in the process are limited. This is important in and of itself, but to end the conceptualisation of the transitional justice citizen here would do a huge disservice to the citizens themselves and would ignore the multitude of ways in which they actively seek justice and push the boundaries of who can make claims, what claims can be made, and how claims should be made. It is for this reason that Part 2 turns to acts of citizens as justice seekers. It is by taking seriously the alternatives to the imagined citizen that we can go a step further than the deconstruction and critique of Part 1. We are able to see how boundaries around who can act, what claims can be made and how claims should be made, are pushed and contested by the transitional justice citizen themselves in ways which potentially create new understandings of what counts as justice following large-scale violations of human rights.

In her work on the conceptual foundations of transitional justice, Murphy defines transitional justice as distinct from criminal, corrective or distribute justice in its 'just pursuit of societal transformation' (2017: 119). This is a transformation which she sees as relational, altering 'the terms of political interaction among citizens, and between citizens and officials' (2017: 119). This is a definition of transitional justice which is normative – how it *should* operate – and distinct from the actual discourses and policies of transitional justice as the global norm and international bureaucracy which was the focus of Part 1. The acts of citizens which were the focus of Part 2 move us towards such ideas of transformation. Isin writes of the ways in which acts of citizenship create new scripts, transform subjects into citizens, and create new sites and scales of struggle (2008). The transformative potential of transitional justice, so often unrealised as we saw in Part 1, can perhaps only be realised once the transitional justice subject is transformed into a transitional justice citizen through acts of disruption and ongoing or new struggle. These are the elements which have been marginalised from the discourses and policies discussed in Part 1. Part 2 seeks to render them visible through concrete examples of acts of inclusion, acts of expansion and acts of disruption. In Part 1 we have seen how claim-making is confined to a series of specific engagements with transitional justice interventions designed to satisfy current claims and to foreclose the possibility of future ones. In Part 2 we see how claim-making is, and indeed should be, part of an ongoing process of struggle and continual debate over what justice is and could be.

5.   We can make claims too: acts of inclusion in Côte d'Ivoire[1]

Côte d'Ivoire gained independence from France in 1960, and the post-Independence leader Felix Houphouët-Boigny was credited with bringing peace and stability to the country during his 33-year reign (Diallo 2005). During this time democratic freedom was eschewed for economic growth and political stability, with the Democratic Party of Côte d'Ivoire (*Parti Démocratique de Côte d'Ivoire*) squeezing out or absorbing political rivals and dominating the associational space (Faure 1982, Marie 1998). The role that an active civil society had played in the anti-colonial struggle was reversed and redirected into supporting one-party rule. In 1990 multi-party politics was introduced, with 14 parties formally recognised, and between 1990 and 1999 over 264 civil society organizations were registered (PNUD 2004). However, associational space retained the reflexes of the one-party political system, with civil society organizations closely aligned with and influenced by particular political parties. The death of Houphouët-Boigny in 1993 ushered in a series of political crises connected with ethnic divisions, regional splits, and claims to autochthony (Bah 2010). His successor, President Henri Konan Bédié, who was in power from 1993 until 1999, used these divisions to rally political support, mobilizing a concept of Ivoirity (*Ivoirité*) which defined southerners as 'authentic' Ivoiriens, in opposition to 'circumstantial' ones – that is, northerners and immigrants (Adou and Jones forthcoming a). This formed the background for a coup and civil war in 1999 and then a rebellion in 2002. A unity government was created in 2003, and a buffer zone between the north and south of the country was put in place. Political violence continued and in 2007 the Ouagadougou Agreement was eventually signed by President Laurent Gbagbo, Secretary-General of the New Forces (*Forces Nouvelles*)[2] Guillaume Soro, and facilitator and President of Burkina Faso Blaise Compaoré.

In 2010 presidential elections, postponed from 2005, were held with the intention of solidifying unity and marking a formal end to the peace process. However, contested results in the second round led to both the incumbent Laurent Gbagbo and his opponent Alassane Ouattara declaring victory. The Ivoirien Constitutional Council had declared Gbagbo to be the winner, while the Electoral Commission announced that Ouattara had won. The former was controlled by Gbagbo's political party and had invalidated about 600,000 opposition votes from the north of the country in order to claim a Gbagbo victory (Piccolino 2012: 21). The UN Security Council intervened to declare Alassane Ouattara to be the winner, along with support from the African Union (AU) and the Economic Community of West African States (ECWS) . A 'period of difficult coexistence was inaugurated between an internationally recognised President, entrapped in the Hotel du Golf under UN protection, and a self-proclaimed one who continued for some time to control the security forces in the south' (Piccolino 2012: 21). The contradictory declarations of victory led to post-election violence from 2010-2011, during which 3,000 people died and 5,000 were displaced (Tawa and Engelsdorfer 2017: 1). The crisis finally 'ended' on 11 April after the capture and house arrest of Laurent Gbagbo following a month-long military campaign to oust him facilitated by the New Forces (*Forces Nouvelles*), a former insurgent group, the United Nations Operation in Côte d'Ivoire ()and the French mission 'Unicorn' (*Licorne*) (Piccolino 2018: 486). The following transitional justice process led by President Ouattara was put in place quickly; and, aided by international partners, it focused on the UN pillars of transitional justice – truth, justice, reparation, guarantees of non-recurrence – fitting squarely into the mould of the global norm discussed in Chapter 2.

The transitional justice process, however, has been clouded by accusations of victor's justice and ongoing political tensions. The focus of this chapter is on the acts of citizenship of supporters of the former President Laurent Gbagbo and his political party the Ivoirian Popular Front (*Front Populaire Ivoirien*, FPI). Their lobbying, protests, and alternative programmes of action expanded the framing of who could make claims. In Chapter 2 we saw how transitional justice can place boundaries around who is entitled to make claims, with entrepreneurs and experts dominating the framing of the justice on offer. The result of this is that views which fall outside of the global norm are marginalised, with certain actors excluded from the process. This is certainly the case in Côte d'Ivoire where those who were seen as being on the 'wrong' side of justice were not seen as credible or legitimate interlocutors in the justice debate. For the Ivoiriens whose acts I analyse in this chapter, this is a question of democracy, inclusion, and the right to participate in defining what justice should look like.

5.1 CITIZENSHIP, INCLUSION AND POLITICAL VIOLENCE IN CÔTE D'IVOIRE

Writing before the 2010/11 post-election violence, Obi states that

> Peace in Côte d'Ivoire ultimately depends on Ivorian people and the factions of governing elite, who will have to reach a new social contract on which a broadly

acceptable and inclusive notion of Ivoirian nationhood, political representation and citizenship can be (re)created and nurtured. (2007: 8)

Such a social contract has been under strain and under-realised in Côte d'Ivoire due to a history of inter-ethnic conflict, tensions between the local/indigenous populations and immigrants/settlers, and north–south ethnic/religious cleavages (Almas 2007: 10). Indeed, the root causes of civil war and electoral crisis cannot be understood outside of unresolved national and citizenship questions (Yere 2007: 50) and the conflict has been described as 'largely driven by concrete political and social grievances over citizenship' (Bah 2010: 597). In her tracing of the debate over 'who is who' in Côte d'Ivoire prior to the 2010 election violence, Marshall-Fratani argues that 'what is at stake […] is not only a struggle for state power, but also, and more importantly, the redefinition of the content of citizenship and the conditions of sovereignty' (2006: 11).

Under the French colonial administration (18931960), as for many other colonies, Côte d'Ivoire was seen through a lens of ethnic and racial hierarchy, with a policy of creating administrative units based on 'pure autochthonous races', delineating between different categories of labour in the plantation economy (Marshall-Fratani 2006: 1415). This project of fixing and categorizing labour populations occurred alongside a large-scale labour migration programme (Marshall-Fratani 2006: 15) which moved populations within the country and also moved immigrant labour from the area which is now Burkina Faso to work on the plantations in the south of Côte d'Ivoire (Almas 2007: 12). Economic prosperity following independence continued to attract immigration from poorer countries in the region. During Houphouët-Boigny's reign (1960–1993) there had been a liberal and open attitude to immigration under his policy that 'the land belonged to the one who worked it', leading to a large immigrant population in the country – primarily from Burkina Faso but also from Mali, Guinea, Niger, Benin, Ghana, Liberia, Mauritania, Nigeria, and Senegal (Almas 2007: 12). During this time, associations were formed based on ethnic group interests, crystallizing early civil society as embedded in the various claims to autochthony, and from 'this point on, territoriality and citizenship would become organically linked in political discourse' (Marshall-Fratani 2006: 17). The political history of the country thus needs to be understood as being intimately linked to its immigration history (Almas 2007: 12); a history of contradiction. On the one hand there is the valorization of immigration as key to the country's economic success and an important indicator of values of Pan-Africanism, fraternity, and generosity; on the other hand, themes of immigrants' lack of gratitude and their greed have increasingly been evoked since the 1990s (Marshall-Fratani 2006: 19).

Once multi-party politics were introduced in 1990, ideas of 'belonging' defined political jostling and the political process. In the first presidential elections, for example, Ouattara faced opposition based on his 'non-citizenship' which was said to result from having a father from Burkina Faso. Framed as an 'intruder' in Ivoirien politics, his legitimacy as a candidate was called into question (Almas 2007: 13). Henri Konan Bédié won the election and quickly began to implement a political strategy of Ivoirity (*Ivoirité*) which led, among other things, to radical changes in the country's citizenship policy. In December 1994 the National Assembly passed a new electoral code which restricted the right to vote to Ivoirien nationals, and stated that presidential candidates must be Ivoirien by birth (with both parents also being Ivoirien by birth), must not have not been living outside of the country for the last five years, and must have never renounced their Ivoirien citizenship or taken the nationality of another state (Almas 2007: 14). This was a stark shift from a previously fluid concept of national identity and citizenship, which had proved useful in a multi-ethnic and high immigration society, and which had allowed migrants to vote, to own land, and to participate in politics as members of government (Riehl 2007: 33). It was also a move from citizenship as juridically based to a national citizenship based on birthright (Akindes cited in Yere 2007: 57), interweaving anti-foreigner and anti-northerner sentiments (Bah 2010: 602). In essence, Ivoirity (*Ivoirité*) 'meant the forced exclusion of indigenes from the north and immigrants from Côte d'Ivoire's northern neighbours from elections and land ownership'. 'As a result, more than twenty percent of the Ivorian population were no longer politically and juridically citizens of the country' (Riehl 2007: 34). This created, de facto, two types of citizen: those of 'pure' Ivoirien origin and those of 'mixed heritage' (Marshall-Fratani 2006: 23).

In the years that followed, there was a political history of exclusion – either exclusion of the opposition by the regime in power, or self-exclusion by opposing powers who refused to participate (Adou 2018: 23). The three leaders after Houphouët-Boigny – Bédié, General Gueï, and Gbagbo – all used Ivoirity (*Ivoirité*) as a political strategy while Ouattara and his supporters mobilised ethnic identity and feelings of exclusion to gain support from 'northern' Ivoiriens (Almas 2007: 16). Guillaume Soro, leader of the rebel forces in the North responsible for the 2002 attempted coup, traced their actions to dissatisfaction with political exclusion based on the concept of Ivoirity (*Ivoirité*), which he described as follows:

> Ivoirity is no more nor less than a xenophobic concept. The Ivoirity word in its true sense means nothing other than: "Côte d'Ivoire to Ivorians", which is to clearly say, according to those from the south northerners are considered foreigners in their own country' (*n'est ni plus ni moins qu'un concept xenophobe. L'ivoirité est un mot dont le vrai sens ne signifie rien d'autre que: "la Côte d'Ivoire aux Ivoiriens", c'est-à-dire, en clair, à ceux qui sont originaires du Sud, les Nordistes étant considérés comme étrangers dans leur propre pays*. (cited in Bah 2010: 604, translation taken from original)

Discourses of 'foreignness' were overlaid onto internal migratory patterns, which had seen ideas of the 'foreigner' applied not only to migrants coming from outside of the country but also to people moving from one part of the country to another (Yere 2007: 56). Successive peace agreements failed to address these contentions about the definition and proof of citizenship, reducing them to a mere struggle for power between different political forces (Bah 2010: 607). This was remedied to some extent by the Ouagadougou Agreement of 2007 which recognised that 'the identification of the Ivorian and foreign populations living in Côte d'Ivoire is a major concern. The absence of a clear and standard identity document and of individual administrative documents attesting to the identity and nationality of persons is a source of conflict' (Article 1 cited in Bah 2010: 610). Under the agreement there were provisions for providing credentials to all Ivoiriens, for mobile courts supplying birth certificates, and a definition of Ivoirien citizenship as any person born to at least one Ivoirien parent or someone born in Côte d'Ivoire to unknown parents (Bah 2010: 611). However, the continued crisis and violence which preceded the 2010 election were underpinned by the complex interaction between discourses of autochthony, belonging, and citizenship which sought to exclude 'foreigners' from outside of the country as well as within it.

5.2   TRANSITIONAL JUSTICE IN CÔTE D'IVOIRE

The transitional justice process implemented in Côte d'Ivoire, following the post-election violence of 2010–2011, maps well onto the global norm consolidated in the UN pillars and supported by a network of international transitional justice entrepreneurs and advocates. In 2011, shortly after taking power, President Ouattara announced a series of transitional justice measures. The process comprised ICC indictments, national prosecutions, a Commission of Dialogue, Truth, and Reconciliation (*Commission Dialogue, Vérité et Reconciliation*, CDVR), a National Commission of Inquiry (*Commission Nationale d'Enquête*), and a National Commission for Reconciliation and Compensation of Victims (*Commission Nationale pour la Réconciliation et l'Indemnisation des Victims*, CONARIV). While transitional justice in Côte d'Ivoire meets in many ways the standard template of the global norm of transitional justice, it has been controversial and contested and cannot be seen as existing in a vacuum, separate from the social and political contexts outlined in the previous section. Accusations of victor's justice are well documented, excluding those who are on the 'wrong' side not only from justice debates and dividends but also from shaping the political and social future of the country.

The legal justice pursued in Côte d'Ivoire includes three cases at the ICC as well as national trials. At the time of the violence, Côte d'Ivoire was not a member state of the ICC, but it had accepted the court's jurisdiction in 2003 and reconfirmed this acceptance in December 2010 and May 2011, ratifying the Rome Statute on 15 February 2013 (Tawa and Engelsdorfer 2017: 3). Laurent Gbagbo, Simone Gbagbo and Blé Goudé were all indicted by the ICC. Only Laurent Gbago and Blé Goudé[3] were transferred to The Hague for trial, with Simone Gbagbo tried in a national court following public statements by Ouattara that he would not transfer any more Ivoiriens to the ICC (Tawa and Engelsdorfer 2017: 14). Laurent Gbagbo's and Blé Goudé's cases were joined on 11 March 2015 with the trial beginning on 28 January 2016. On 15 January 2019, Trial Chamber 1 acquitted them both of all charges of crimes against humanity, a decision which was appealed and then upheld on 15 January 2019.[4] Analysis of the ICC cases in Côte d'Ivoire by Human Rights Watch finds that 'the one-sided focus of the ICC's cases ... has helped to polarise opinion about the court and undermined perceptions of its legitimacy' (Human Rights Watch 2015: 5). Simone Gbagbo was convicted in an Ivoirien court of the crime of undermining state security on 10 March 2015 and was sentenced to 20 years in jail. She was then granted amnesty on 6 August 2018 as part of an extensive amnesty marking the 58th anniversary of independence from France.

Despite this recent amnesty there are still strong claims by domestic and international actors of victor's justice, as not a single pro-Ouattara individual has been tried or convicted (Baldo 2011, ICG 2011). A statement by a member of the FPI encapsulates the opposition's frustration with this victor's justice, propped up by international support:

> We are an independent state. The intervention of the ICC suggests that our independence is not complete. We do not need this Court, which is an imagination from Western countries to regulate politics in Africa and eliminate African nationalists. If the Court's objective is to render fair and impartial justice it should trial Ouattara's supporters and former rebel's leaders. (cited in Tawa and Engelsdorfer 2017: 4)

In addition, the number of cases being tried in the national courts has thus far been limited even though dozens of Gbagbo supporters are currently detained awaiting trial (Adou and Jones forthcoming b). As Piccolino observes:

> by rewarding former FN leaders and sheltering them from potential prosecution, the president and his collaborators have been forced to make choices that have preserved short term stability, but that might have jeopardized other goals. In particular, these choices have further alienated the vanquished of the post-election crisis – the supporters of former president Laurent Gbagbo. (Piccolino 2018: 497).

The non-legal justice on offer includes the CDVR which was created on 13 May 2011 (Piccolino 2018: 500). The mandate of the CDVR was:

(a) to develop a typology of the human rights violations that may be the subject of its deliberations;
(b) to seek the truth and place responsibilities on past and recent national socio-political events;
(c) to hear the victims, to obtain the recognition of the facts by the perpetrators of the violations, and to foster forgiveness;
(d) to propose means to heal the trauma suffered by the victims;
(e) to identify and make proposals for their implementation of actions likely to strengthen social cohesion and national unity;
(f) to identify and make proposals aimed at combating injustice, inequalities of all kinds, tribalism, nepotism, exclusion and hatred in all their forms;
(g) to educate for peace, dialogue and peaceful coexistence;
(h) to contribute to the emergence of a national consciousness and the adherence of all to the primacy of the general interest; and
(i) to promote respect for differences and democratic values. (Adou and Jones forthcoming c)

Critics have suggested that this mandate was vague, broad, and overly ambitious (Piccolino 2018: 500). Despite calls from the FPI to boycott the CDVR, it gathered in total 72,483 victim testimonies from different regions of the country as well as from the Ivoirien diaspora in three platforms in New York, London, and Paris. It finished its work in December 2014, but its work has been controversial due to a lack of transparency in the methods used to identify victims, and the political ambitions of the CDVR President Konan Banny (Adou and Jones forthcoming b). While its report was presented to Ouattara on 15 December 2014, it was only made public on 25 October 2016, 'in a version where the passages more critical towards Ouattara and his regime have been deleted' (Piccolino 2018: 501). Population surveys suggest that most Ivoiriens see the CDVR as a failure (Piccolino 2018: 500).

One recommendation made by the CDVR was to establish the CONARIV which was active between 24 May 2015 and 22 December 2016. It was responsible for offering compensation to the victims of successive crises in Côte d'Ivoire. The CONARIV undertook a census of the victims, following the one already completed by the CDVR. Out of 874,056 cases, the CONARIV validated 316,954 (that is, 36 per cent). It rejected many victims because of a lack of evidence such as a death certificate, inaccurate contact telephone numbers, and incomplete information. Individuals recognised as victims were compensated for abuses suffered between 1990 and 2011 (Adou and Jones forthcoming a). The work of the CONARIV in registering victims and developing a reparations policy was hampered by a lack of coordination with the National Programme for Social Cohesion (*Programme National pour de Cohésion Sociale*) which had been mandated to implement the reparations programme. Political rivalry between the leaders of the two organs was a serious issue, and so once the CONARIV had completed its mandate the government established a Ministry of Solidarity, Social Cohesion and Victims Compensation (*Ministère de la Solidarité, de la Cohésion Sociale et de l'Indemnisation des Victimes de Guerre*), dedicated to victims' reparations. Hopes that this would speed up the reparations process have unfortunately not been realised (Adou and Jones forthcoming a). Moreover, the CONARIV has been criticised for reducing reconciliation to a technocratic process of victim registration and economic reparations (Piccolino 2018: 501).

Throughout the transitional justice process there has been ongoing political violence, related to some of the tensions already referred to in this chapter. Indeed, the transitional justice process is 'anchored in the ongoing political contestation in Côte d'Ivoire' which is more nuanced than a simple 'two camps' analysis of pro-Ouattara versus pro-Gbagbo (Adou 2018: 17). Since the introduction of multi-party politics in 1993 there has been consistent political violence which 'now pervades daily life' (Vidal 2003: 45). In 2012, during the first year of operation of most of the formal institutions of transitional justice, there were ten pockets of armed violence across the country, interpreted by the government as 'acts of terrorism' and by pro-Gbagbo actors as a strategy to discredit them and legitimise their arrest (Adou 2018: 21–22). Divisions between ethnic groups, different regions, and different political parties intersect and are reinforced and simplified by the transitional justice process which places decisions about justice firmly in the hands of some actors. This leads to inevitable resentment from those who feel excluded, as these words spoken by the President of the FPI upon being released from prison illustrate:

> Today there are two Côte d'Ivoires. The Côte d'Ivoire of the defeated and that of the victors. And as long as we do not complete reconciliation, it is deluded to think that the defeated who have been thrown in prison, who have had their accounts frozen and their homes occupied, who have gone into exile, will join in the initiatives of the victors. The defeated suffer in silence. (cited in Adou 2018: 24)

This speech contrasts with that of Ouattara when he outlines his vision for the future of the country:

> Being reconciled is first for me, to have a peaceful country, where people live in harmony with the same equalities of opportunities and I can tell you that this is the case. There are no areas reserved for any ethnic group. In all districts of Abidjan, all ethnic groups are together. Can we better reconcile than that? If you go to Korhogo, Gagnoa, etc., you will find people of all ethnic groups. Basically, it should not

mislead the notion of national reconciliation as to link it to a person or an event. [...] The post-election crisis was very serious. More than 3,000 people were killed. It is necessary that those involved be tried here or elsewhere. Besides, if we do not, international courts will do it one day. Everyone will be judged here [...] There is a key element in what I have read about reconciliation. This is the well-being of the population. This is what we are doing: a growth rate of 8 to 9%, reducing poverty, building schools, cleaning up the environment, etc. Once we will finish all this, tensions will drop.[5]

For Ouattara economic success underpins and engenders social cohesion which will reconcile the country (Piccolino 2018: 502). This is a liberal vision of peace where economic liberalization and liberal democracy go hand-in-hand and provide a foundation for a sustainable peace, reminding us of the discussions in Chapter 1 regarding the liberal-legalist paradigm of the transitional justice global norm. The dominance of the government's liberal framing of justice, reconciliation, and peace has 'sent strong signals to the international community and to the Ivorian society of their determination to write a new page in the history of Côte d'Ivoire'; but it has also 'provided little room for negotiation among the various stakeholders' (N'Da and Fokou 2021: 79) . This is a challenge for Ouattara's leadership which continues to the present day: 'Ouattara and his associates have won and do not want to make substantial political concessions to pro-Gbagbo leaders, but they cannot completely ignore the fact that a substantial portion of the population regards the current regime as illegitimate' (Piccolino 2018: 501). Transitional justice thus occupies two spaces and identities. On the one hand, it is a technical solution which promises to order and harmonise society according to the global norm and liberal vision of justice. On the other hand, it is a focal point for continued discussions over the complex history of socio-political crises related to citizenship, autochthony, and economic collapse (Akindes 2004). It is at the point of friction between the two identities of transitional justice that the acts of citizenship of those excluded from the process gain traction. As Piccolino writes of the actors to be discussed in the next section, 'Gbagbo's former supporters continue to hold their resentment. While unable to challenge the government violently, they manifest their discontent by boycotting elections and by keeping alive their alternative narrative about the Ivoirien civil war and post-election crisis' (Piccolino 2018: 502).

5.3   IVOIRIEN 'DEVIANTS' AND THEIR ACTS OF CITIZENSHIP

Once the transitional justice process was underway there was a sense of a divided civil society, between those organizations that supported and advocated for the process and those that opposed (Jones and Fatogoma 2018: 5).

Organizations that supported the process connected their activities with a sense of duty being fulfilled: by 'wanting to end impunity'[6] and by going 'into the field, we collected opinions and we did our research…so it is to say that in reality civil society is doing its job'.[7] This chimes well with the framings in Part 1 of the book of a dutiful transitional justice citizen who not only accepts the justice on offer but also actively supports the process without making additional claims. This justice *receiver* emerges as the legitimate actor, eclipsing those who are marginalised from the process due to differing views. In Côte d'Ivoire the transitional justice process, dominated by the political victors in the conflict, placed boundaries not only around what kinds of claims could be made but also around who could make them.

Supporters of the former President and his political party came to be associated with a discredited political force, and thus became synonymous with the violent past with which the transitional justice process was supposed to make a break. To have a space in the justice claims of the present these actors were thus expected to also make a break with their political allegiances and views. Such expectation is the result of the dominant framing of transitional justice as a linear process between a 'bad' past and a 'good' future, as discussed in Chapter 1. In this earlier chapter I contrasted the realities of the non-linearity of struggle with the neat idea of transition contained in the dominant global norm of transitional justice. This is an idea of transition which moves towards an end point of closure, a definitive break with the past. This is not an incremental or messy process of social and political transformation. Early ideas in the field of 'short-term, corrective measures during a brief window of a transitional opportunity' (Ní Aoláin and Campbell 2005: 77) have indeed evolved into more nuanced discussions in the transitional justice literature of the exceptionality of the transitional moment and of calls for more focus to be placed on transformation rather than linear transition (Gready and Robins 2014). However, as is clear from the relatively recent case of Côte d'Ivoire, the early dominant framings of transition still prevail in policy and practice. Justice claims, and their claimants, which fall outside of this dominant framing are thus too easily dismissed as 'deviant', as I have discussed elsewhere (Jones and Bernath 2017). This makes it difficult, if not impossible, for such actors to participate in shaping what justice could and should be.

Without wanting to make normative statements about which views, and which justice claims are legitimate in Côte d'Ivoire – for it is not the purpose of this book to make such judgements – it is important to note that the *de facto* exclusion of certain claim makers because of their association with the 'bad' past has political effects. It helpfully contributes to the consolidation of political support for, and position of, the new President and his supporters. As discussed in Chapter 1, transitional justice has indeed often been used to consolidate the authority of new individuals and governments in power (Ilif 2012), and Côte d'Ivoire's transition has been described as 'marked by the gradual reinforcement of President Ouattara and his power' (Piccolino 2018: 493). The temporal and moral separation of the past from the present thus ensures that the holders of power during a transitional justice process can distance themselves from past injustices. By presenting Ouattara as pro-transitional justice, and importantly pro the global norm version of transitional justice, it becomes harder to disassociate the actors in Ouattara's 'camp' from the assumed inherent 'good' of the transitional justice process. The more this link between particular views, actors, and transitional justice is strengthened, the more the opposite becomes true – that *other* actors and *other* views are *de facto* against transitional justice and therefore cannot be included in the implied promises of the future good life. For Ouattara this is justice though economic prosperity and social cohesion, and his transitional justice process – implemented quickly and with an international audience in mind – demanded that Ivoiriens accept the justice terms on offer or risk being excluded as justice claim-makers.

Importantly, despite such framing of the transitional justice citizen as a justice *receiver*, there are actors who expand the boundaries of inclusion and insert themselves into the debates, demanding that they be seen as those who should be able to make justice claims. In Côte d'Ivoire one such set of actors are those aligned with the political views and power of the former President Laurent Gbagbo. As Piccolino observes: 'Ivorian actors who perceived themselves as "vanquished" in the aftermath of 2011 are a diverse group' of Gbagbo's political party, "patriotic" organizations, militia groups, and ordinary voters, particularly 'students and urban intellectuals, who are sympathetic to the anti-French and ostensibly anti-colonialist discourse of the "patriotic galaxy"' (Piccolino 2018: 498). In interviews with actors who were publicly seeking to be included by making justice claims 'from the fringes', I spoke to members and representatives of the diaspora group Committee of Actions for Côte d'Ivoire – USA (CACI-USA), the Abidjan-based National Congress for Resistance and Democracy (*Congrès National pour la Résistance et la Démocratie*, CNRD) and the FPI. The actors developed an online presence with Facebook groups and discussions, produced leaflets to promote their views, spoke publicly when possible, and boycotted parts of the transitional justice process. In the interviews, which I have also analysed elsewhere as acts of resistance (Jones 2017), I was particularly interested in how the actors understood these acts themselves. This was important as an approach, because it allowed me to look beyond their *de facto* exclusion as interlocutors, and to analyse their mode of claim-making and its implications for the politics of transitional justice.

What was clear from the interviews was that Ouattara did not seek coalitions of support for the transitional justice process beyond his own supporters and the transitional justice advocates and entrepreneurs among international actors.

There was limited, if any, consultation, and this led to the boycott of key mechanisms by the actors I interviewed. CACI-USA and the Abidjan-based CNRD refused to participate in the activities of the CDVR, including the diaspora platforms or in-country testimony gathering. In contrast to the civil society organizations quoted above, which saw themselves as 'doing their job', i.e., duty, my interviewees understood their duty very differently. For them it was their duty to call into question the political process by which Ouattara had become president, and which subsequently gave him the authority to implement transitional justice. According to a CACI-USA interviewee: 'there will be no reconciliation with a regime that is illegitimate, that is in violation of the constitution, and that is what we are denouncing, this is our baseline of approach ... any organization that was set up by the illegitimate president of the Ivory Coast, Mr. Alassane Ouattara, we have stayed away [from] because we don't trust the way it was put together, one, and we don't trust the mission'.[8] Following the contested election result, and intervention by both the UN and French troops, one might have assumed that Ouattara would first engage with the political opposition to create a solid foundation on which to pursue transitional justice. Instead, he moved ahead quickly and with a bias towards holding to account those who had opposed his election.

This has clouded the transitional justice process and was cited by many of my interviewees as a reason for their boycott of the process, as this quote from a representative of the FPI illustrates:

> Look at how the CDVR's make-up and mandate was taken over. This commission is not at all transparent. Instead of instilling conditions for trust, we proceed to the hearings of those they call victims. This operation is premature. The commission should have first created an environment of trust so that everyone could speak freely. Instead, this commission carries out its work alone.[9]

It has also motivated those who felt targeted by the justice process, at the same time as being excluded from shaping it, to act to reinsert themselves into the public debate. This was very difficult due to the shift which had come after the 2010/11 violence and the pursuit of the transitional justice process to hold to account the 'bad' actors of the past while the 'good' actors now in political power could build the future. As one interviewee from CACI-USA explained:

> During the time of the elections I was invited by Voice of America to give a position, and to speak on behalf of what we call quote unquote the pro-Gbagbos. And many times I had an opportunity to do that and I was interviewed also in a contra-dictors debate with other people. But right after April the eleventh all those doors were shut [...] so there was a tacit boycott of anything that would be representing the views or dissenting views.[10]

This was reinforced by another interviewee who expressed concern that the views of the political opposition and the experiences of their supporters were being eradicated from the broader public memory.[11] A representative of the FPI told me:

> You know, the other form of death that Alassane Ouattara's form of governance is bringing upon Ivorian society is much more pernicious. It is neither quantifiable, nor perceptible to the naked eye. A few years have yet to pass to be able to experience and assess its destructive consequences. For want of a precise name, we call it symbolic death, its first form was 'de-Gbagboization'. That means symbolically killing President Gbagbo in order for him to be forgotten. In order to 'de-Gbagboise' Côte d'Ivoire, everything was orchestrated to erase anything that can be a reminder of Gbagbo, to remove the traces of his official acts and forbid him from a future place in the collective imagination. In the first months of the Ouattara regime, it consisted in demolishing monuments, in repealing the decisions taken during his mandate.[12]

There are indeed accounts of a retreat from more public spaces since the discrediting of Gbagbo supporters following his defeat in 2010. The 'agoras' and 'parliaments', popular gathering spaces used by pro-Gbagbo militants to disseminate their ideas, had to become more discreet (Jones and Fatogoma 2018: 7) and hidden for fear of reprisals.[13] In the diaspora, CACI-USA was able to mobilize more visibly, being established:

> [O]n the May 13th 2012 in Washington D.C, Silver Spring in Washington D.C. United States. It was thought to be a platform or a coalition of Ivorian organizations in the United States and most of, or all of those organizations, were concerned and disapproved of the way in which the international community handled the 2010 election and the results of the 2010 election.[14]

As can be seen in this quote, the concern which evolved into a boycott of the transitional justice process began as a concern with the way in which the election itself had been handled and the extent to which non-Ivoirien actors should have been involved. The act of mobilization and insertion into the public debate about transitional justice in Côte d'Ivoire was connected, for these actors, to a historical experience of colonialism and pre-existing concerns over the influence of France:

> [I]t is also important to mention that prior to coalescing and coming together some of these groups you know already existed in 2002, when the rebellion broke out in the Ivory Coast. So if you want, with the former President being still in power they were a kind of a quote unquote informal gathering of Ivoirians. I remember for example the first rally that in the diaspora we had either at the United Nations Headquarters or in front of the White House or in front of the French Embassy right after the rebellion broke out in September of 2002. And on and on we had rallies protesting the rebellion and the other factors both national and international that

helped fuel the situation. We also had gigantic rallies for example to denounce the
involvement of the French army or the French authority.[15]

Ivoirien-based organizations also framed their activism in terms of an extension of the colonial struggle, telling me that 'Alassane Dramane Ouattara was
forced on Côte d'Ivoire by the French army'[16] or that he was 'put there by
a French coup d'état' as part of a 'menace of re-occupation'.[17] In this sense the
interviewees understood their activism as a democratic and patriotic act, with
one describing 'the combat for the liberation of Laurent Gbagbo is a combat for
the return of democracy'.[18] This democratic struggle transitioned seamlessly
from that of the independence struggle to opposition against Ouattara (Jones
2017: 44). Even before Gbagbo's defeat in 2010, he and his supporters had
portrayed the crisis 'as a "war of second independence"against an all-powerful
France and its Western and African allies, rather than as a domestic political
battle for control of the state' (Piccolino 2012: 2). This framing of 'foreigners'
as the menace of the nation, Piccolino asserts, must be seen in the context of
the Ivoirien debate over citizenship (Piccolino 2012: 6) which was discussed
earlier in this chapter.

Since the 2010 presidential election we have seen two more elections which
Ouattara has won easily, not least because of other candidates not running in
protest (Jones 2017: 48). The most recent election in 2020 saw some pockets of
violence sparked by Ouattara running for a third term as he retains his firm grip
on political power in Côte d'Ivoire.[19] However, the 2021 legislative elections
saw a return of opposition parties to the competition for political power and an
end to a boycott which had been in place since the arrest of Laurent Gbagbo
in 2011 and his transfer to The Hague.[20] The trial of Laurent Gbagbo had been
a focal point for protesters, as one commentator wrote:

> Hundreds of Gbagbo's supporters gathered outside as the hearing began, demanding
> the release of a man they say is a victim of neo-colonial meddling by former colonial
> power France. Presiding Judge Cuno Tarfusser insisted the court would not be used
> for political grandstanding during the trial. (cited in Jones and Fatogoma 2018: 7)

Pro-Gbagbo press saw the protesters as Ivoirien democrats trying to have their
voices heard:

> All in the Hague, January 28, 2016 to support President Laurent Gbagbo and the
> Minister Charles Ble Goude, the official opening of the trial of Shame by the ICC,
> and to maintain pressure so that the truth can triumph and be set free. One day:
> Thursday. Date: January 28. A City: The Hague. A cause: support for the President
> of Ivory Coast Laurent Gbagbo Koudou and Minister Charles Ble Goude battling
> imperialist institution of modern times. Ivorian patriots, Africans, friends of Africa
> and Côte d'Ivoire, the time of mobilization is here. Do not be telling the story of
> Africa that is written under your eyes. (cited in Jones and Fatogoma 2018: 7)

By contrast, coverage of the trial by pro-Ouattara press focused on the wrong-doing of Gbagbo's regime: 'ICC 2nd day of the trial of Gbagbo and Ble Goude. The shock of horror. The world discovers the ugly face of a bloody regime'[21] and 'Lawyers of the devil come in. How they tried to turn the executioners into victims. Frequent manipulation and lying this morning'.[22]

The choice of language is telling here. For those seeking to delegitimize Gbagbo and his supporters, comparison to 'the devil' is vivid. My interviewees also carefully chose their language, always referring to Ouattara as 'Mr' if using a salutation, and to Gbagbo as 'President' despite his loss in the election. As with their boycott of the transitional justice mechanisms and protests outside the ICC in The Hague, these discursive acts (Jones 2017) are powerful in sending a message not only that justice on offer is incomplete, but also that those who have been excluded and delegitimised also have a right to be justice claimants.

Another way of making justice claims came through the proposal of alternatives. During the height of the transitional justice process the FPI presented a proposal to base the transitional justice process on the 'Estates-General of the Republic' 'in order to put aside the successive electoral conflicts and lay a consensual path for the political future of Côte d'Ivoire' (Adou 2018: 23). As it was described to me, 'it is with reconciliation through sincere and inclusive political dialogue, and the estates-general of the Republic, that the FPI proposes to resolve all the disputes born of the violent power struggle'[23]. The Estates-General proposal included six different commissions: (i) the truth, justice, and damage reparations commission; (ii) the constitutional, institutional, and electoral reform commission; (iii) the rule of law, freedoms, and democracy commission; (iv) the secularism, republican ethics, social cohesion, and national conscience commission; (v) the security sector reform commission and; (vi) the territorial administration and decentralization commission.[24] According to the proposal three categories of stakeholders should take part:

(1)   Representatives of the government and institutions of the Republic, of political parties, of civil society, representatives of regions, communities and traditional authorities, religions, union and employer organizations, representatives of the diaspora, representatives of youth and women's movements, representatives of constitutional bodies.
(2)   National and international experts.
(3)   Stakeholders of the crisis i.e. leaders of the three main political parties involved in the quest for power, the presumed perpetrators of the crimes and human rights violations, victims of socio-political events, and witnesses of the events. (Adou 2018: 24)

Reflecting on such engagement, Piccolino says that: 'The challenge of dealing with the defeated enemy is a complicated one for the Ouattara government, because the pro-Gbagbo camp includes revengeful and potentially disruptive actors, but also advances legitimate political demands'(Piccolino 2018: 499). The citizenship acts of the 'deviant' Ivoiriens thus spanned a spectrum from boycott to constructive engagement with the transitional justice process. Their acts were in constant tension with their exclusion as legitimate interlocutors in the process, placing demands to be recognized as legitimate justice claimants, as *justice seekers.*

5.4   ACTS OF INCLUSION: WHO CAN SPEAK AND WHO IS HEARD

In Chapter 2 we saw how boundaries are placed around who can make claims, with the dominant norm of transitional justice imagining a vulnerable, individual victim in need of protection. Transitional justice experts and advocates work supposedly on behalf of the victim, determining the type of justice on offer which is to be (gladly) received by the victim. This is one part of the framing of the transitional justice citizen as a *justice receiver,* with the other parts elaborated in Chapters 3 and 4 on duties and virtues. Chapter 2 also highlighted the tendency for transitional justice processes to forget the struggles which put it on the agenda in the first place, its indebtedness to struggle which is eclipsed by a dominant liberal norm. This is primarily because the transitional justice dominant norm requires a vulnerable, and disempowered victim. The dominant norm also determines which crimes are to be considered as part of the transitional justice process, eclipsing historical struggle, collective struggle and wider claims to justice which go beyond that on offer (see also Chapters 2 and 6). This, in turn, excludes certain justice claimants who do not fit with the framing of the *justice receiver* and instead actively *seek* justice.

In this chapter transitional justice in Côte d'Ivoire has been described as a primarily elite-led process dominated by the political victors and designed with an international audience in mind. There was no broad consultative process; nor was there bridge building with the political opposition. The temporal and moral break with the past, which transitional justice claims to be, has helped to consolidate the power of President Ouattara and to delegitimise his opponents now associated with a 'bad' past. This is not to deny the violence and crimes committed by both 'camps' or to act as an apology for the continued insistence of the illegitimacy of the Ouattara government. President Ouattara did win the 2010 election. However, the marginalization of the justice claims made by those associated with Gbagbo pushed these actors into acts of boycott, protest, and contestation. The absence of a political compromise and bridge building has led to a situation where,

> The Ouattara regime has appeared too strong to make concessions, and opposition leaders, with little perspective to improve substantially their situation and gain state power in the short term, have been locked into a rhetoric of victimization and maximalist demands. (Piccolino 2018: 498)

While the interviewees quoted in this chapter have indeed denied the legitimacy of the Ouattara government, the complicated ethics of a transitional justice context renders simplistic notions of 'good guys' and 'bad guys' false. The 'good', 'innocent' victim of Chapter 2 does not exist, and it is not clear why those who are associated with the 'bad' past should have no say in the justice meted out or the vision of the future. Indeed, the more reasonable claims of the actors I interviewed – that the CDVR was not transparent, or that an Estates-General could offer an alternative model for justice – have been dismissed, not because of the content of the claims but because of *who* is making them. The acts analysed in this chapter illustrate that the agenda is not only about delegitimizing the government, but also about pushing to expand the boundaries placed around who can make justice claims. These are acts of *seeking* justice and demanding to be recognised as interlocutors in the justice debate, regardless of how successful such acts are. In this way we are reminded that the justice experts are not only the entrepreneurs of transitional justice but also the supposed beneficiaries of the process.

The Côte d'Ivoire case illustrates the importance of history and context in understanding these acts of justice claim-making, of the transformation of the struggle for independence into a struggle over democracy and belonging, and of continuing tensions and contradictions over who is autochthonous and who is foreign. The liberal victor's justice of President Ouattara and his government has not grappled with this longer history of struggle and has disconnected transitional justice from the ongoing debates and contestations. It has addressed the global norm but not the local context, with limited room for negotiation and the side-lining of the vanquished (Piccolino 2018: 506). This may be the price to pay for stability, but it is not clear that the long-term future of peace can be assured.

NOTES

1. This chapter builds on work that I have already published on Côte d'Ivoire and which is cited throughout the chapter, namely Jones, B. (2018) 'Seeking a "Just Justice": Discursive Strategies of Resistance to Transitional Justice in Côte d'Ivoire' in Jones, B. and Bernath, J. eds. *Resistance and Transitional Justice*. London and New York: Routledge; and Fatogoma, A.D and Jones, B. (2018)

'Reading the 'Uncivil' in Civil Society Resistance to Transitional Justice in Côte d'Ivoire', *Political Geography* 67: 135–144.
2. A political coalition that had been formed in 2002 between rebel movements.
3. Leader of the Young Patriots (*Jeunes Patriots*), a group active in opposing the presence of French troops and the UN in Côte d'Ivoire and supportive of Laurent Gbagbo and the FPI political party.
4. See https://www.icc-cpi.int/cdi (last accessed 19 November 2021).
5. President Ouattara's speech, *Fraternité matin, vendredi 26 juin* 2015. N° 15164 p 6 and 7.
6. Interview 1113.
7. Civil society representative and workshop participant, held at the Swiss Centre for Scientific Research (*Centre Suisse de Recherche Scientifique en Côte d'Ivoire*) on 5 November 2014.
8. Interview 290514.
9. Interview 120414.
10. Interview 290514.
11. Interview 260314.
12. Interview 120414.
13. See https://www.lemonde.fr/afrique/article/2020/02/06/en-cote-d-ivoire-la-ferveur-retrouvee-des-fideles-de-laurent-gbagbo_6028685_3212.html?xtor=EPR-33280896-[afrique]-20200208-[zone_edito_1_titre_1] (last accessed 26 November 2021).
14. Interview 290514.
15. Interview 290514.
16. Interview 260314.
17. Interview 131014.
18. Interview 131014.
19. See https://www.reuters.com/article/us-ivorycoast-election-idUSKBN27E2MO last accessed 26 November 2021.
20. See https://www.africanews.com/2020/12/24/gbagbo-s-party-ends-boycott-of-ivory-coast-elections/ (last accessed 26 November 2021).
21. *Le Patriote*, Saturday, 30 January 2016. No. 4741.
22. *Le Patriote*, 1 February 2016.
23. Interview 120414.
24. Interview 120414.

6. These claims should be included: acts of expansion and Tunisian Black activism

Transitional justice in Tunisia was implemented following the ousting of President Zine El Abidine Ben Ali and the end of his authoritarian rule in 2011. It came as a result of the wave of popular uprisings known as the 'Arab Spring'[1] which began in 2010 in Tunisia when 26-year-old street vendor Mohamed Bouazizi self-immolated in protest at his treatment by local officials. The protest movement and revolution that his act spawned spread throughout the country and on January 14 2011, Ben Ali fled the country. The transitional justice process which followed was a moment of opportunity. It offered the possibility of addressing past grievances, especially those related to socio-economic injustice and crime, and of paving the way for a peaceful, democratic future. As Hoddy and Gready have observed, 'its premier slogan – employment, freedom, dignity – illustrated the indivisibility of political and socio-economic concerns' (Hoddy and Gready 2020: 562). Tunisia has come to be regarded as the poster child for the Arab Spring (Salehi 2021: 6) and has been lauded for its early adoption of transitional justice measures designed to address past injustice and violence, and for managing to keep democratic advances on track (Mahmoud and Ó Súilleabháin 2020: 101). This is in no small part due to a 'vigilant and vibrant civil society' (Mahmoud and Ó Súilleabháin 2020: 102) which has blossomed after the revolution in such forms as new associations, protests, and social media campaigns.

This chapter focuses on the citizenship acts of Black Tunisian activists who, 'emboldened by the Tunisian Revolution's promises of restoring dignity and equality ... came out in the public sphere ... as "full citizens" asking for an end to what they called "silent racism" perpetuated against them for centuries' (Mzioudet 2018a: 4). I draw on desk-based research as well as interviews with Black Tunisian activists, representatives of local NGOs, and representatives of international NGOs conducted in 2021. Having faced historical discrimination and racism, Black Tunisians used the transitional justice moment to expand the justice claims being made and to actualise themselves as equal citizens. Their campaign led to the submission of a file to the Truth and Dignity Commission (*Instance Verité et Dignité*, IVD) in 2016 and later to a historical new anti-racism law in 2018. Pushing to have their experiences of injustice recognised, and demanding legal reform, constitute important acts of citizenship. Chapter 3 focused on the duties of the transitional justice citizen, and the boundaries placed around what claims can be made. In this chapter, I focus on the expansion of claims through citizenship acts which seek to use the opportunity presented by transitional justice to expand both the range of injustices which are recognised, and the content of justice on offer. This case of Black Tunisian activism reminds us that the transitional justice citizen is also able to contest these limits, and that transitional justice processes provide openings for claims which may not have been expected or planned for.

6.1   RACISM IN TUNISIA

Black people have lived in Tunisia for millennia, along with the autochthonous Amazigh population. Some observers describe the history of the black population as mostly linked to the history of the trans-Saharan slave trade in 1705–1881 (Quattrini 2020: 75), while others disagree (Mzioudet 2018a: 6). However, the national imagination which associates Black Tunisians with a geographical origin in the south of the country as well as Sub-Saharan Africa intimately links Black history with that of slavery (Pouessel 2018), problematically associating Black Tunisians with servitude. As one activist told me, the perception of Black Tunisians as slaves 'translated into the society in terms of a stratified or classified society, where in most cases black persons, black Tunisians in particular, they have the role of servant rather than full citizens' leading to them being 'invisibilized'[2] despite constituting between 10 and 15 per cent of the population (Quattrini 2020: 75). Tunisia abolished the slave trade in 1841 and slavery itself in 1846, the first Arab country to do so (King 2021). Following successful lobbying by activists (Scaglioni 2020: 201) 23 January every year is commemorated to mark the abolition of slavery (Pouessel 2018), with the official commemoration used to present Tunisia as a 'beacon of modernity' in contrast to other countries in the Arab-Muslim world (Oualdi 2021: 3).[3] However, following the end of the slave trade, Black individuals were 'engulfed in patronage and slavery-like relations which provided them with protection and legitimation of their lineage, but crystalised subaltern social relations' (Scaglioni 2020: 214). In addition to the national imagination which links Black Tunisians with slavery and servitude, there are concrete practices which mark the legacy of slavery in the country. Birth certificates provided by state institutions include 'slave' (*abid*) or 'freed person' (*atig*) and the village of El Gosba in Southeastern Tunisia has separate school buses for 'Whites' and 'Blacks' (Mzioudet 2018a: 5). Descendants of African slaves, and also of free African migrants, are kept in subordinate positions socially and economically (Oualdi 2021: 3). There are also varied types of more recent immigration which some describe as 'elitist' with Black students coming to study in private schools in Tunisia or professionals to work for the African Development Bank (Pouessel 2018). In addition, irregular migration from Sub-Saharan Africa is associated with seeking employment, with many domestic workers coming from Côte d'Ivoire (Pouessel 2018). This has led to a varied set of histories and experiences of Black Tunisians who certainly do not form one homogenous group in society.[4] Anthropologist Pouessel observes that it is difficult to identify one black identity, black culture, or common background that could delineate a Black Tunisian group.

The public collection of statistics on the numbers of Black and White Tunisians was stopped at the beginning of the twentieth century and, after independence, in 1956, the state ceased to operate a distinction between Arabs, Berbers, Blacks or Jews. This was a project of modernization (Scaglioni 2020: 193) as well as of nationalism in line with the forging of new states in the region at the time along secular lines (Dali 2015: 63). Indeed, the Bourguiba regime's construction of 'Tunisianness' in post-colonial Tunisia (1856–1987) rejected all other identities and 'Black or Amazigh identities, Jewish or Ibadi religious identities had to blend into the Sunni Arab-Muslim identity constructed by the state' (Fassatoui 2021). Bourguiba was fighting for national unification and thus tried to annihilate affiliations resistant to the unity of the nation (Pouessel 2016: 53). As Scaglioni observes: 'Counting people and measuring diversity meant creating it, and inculcating it with political meanings' (Scaglioni 2020: 193). This also meant that when post-2011 activists began to publicly tackle the issue of racism and Black rights, they had to construct a category of 'Blacks' to mobilise around (Scaglioni 2020: 193) (see section 6.3 below).

Bourguiba's model of universal education and secularization, and moves towards Arabization and nationalism were hailed as a success in the West, but 'hid the ugly reality of systematic discrimination against minorities' (Mzioudet 2018b). Any accusations of racism by the state were labelled subversive and not tolerated (Dali 2015: 62) while at the same time such oppression was hidden behind a façade of controlled pluralism (Scaglioni 2020: 195). Black Tunisians were, in fact, excluded from Bourguiba's vision of modernity, absent from the political space, development projects and his political activities and speeches (Scaglioni 2020: 197). This was partly a function of their 'othering' through the regime's framing of Black Tunisians as exogenous to the country, despite centuries of integration of former 'slaves' as well as 'free' individuals (Scaglioni 2020: 197). As one activist described it:

> Tunisia had a very unified discourse around what it means to be Tunisian, so you have this image of a Tunisian that is standard, that is Arab and Muslim, and there was invisibilization of all, of all diversity, whether it's, you know, black Tunisians or religious minorities.[5]

Under Ben Ali (1987–2011) this marginalization continued, as did the denial of racism, and he prevented the establishment of anti-racism organizations and refused legal reforms to address racism (King 2021). This conformity and obedience which were required of Black Tunisians by the state led to the silencing of their voices and fostered the denial of racism in the country (Dali 2015: 61). At the same time, Black Tunisians were marginalised in society, with a limited role in politics, education, or public life.

While discrimination against Black Tunisians has not been an official policy of the state, it is the result of state silence as well as social and cultural norms and the inaccurate association of Black Tunisians with slavery and Sub-Saharan Africa (Dali 2015: 64). Black Tunisian activists identify different forms of racism which they still suffer today: pejorative names, a limited presence in the media and politics, and a lack of support for inter-racial marriage (Pouessel 2018)[6]. The question of racism also has regional and social distinctions, with the centre and the south of the country more marginalised, and accents from these regions stigmatised. In 2017 the Association for African Students and Interns in Tunisia confirmed that almost half of the 12,000 sub-Saharan students in Tunisia had left in recent years as a result of public humiliation or verbal and physical assault (Quattrini 2020: 76). As I was told by one activist:

> So, the condition of Black people in Tunisia is still a total absence. The total absence in all areas, whether cultural, social, economic, there is still no political opinion, even public, as to how to integrate Tunisian Blacks, to ensure their living conditions, but also to know Tunisia, its constituent parts [...] Tunisia is still [...] In the political field, there is still an absence of all minorities.[7]

This situation has affected Black Tunisians both in material terms of livelihood and in terms of their place in the public national imagination.[8] It was the transitional moment which activists identify as pivotal in 'the fact that people started speaking up and were able to be visible...Whereas before, you would see, like, maybe there is one black Tunisian here and there, but that's just one percent of the population, but that's not actually the case'.[9]

Mahmoud and ÓSúilleabháin observe that 'While Tunisians have a rich sense of their shared culture and lifestyle, they have not long identified as citizens of the state'. The post-revolutionary moment was important in terms of shaping a new citizen-led social contract in general (Ibid 2020) as 'a period of "real" citizenship for all Tunisians was experimented with and aspired to after decades of authoritarian regimes, from the colonial period to the 2000s' (Oualdi 2021: 5). Black Tunisian activists were also able to capitalise on this post-revolutionary moment of citizenship, by using the transition to claim their equal citizenship and demand justice. Importantly, these claims have a longer history of anti-racism struggle including through music, public testimony, education and migration (Oualdi 2021: 6). They found a new opportunity however, following the 2011 revolution, exemplified in the establishment of new anti-racist associations and social media profiles. Two months after the revolution the Facebook page Guarantee of Citizenship without Colour Discrimination[10] was established, with the tagline 'if you do not fight for your rights and your dignity then no-one else will do it for you'.[11] This group describe their situation as one of 'second-class citizens' or 'marginalized citizens', reflecting the wider movement of Black Tunisian Activism's desire to express their sense of social subordination and aspiration for equality (Pouessel 2016: 60).

6.2　TRANSITIONAL JUSTICE IN TUNISIA

The activists I interviewed understand the transitional justice 'moment' as fundamental to the Black Tunisian cause and its struggle for the recognition of racism in the country as well as a recognition of Black Tunisians as full and equal citizens.[12] Indeed, the activists in general deliberately positioned themselves as being invested in a struggle for equality between citizens rather than a struggle for recognition of a minority (Pouessel 2016: 62). As one told me: 'What is the image of a Black Tunisian? It is always that they are in second place, not a citizen.'[13] This window of opportunity of the transition served both the early adoption of a comprehensive transitional justice process, and an increase in political engagement in general (Salehi 2021: 6). As Govantes and de Larramendi observe, the Tunisian revolution is a success story of 'outsiders', the economically marginalised and disaffected (Govantes and de Larramendi 2021: 5). The fall of Ben Ali's authoritarian regime meant that the creation of civil society associations was possible, a key motor in Black Tunisian activism, as I was told by one NGO employee.[14] According to this employee, it was civil society associations which, after 2011, brought the racial discrimination debate into the public space and began to break down and contest the previous national imaginary of 'Tunisianess' as Arab and Muslim.[15] According to another activist I interviewed, the accompanying transitional justice process itself did not directly engage with the issue of racial discrimination as a prominent issue;[16] it was instead the activism of Black Tunisians which expanded the claims to justice being made and which brought historical and contemporary racism into the discourse and actions of the transitional moment.

Following a series of more *ad hoc* measures in the immediate aftermath of the revolution, with institutionalization of the political system prioritised (Govantes and de Larramendi 2021: 8), the Tunisian government then acted quickly and in line with international treaties and global human rights norms to implement a comprehensive approach to transitional justice (Preysing 2016: 106–107). One NGO employee told me it was 'overambitious' but reflected the intensive training by organizations such as the ICTJ before and in the aftermath of the revolutions.[17] The transitional justice process in Tunisia comprised several key mechanisms mandated to address almost 60 years of repressive rule and human rights violations (Salehi 2021: 7); and, importantly transitional justice was included in Article 149 of the new constitution of 2014 – a move which one interviewee described to me as 'incredible'.[18] In April 2012 a National Dialogue on Transitional Justice was launched, comprising a country-wide consultation process and a technical commission of 12 representatives from government, civil society and the international community (Preysing 2016: 108). Reminiscent of the problems identified with consultations in Chapter 3, the Tunisian consultations

> were framed from the outset in a way that they focused on the following five pre-determined topic areas: 'the revelation of truth and preservation of memory', 'material and moral compensation and the rehabilitation of victims', 'fight against a culture of impunity dedicated to accountability and the primacy of law', 'guarantees for non-recurrence and institutional reform' and 'reconciliation'. (Preysing 2016: 111)

The types of claims to justice which could be made were determined from the start. This dialogue provided the basis of the Transitional Justice Law passed by the National Constituent Assembly in December 2013 (Salehi 2021: 7). This law defined the transitional justice approach to be taken in the country in the following way:

> In this law, Transitional Justice shall mean an integrated process of mechanisms and methods used to understand and deal with past human rights violations by revealing their truths, and holding those responsible accountable, providing reparations for the victims and restituting them in order to achieve national reconciliation, preserve and document the collective memory, guarantee the non-recurrence of such violations and transition from an authoritarian state to a democratic system which contributes to consolidating the system of human rights. (Republic of Tunisia 2013: Article 1, unofficial translation by ICTJ)

With this comprehensive vision of transitional justice, the law called for the establishment of the IVD, Specialised Chambers in the Tunisian court system (Mahmoud and Ó Súilleabháin 2020:112) and a reparations fund (Salehi 2021: 7). The law itself mentions various categories of particular attention, including the elderly, women, children, and those with special needs (Republic of Tunisia 2013: Article 4, unofficial translation by the ICTJ). It does not, however, refer to Black Tunisians as a special category or to racism as a violation suffered under the previous regime.

The IVD was created with high expectations. Tunisia is the only country to have established a national truth commission in the wake of the Arab uprisings (Human Rights Watch 2019). It was expected to address distrust and disillusionment by promoting national reconciliation (Mahmoud and Ó Súilleabháin 2020: 112), to compensate victims of state-sanctioned human rights violations and corruption which occurred between 1955 and 2011, and it was part of a series of actions designed to get Tunisia out of the political 'danger zone' and protect the transition towards democracy (Govantes and de Larramendi 2021: 12). The IVD was originally given a four-year mandate, with a potential one-year extension that was never granted in full. At its peak it had 676 staff members and consultants with a budget of 58 million Tunisian dinars. In total, over 600,000 people submitted their files to the IVD, with the commission conducting almost 50,000 closed hearings before political quarrels forced the termination of its operations at the end of 2018 (Salehi 2021: 8). The final report was handed over to the legislative and executive branches in early 2009 (Mahmoud and Ó Súilleabháin 2020: 112), made public on the commission's website on 26 March 2019, and published in the country's official journal in June 2020 (Salehi 2021: 8). In the report the commission documented abuses against political opponents and their families, named officials responsible for the crimes (including the President at the time, Beji Caid Essebsi) and called for apologies (Human Rights Watch 2019).

The work of the IVD, while lauded as having a holistic and comprehensive mandate, was beset by political animosity and institutional resistance (Mahmoud and Ó Súilleabháin 2020: 112). With regard to the former, one interviewee described it as a lack of oversight in the process of selecting commissioners for the IVD:

> [E]ven though the law provided for us to give objections, or to express objections about some candidates [...] the National Constituent Assembly received those objections, they listened [...] they invited those candidates who are objected to, they listened to them, and then they ignored the objections' meaning that the political appointments led to internal divisions 'and they couldn't even work as a team because they were [...] everyone has his own affiliation, political background, even though they looked independent'.[19]

Compounding this, the lack of institutional support for the IVD and its President Sihem Bensedrine was significant and impeded its work (Govantes and de Larramendi 2021). I was told by an employee of one Tunisian NGO that Bensedrine has been a 'very difficult person to work with' and it was this which explains the unsatisfactory relationships and lack of support.[20] Another interviewee, who had been working for an international NGO supporting the process, referred to 'mistakes [...] they had nice cars and [...] there were rumours of corruption'.[21] Whether or not this was the case, there is a sense

of the IVD's work being compromised. The final report was published multiple times on the website of the IVD, and each time it was changed, raising
suspicions.[22] Both the security and judicial authorities had blocked access to
evidence in archives and to the identities of police officials implicated in abuse
(Human Rights Watch 2019). The same authorities that obstructed the work of
the IVD are now responsible for implementing its recommendations, and we
are yet to see substantial progress in this regard (Human Rights Watch 2019).
In September 2017 the Tunisian Parliament adopted a law which removed
certain economic crimes from the commission's purview (Human Rights
Watch 2019) and exempted from prosecution some categories of Ben Ali-era
government officials accused of corruption, despite significant civil society
opposition (Mahmoud and Ó Súilleabháin 2020: 112).

The broader social and economic root causes of the revolution have also
not been tackled. Young people, who led the movements that helped spark
the revolution, have since felt excluded from many of the transitional mechanisms, leading to a generational divide and distrust of the state (Mahmoud and
Ó Súilleabháin 2020: 113). There are also high levels of unemployment and
political disaffection among the wider population, with low voter turnout and
ongoing social protests (Govantes and de Larramendi 2021). On 24 December
2018 a young journalist, Abderrazak Zorgui, set himself on fire as Bouazizi
had done in 2010, claiming in a video which he previously recorded that he
wished to keep the revolution alive – a 'reminder that social justice was at the
origin of the revolution' (Govantes and de Larramendi 2021: 22).

6.3   BLACK TUNISIANS AND THEIR ACTS OF CITIZENSHIP

> All citizens, male and female, have equal rights and duties, and are equal before
> the law without any discrimination. (Article 21 of the Tunisian Constitution cited
> in Jebli 2020)

While present-day Tunisia has an active civil society, with a large capacity
to foster debates and put forward social and political proposals, this was not
always the case. Mahmoud and Ó Súilleabháin identify an 'atrophying [of]
any sense of active citizen agency' in the decades following independence
where Tunisia's first President Habib Bourguiba focused on providing basic
needs and developing a dependency on the state. When Ben Ali took power
following a bloodless coup in 1987 the regime 'moved from serving its citizens
to serving the regime', which of course ultimately led to the dissatisfaction
motivating the revolution. After the revolution 'Tunisia became an immense
citizen-led agora' and 'for two years Tunisia became a polity of citizens
without a state' (Mahmoud and Ó Súilleabháin 2020: 103). The following

process of countrywide consultations led to a constitution which created spaces for citizen participation in the governance of their lives and was 'a truly whole of government and whole of society endeavour' (Ibid: 106). Importantly, this democratic political shift 'confronted the Tunisian government to the expression of real diversity – Berber populations and Blacks – not just a historical and fanciful one' (Pouessel 2016: 51).

In this context of a revitalization of civil society activism, beyond the kind of associationism controlled by the one-party state pre-2011 (Scaglioni 2020: 199), Black Tunisians were also more visible in their denouncement of racism and in their claims to justice, with a revitalization of their collective mobilization (Dali 2015: 62). This revitalization was primarily led by three associations – M'nemty, ADAM, and Aqaliyet – working with Black Tunisians as well as other marginalised minorities (Dali 2015: 65), and spearheaded by young, well-educated Tunisians, especially women, originating from the south of the country but often residing in the north (Dali 2015: 66). Earlier activism had been present, particularly spearheaded by certain individuals who already had public profiles. These included the musician Salah Mosbah, who spoke openly about discrimination he had encountered; and the 2004 publication in the weekly newspaper *Young Africa* (*Jeune Afrique*) of a letter by Tunisian dancer Afet Mosbah denouncing racism in Tunisia (Scaglioni 2020: 200). But the new activism post-2011 was more widespread and gained more traction. In the first instance following the revolution the priority was to put pressure on the ongoing writing of the new Tunisian constitution (Pouessel 2016: 61), but the work of the associations and the movement in general continued to grow and expand the justice claims being made. Previous activism had been met by repression and imprisonment, and when Black Tunisian activists began to '[lift] the veil on silent discrimination and on the violent racist attacks that often take place', they were also met 'by strong opposition from the mainstream population' (Mzioudet 2018a: 4). Gradually, talk shows, social media and protests began to acknowledge and discuss historical and ongoing racism, a freedom of speech made possible by the revolution (Pouessel 2018). Street activism was particularly important in this regard – for example the March for Equality against Racism on 18–21 March 2014 (Mzioudet 2018a: 4), as well as the use of social media by Black Tunisian youth to report on racism and to affirm a Black Tunisian identity (Dali 2015: 61–62, 65). Social networks in general were particularly important for connecting the activists living in the north with Black Tunisian populations in the south (Scaglioni 2020: 200).

The initial focus of activism on the racism experienced by Black Tunisians evolved into an activist movement incorporating Sub-Saharan students and refugees from Libya (Scaglioni 2020: 203). As mentioned in section 6.1 it was necessary for post-2011 activists to construct a category of 'Blackness' which could be mobilised around. This included identifying certain bodily features as 'Black', identifying a common experience of racism, and identifying 'Black' as a monolithic category which is 'fragile and marginalized' and can be targeted by empowering policies *en bloc*. Into this group category were incorporated varied experiences and classes including slave descendants, students, refugees, and elite migrant workers who had come to work for the African Development Bank (Scaglioni 2020: 206). This provided a powerful base from which to demand the full citizenship rights articulated by the activists. While some activists supported a minority rights approach to tackling racism in the country, prominent activists such as the President of M'nemty, Saadia Mosbah, stressed the importance of fighting for recognition of full citizenship rights (Scaglioni 2020: 203). However, the continued denial of racism by a significant part of the population, and accusations of sowing discord by Arab-leaning activists, led Black Tunisian activists to 'realize that their battle for full citizenship and equality would need to move from the streets to parliament' (Mzioudet 2018b). Black Tunisian activism has thus particularly focused on the legal battle for recognition of the racism suffered as well as for legal reforms (Scaglioni 2020: 217).

The IVD would accept dossiers from individuals as well as civil society organizations, and the latter had an important role in highlighting injustice and making justice claims.[23] On 14 June 2016, NGO M'nemty (meaning 'my dream', in reference to Martin Luther King) (Pouessel 2018) submitted its file to the IVD, a file which contained both a description of the racial injustice suffered by Black Tunisians and demands for redress and reform. As one international NGO employee described it to me 'there was a list of victims of discrimination, both economic and social, as well as human rights violations'.[24] The list of victims was accompanied by demands including the memorialization of historical sites that attest to slavery in Tunisia, regulations to clarify the changing of names with slave connotations, an end to the segregated buses in El Gosba, and action on segregated cemeteries for Blacks and Whites in Djerba (Mzioudet 2018a: 5). The issue of segregated buses in El Gosba had been a huge public scandal, but there had never been an official government response to the issue, claiming it was a 'one-off incident…and not a systemic practice',[25] according to a Tunisian NGO employee that I interviewed. The submission of the dossier to the IVD marked an important shift,[26] as it sought recognition of the practice, and its embeddedness in systemic racism in the country. The submission of the dossier was also pivotal in ensuring that acknowledgement of racial injustice was included in the IVD report, further pushing forward public recognition of it, and leading to later legal changes to be discussed below. Despite the absence of any specific references to racism in the transitional justice law which established the IVD (see above), the final report does include a small section on 'The Fight Against All Forms of Racial Discrimination' (Truth and Dignity Commission 2019: Section 2.3.5) which is worth quoting at length because it demonstrates the importance of the work of the Black Tunisian Activists and the submission of the dossier by M'nemty:

> TDC emphasizes the need to focus on citizenship and to enrish [sic] the choices and ways that prevail the values of tolerance, regardless of color, sex, ethnicity and religious affiliation. The State must provide protection for all citizens without discrimination.
>
> The Commission has not found complaints and lawsuits filed by racial discrimination victims, this is largely indicative of the lack of appropriate legislation, the ignorance of existence of legal remedies or the distrust of the authorities in taking effective judicial action.
>
> TDC requests therefore the State to include the provisions necessary to criminalize racial discrimination in its national legislation and to provide effective legal remedies. As well, the State must raise public awareness on the existence of such remedies with regard to racial discrimination.
>
> [...] The phenomenon of racial discrimination and violence against the different other, especially those of black or brown skin, is still rooted in the Tunisian popular imagination and in the daily discourse. There must be an intellectual revolution that breaks down what has been deeply rooted in the collective consciousness, and endeavors to get rid of racism sequels that has long been entrenched in society.
>
> [...] Therefore, TDC recommends that the State should do the following:
>
> - Tackle and fight against hate speech and ideas or theories of superiority, racial superiority or hatred.
> - Develop a legal framework that protects all victims of discrimination, in accordance with the Tunisian Constitution and the international conventions.
> - Put an end to the impunity of all discriminatory acts or speeches.
> - Include the following acts in the Penal Code as offenses punishable by law:
>   - All dissemination of ideas based on ethnic or racial superiority or hatred, by whatever means.
>   - Incitement to hatred, contempt or discrimination against members of any group on the basis of race, color, descent, national origin or ethnicity.
>   - Threats or incitement to violence against persons or groups on the above grounds.
>   - Insult, mock, defame, justify hatred, contempt or discriminate persons or groups on the above grounds, when it clearly amounts to incitement to hatred or discrimination.
>   - Participation in organizations and activities that promotes and incites to racial discrimination.
> - Take immediate and effective measures, particularly in the fields of education, culture and media, to combat prejudices leading to racial discrimination, and to promote understanding, tolerance and coexistence.
> - Curricula, textbooks and educational materials should inform and address human rights issues and seek to promote mutual respect and tolerance between citizens.

- Take educational and awareness-raising measures to eliminate stigmatization and discrimination against black people, taking into account the particular stigmatization of women.

The framing of racism as a citizenship issue is important, and the report rightly points out that Black Tunisians have been marginalised and disempowered socially, culturally, and economically. This small section in the report is an acknowledgement of the existence of racism and of the relevance of such injustices to the transitional justice process. It also reproduces some of the language used by Black Tunisian activists who have been vocal in framing racism as a question of citizenship, and in framing their struggle as one for equal citizenship. The act of submitting a dossier to the IVD used the transitional justice process to push the boundaries of what should be included as an injustice, and what claims could be rightfully made. As one activist told me:

> The fact that M'nemty submitted a file meant that there was some communication about it, so the media talked about it, so Tunisians understood that there is a community that is discriminated, and they are Tunisians, they are not foreigners. So, first of all, the fact of depositing a file was very important. The fact that the recommendations of the IVD concern the demands of this association is significant.[27]

This work, however, needed to go beyond the transitional justice process. This process, as described above, had not made racism central to the narrative of past violations and the arena of transitional justice did not offer a large enough space for these claims to justice to be made. Activists that I interviewed expressed frustration that the changes requested in the dossier have not been forthcoming, and that the situation of Black Tunisians is not a priority for the state.[28] Black Tunisian activists have had to continue their struggle outside of the formal transitional justice process by lobbying for legal reform and building on the work of submitting the dossier to the IVD.[29] As a result of this act and the momentum of the anti-racism movement a bill was drafted criminalizing racial discrimination. This was a significant moment for Black Tunisian activists who had been lobbying for such a law. Activists had identified a weakness in the formulation of the Tunisian Constitution which, in Article 21, declared the equal status of all citizens. The vague formulation referring to all citizens did not go far enough, in their view, towards either outlawing racism or offering a legal basis for Black Tunisians to defend themselves against racism (Dali 2015: 72). A coalition of M'nemty, associations of Sub-Saharan African students, the OHCHR, and the only Black MP, Jamila Debbech-Ksiksi, worked together to push forward the drafting and presentation of the bill.[30] The new bill was lodged with parliament in July 2016 and, on 26 December, at the National Conference against Racial Discrimination,

Prime Minister Youssef Chahed announced that the bill would be examined by parliament (Mzioudet 2018a: 5).

On 6 June the parliament approved the bill and, on 9 October 2018, Organic Law 50–2018 was adopted – the first of its kind in North Africa and the Arab world (Fassatoui 2021). Prime Minister Youssef Chahed referred to this symbolic moment as when he 'decided to put an end to racist discrimination in Tunisia: the revolutionary, free and dignified Tunisia' (Scaglioni 2020: 211). The law defines racial discrimination according to the International Convention on the Elimination of All Forms of Racial Discrimination; stipulates penalties for those found guilty of racial discrimination; obliges the Tunisian state to undertake various public programmes to raise awareness and educate against all forms of racial discrimination; and allows victims to come forward for reparations (Fassatoui 2021). This was a momentous victory for Black Tunisian activism with 'the comprehensiveness of Law 50 as an impressive admission by the state that anti-Black racism exists in Tunisia and needs to be addressed in state and society' (King 2021). A stark reminder of the importance of the law came shortly afterwards, when the President of the Association of Ivorians in Tunisia was stabbed to death in a suburb of Tunis on 23 of December 2018 (Scaglioni 2020: 211). Falikou Coulibaly was an activist who regularly spoke out against racism in Tunisia, and his murder prompted a mass mobilization of Ivoirians living in Tunisia who marched in the capital protesting violence against Sub-Saharan Africans and the lack of response from the government (Observer and 24 2018).

Aside from the huge achievement of establishing a law against racism, there have been historically important wins for justice connected to Organic Law 50–2018. For example, on 14 October 2020 the lower court in Medenine authorised Hamadan Dali and his son Karim to remove the part of their family name, 'atig', meaning 'freed person' (as discussed in section 6.1) (Fassatoui 2021). Cited in an Arab Reform Initiative online article Hamadan Dali himself said: 'The designation "Atig" is the symbol of an era of oppression and obscuratism for every black person who still carries this shame in their name. I don't want to look back at my past of pain and racism' (King 2021). This act was possible through the support of the NGO M'nemty as well as Minority Rights and using Organic Law 50–2018, and opens the way for other similar proceedings (King 2021). A Minority Rights activist explained to me that they had tried to bring the case prior to the 2018 law but there was a 'lack of competence' and no designated government committee which could deal with the case. They tried again after 2018 when the new law was passed and were this time successful.[31]

It is noteworthy that Minority Rights has also undertaken the training of 150 lawyers on Organic Law 50–2018, as the government has been unwilling to do the necessary training to ensure that the new legal framework is understood and properly implemented. As one activist lamented:

> Until now, the situation for Black Tunisians has not changed, even after the law against racial discrimination. The Tunisian state must take responsibility for training journalists, the media, judges, judicial police, etc. There is no initiative by the state. Frankly, it is a showcase law, designed to demonstrate to the international community that Tunisia is more open, can guarantee human rights, can guarantee justice and equality, but in reality Black Tunisians are still…. frankly, in misery.[32]

There is a strong need and demand for concrete changes to follow after the passing of Organic Law 50–2018. Minority Rights has also been approached by other Black Tunisians who wish to bring a case to have 'atig' removed from their names on official documents. These are all positive developments, but as a representative of Minority Rights told me they are hoping to develop 'a more strategic approach to the issue' and to lobby for the establishment of a government committee responsible for such cases brought under the law. These more structural changes, which are necessary to translate individual legal wins into more widespread transformations, are currently limited by the current political context. The Constitutional Court still has not been created and the Ministry of Human Rights has been dissolved with all human rights issues now going directly to the presidency of the Government.[33] In addition, many victims of racial discrimination lack the financial means to start costly legal proceedings or are hamstrung by the socially unacceptable and unrealistic character of filing complaints against neighbours or family members (King 2021). There are no official statistics on the number of racist attacks; indeed, many victims do not come forward or when they do, do not describe the crimes as racist (Blaise 2018). Some observers see racism as on the rise in Tunisia (Fassatoui 2021), saying:

> [T]here are still intolerable acts of discrimination in the south of the country with buses and cemeteries for Blacks in several cities, and entire villages created to isolate black citizens. The fact is that Blacks are not considered a full and equal component of Tunisian history and culture. (Zied Rouine cited in King 2021)

As a high-profile example, Tunisia's only female Black parliament member, Jamila Debbech-Ksiksi, has been subject to an online racist campaign (Jebli 2020). The unravelling of 400 years of prejudice is not easy, especially given the cultural, political and structural forms it takes in the face of high levels of denial (Blaise 2018). As Yamina Thaber, president of the Tunisian Association for the Support of Minorities, is quoted as saying in 2018: 'In recent years, we have mainly fought against denial, to make the authorities recognise that racism does exist in Tunisia. Now the real fight for rights begins!'[34]

6.4   THE EXPANSION OF CLAIMS: WHERE HISTORICAL INJUSTICE MEETS CONTEMPORARY JUSTICE

Scaglioni has written that: 'Undeniably, the biggest achievement of black rights associations is bringing to the fore the issue of racism' (Scaglioni 2020: 212). Black Tunisians focused their activism on rendering visible historical racism, its institutionalization in Tunisian politics, economy and culture, and its widespread denial by the wider Tunisian population (Mzioudet 2018a: 5). Their activism was an explicit attempt to bring historical injustice into the frame of contemporary transitional justice processes. Their acts of citizenship also demonstrate that they are justice *seekers* and not only justice *receivers*. This stands in contrast to the analysis presented in Chapter 3 where the transitional justice citizen is rendered passive, even through programmes of consultation and outreach, by the limits which are placed on 'legitimate' claims. The case of Black Tunisian activism reminds us that the transitional justice citizen is also able to contest these limits, and that transitional justice processes provide openings for claims which may not have been expected or planned for. As Mzioudet describes:

> By appealing to transitional justice, in particular through the IVD, the movement has waged a legal battle for an end to systemic discrimination against Blacks, exercising judicial pressure on policy makers to overcome the culture of denial of racism in Tunisia. (Mzioudet 2018a: 6)

Indeed, we might think of transitional justice as an arena where different actors try to make claims. The key question is whether the arena is helpful.[35] As we have seen in this chapter, the transitional moment presented an opportunity for Black Tunisian activists to connect historical injustices with contemporary claims to justice and to bring the issue of racism to the fore. However, this was not a focus of the transitional justice process and, despite the inclusion of a small section on racism in the final report of the IVD, my interviews suggest that justice for historical racism was not a focus of the justice process, nor was knowledge of the dossier submitted by activists to the IVD widespread. As one representative of an international organization which was significantly involved in the process told me: 'I've never heard of these Black Tunisian Activists... This is the first time I'm hearing of this'.[36] Another interviewee who works for an international NGO focused on discrimination of different kinds admitted: 'I mean I have to be honest I didn't know that there were demands around racial discrimination until quite recently ... I never discussed it with the President of M'nemty. And we worked, like, very closely together since 2016, so I'm not really sure what the dynamics behind that were.[37] Another working for a different NGO said that racial injustice was not included in transitional justice because 'the focus was on the classical types of victims' and 'the issues that we all knew'.[38] This is a concerning lack of awareness among key organizations working with and shaping the transitional justice process. In the last quote we can see how such a blind spot may result from a tendency for transitional justice advocates and experts to acknowledge as injustices those which are recognizable in the context of previous work and the international norm of transitional justice. This chapter has certainly shone a light on, and perhaps amplified, the acts of Black Tunisians in expanding justice claims. As I recognise, Black Tunisians are not one homogenous group, and the activism was spearheaded by a set of activists mainly located in the north of the country. However, regardless of the size of the activist movement, their acts are important and illuminating, not least because of their successful lobbying for Organic Law 50–2018. In addition, they demonstrate that there are multiple pathways for the transitional justice citizen and their struggle. These pathways may be included within a transitional justice process but also and importantly exist outside of it, as the transitional justice citizen finds alternatives for making claims and seeking justice.

In Chapter 3, the transitional justice citizen as a duties bearer was elaborated. Transitional justice processes tend to frame participation and consultation as about generating 'buy-in' to the justice on offer, with the expectation that it will be accepted by the population at large. The justice offer is also clearly demarcated by a boundary around what claims to justice can be made. In the Tunisian case we see this clearly. Racism as a historical and ongoing injustice was not on the transitional justice agenda until the Black activists themselves acted to expand what claims could be made. The submission of a dossier to the IVD, and the lobbying for an anti-racism law, are all acts which make clear that racial justice should be included in the transitional justice offer. The activists moved between formal participation, submitting a dossier and informal awareness raising and activism to make their case for the expansion of claims. The impact of this work is still ongoing of course. Since the revolution there has been a strong movement by the citizenry in general to take a lead in shaping the new social contract and making demands from the state (Mahmoud and Ó Súilleabháin 2020). However, the economic crisis and the fundamental question of redistribution of resources have not been addressed in post-revolutionary Tunisia (Hoddy and Gready 2020, Oualdi 2021: 12). Many Black communities in the south of the country prioritise employment over the legal fight of the Black activists (Scaglioni 2020: 218) and this is a challenge for the future. But what can be said about this case is that the acts of citizenship by Black Tunisians concretely expanded the claims to justice being made and beyond that which had been on offer through the transitional justice process as envisaged by the elite.

NOTES

1. This is a contested term – see, for example, https://blogs.lse.ac.uk/mec/2021/01/20/talkin-bout-a-revolution-four-reasons-why-the-term-arab-spring-is-still-problematic/ (last accessed 12 July 2022).
2. Interview TL01.
3. This 'beacon of modernity' narrative goes beyond the issue of slavery to include the reputation of Tunisia as progressive in terms of women's rights. See, for example, this commentary: https://carnegieendowment.org/2018/11/30/what-tunisia-can-teach-united-states-about-women-s-equality-pub-77850 (last accessed 17 February 2022).
4. Interview TA02.
5. Interview TL01.
6. Interview TA02.
7. Interview TA02.
8. Interview TA02.
9. Interview TL01.
10. *Assurance de la citoyenneté sans discrimination de couleur.* Translation in the source cited.
11. *Si tu ne luttes pas pour tes droits et ta dignité peronne le fera à ta place.* Translation by the author.
12. Interview TL01.
13. Interview TA02.
14. Interview TL01.
15. Interview TL01.
16. Interview TA02.
17. Interview TL06.
18. InterviewTL07.
19. Interview TL06.
20. Interview TI06.
21. Interview TL07.
22. Interview TL06.
23. Interview TI03/4.
24. Interview TI03/4.
25. Interview TL01.
26. Interview TI03/4.
27. Interview TI 03/4.
28. Interview TA02.
29. Interview TI 03/4.
30. Interview TL01.
31. Interview TL01.
32. Interview TA02.
33. Interview TL01.
34. Original in French, translated by the author.
35. Thanks go to Mariam Salehi for this point made during a discussion we were having about transitional justice in Tunisia.
36. Interview TI07.
37. Interview TL01.
38. Interview TL06.

7.   We can make claims in this way: acts of disruption and education reform in Brčko District, Bosnia-Herzegovina[1]

The 1992–1995 Bosnian war was part of the broader disintegration of the Socialist Federal Republic of Yugoslavia (SFRY). Bosnia-Herzegovina was the most ethnically mixed state of the SFRY, but throughout pre-war Yugoslavia there was an 'importance of mixing as a form of public sociality, nationhood, and popular politics' (Hromadzic 2012: 32), including through inter-communal living and mixed marriages (Weine 1999: 18–19). Wary of overly romanticising or simplifying mixing between ethno-national groups (Hromadzic 2012), it is important to note that modes of living were destroyed in the 1992–1995 violence. During the war there were high levels of violence between the three main ethno-national groups – Bosniaks, Bosnian-Croats, and Bosnian-Serbs – and it is estimated that 1.2 million Bosnians became refugees, 1.1 million became internally displaced people (Bieber 2006: 29) and 100,000 were killed.[2] On 1 November 1995, the Dayton Peace Agreement was signed by Alija Izetbegović (then President of the Republic of Bosnia-Herzegovina), Slobodan Milošević (then President of the Federal Republic of Yugoslavia), and Franjo Tuđjman (then President of Croatia). This set the stage for the tripartite power sharing that defines post-Dayton Bosnia, and which has been blamed by the International Crisis Group for creating a 'straitjacket' which has been hampering the reconstruction and reconciliation process ever since (ICG 2007: 9).

Post-Dayton Bosnia-Herzegovina is a consociational democracy, which means that it recognises group differences and group rights in addition to individual rights (Smooha 2002: 424),[3] alongside elite cooperation at the centre with elections and proportional representation to ensure protection of group interests (Sisk 1996). Following this model, Bosnia-Herzegovina has a two-entity state with the Federation of Muslims and Croats (FBiH)[4] occupying 51 per cent of the territory, the Serb Republic (SR)[5] occupying 49 per cent of the territory (Belloni 2005: 164), and a third autonomous district of Brčko District owned by both entities in condominium (Becker 2017: 127). Mujkić has referred to this arrangement as the 'ethnopolis', meaning 'a political context where a person's citizenship is predetermined by her or his kinship, or her or his belonging to this or that group of mutual blood origin' (Mukic 2008a: 20). Indeed, the 'unique way in which Bosnia's Constitution has been realised allows ethnicity to become the most salient identification marker in political life … The participation of the individual citizen in the political community depends on their kinship to an ethnic status' (Piersma 2019: 937).

In contrast, in Brčko District in the northeast of Bosnia-Herzegovina there was a separate set of circumstances which allowed for a different post-war trajectory and multi-ethnic reform to be pursued. Return, integration, and institutional reform were the pillars of the transitional process in this third political entity, promising justice through a return to a multi-ethnic society and protection of each ethnic group. It is particularly interesting to look more closely at this post-war 'success story' in Bosnia-Herzegovina, where the political blockages and ethno-national wrangling that beset the rest of the country are widely believed to have been avoided. As the chapter will outline, there is a strong narrative of a good, multi-ethnic citizen of Brčko District, and high levels of expectations placed on the residents of Brčko District to perform their role in supporting and making possible multi-ethnic reintegration. This reflects the discussion in Chapters 2 and 3 around duties and virtues. The imagined Brčko District citizen is expected to play their role by accepting the justice on offer and by channelling justice claims through the formal transitional justice process. However, in the case discussed in this chapter we see a more disruptive and informal way of making justice claims, seeking not only to expand the justice on offer but also, importantly, to demonstrate that justice claims can be made outside of the formal transitional justice process.

When multi-ethnic schooling was reintroduced in Brčko District, as part of the transitional reforms aimed at reintegration and reconciliation, there were student protests which led to the closure of secondary schools for one month. This act of protest by the student body used the opportunity presented by the implementation of integrated schooling to articulate varied concerns with the mode of reconciliation and justice which had been designed 'from above'. While the expectation of the policy designers and advocates was clearly that the student body would accept the changes and participate willingly in the multi-ethnic vision for Brčko District, the protests claimed a more disruptive space. As discussed in the introduction to this book, such disruption may well be important for democracy, and even part of what should be seen as a normal politics during periods of transitional justice, but it stands in tension with the impulse to order in transitional justice and the framings of the transitional justice citizen. In Chapter 4 we explored the virtues associated with the imagined transitional justice citizen and the connected narratives of the 'good' and 'bad' victim. This framing of the ideal transitional justice citizen de-legitimizes claim-making acts which do not sit easily with the impulse to order. In this chapter we thus focus on the expansion of different ways to make justice claims, and how the justice seeker uses disruptive acts to do so.

7.1 THE SPECIAL CASE OF BRČKO DISTRICT: THE MAKING OF THE MULTI-ETHNIC CITIZEN

The history of ethno-national relations in Bosnia-Herzegovina has been conceptualised as ancient hatreds (Kaplan 2014), as an almost utopian multicultural living (Carla 2005: 284), and as the result of manipulation by the fanaticism of nationalists (Donia and Fine Jr 1994: 8). Others have suggested a less polarised position

> [t]hat hatred and rivalries existed in Bosnia's past is certainly true; those writers that have reacted...by portraying Bosnia as a wonderland of permanent inter-religious harmony have over-reacted. But a closer inspection of Bosnia's history will show that the animosities which did exist were not absolute or unchanging. Nor were they the inevitable consequences of the mixing together of different religious communities...The main basis of hostility was not ethnic or religious but economic: the resentment felt by the members of a mainly (but not exclusively) Christian peasantry towards their Muslim landowners...These animosities were not permanently built into the psyches of the people who lived in Bosnia; they were products of history, and could change as history developed. (Malcolm 1994: xxi)

Based on ethnographic fieldwork in Bosnia-Herzegovina, Bringa concurs with this general position: '[T]here was both co-existence and conflict, tolerance and prejudice, suspicion and friendship' (Bringa 1995). Negotiating the spectrum of approaches which range from the primacy of ethnicity to its relative unimportance to its political invention, authors have discussed how and in what ways ethnicity is relevant. It has been highlighted how memories of violence between different ethnic groups throughout time have been absorbed, commemorated, contested, and reproduced by the different narratives of each group in their everyday lives (Miller 2006), by academics (Dzaja 2005), and by politicians (Stubbs 1999: 4–7). The relative importance placed on ethnicity differs, but key authors caution against a simplistic overemphasis. *The New Bosnian Mosaic: Identities, Memory and Moral Claims in Post-War Society* (Bougarel, Helms et al. 2007a) is a collection of mainly ethnographic work which challenges the bias towards ethnicity as explanatory in accounts of Bosnia-Herzegovina history, violence, and peace:

> [T]he Bosnian 'mosaic' has always been and continues to be multi-layered: while there are still some forms of interethnic coexistence in Bosnia, the war has not only affected ethno-national identifications but also a large array of other categories such as urbanity and rurality, gender, gentrification, class and occupation...It is not enough to presume that ethnic nationalism informs every aspect of Bosnian political

and social life. Nor can memories and narratives of the war be reduced to Serb, Croat and Bosniac 'versions', as if these were uniform and uncontested. (Bougarel, Helms et al. 2007b: 2 and 19)

Other scholars support such analysis, for example Wilmer states: 'one of the problems with defining the Yugoslav war in purely terms of "ethnic conflict" is that it turns individual people into "members" of a group that is then portrayed and discussed in monolithic, universalistic terms (Wilmer 1997: 13).'

There is a significant body of similar work which suggests that the relationships between people have been conditioned throughout history by different identities and experiences, sometimes ethnic, but not always. Vetlesen suggests that the important point in the case of the 1992–1995 war is that there was a mismatch between identities as constructed by the acts of violence, that is to say one criterion of ethnic group allegiance, and the reality of identities as lived by the majority of Bosnians, that is to say hybrid (Vetlesen 2005: 156–157). The 1992–1995 war has been described as an 'explosion of new and old nationalisms' (Dzaja 2005: 127) following a re-definition of the basis of citizenship in the 1980s and 1990s when:

> [t]he socialist conception of the state as providing material protection was replaced with the concept of the nation as the protector and refuge for members of a single national community, to the exclusion of others – first in terms of economic rights and privileges, then in cultural expression, and finally in purely physical terms of survival. (Woodward 1999: 156)

In the case of Bosnia-Herzegovina, where the territory was inhabited by a mix of peoples, the positionality of one individual in relation to another, when re-defined in terms of ethnic group allegiance, became key to ensuring or removing the enabling condition of citizenship. According to Oommen, the struggle for dominance by any of the collectivities within Bosnia-Herzegovina during the 1992-1995 war automatically delegitimised the other collectivities vis-à-vis the state and attendant territory, instantly creating them as outsiders (Oommen 1997: 81).

We can see the effects of this on territory and political representation in the post-Dayton arrangements. As described above, post-Dayton Bosnia-Herzegovina is split into two entities. Most municipalities within these two entities are dominated by one ethnic community, threatening to undermine the formal legal status of Bosniaks, Bosnian-Croats and Bosnian-Serbs as equal 'constituent people' (Bieber 2005: 421). One exception to this is the autonomous district of Brčko situated in the Posavina region of northeast Bosnia-Herzegovina close to the borders with Croatia and Serbia. After being ethnically cleansed of Bosniaks by Bosnian-Serbs, this territory is now shared between the two groups alongside a smaller Bosnian-Croat population, and is seen by the international community as a success story of intervention and a victory for moderate politics (ICG 2003, Bieber 2005: 427). As the High Representative[6] Paddy Ashdown declared in 2003:

> This city, which was once well-known as a 'black hole', is steadily becoming a model for the whole of BiH. When the rest of the country accomplishes what has been accomplished here, BiH will be a much more developed country. (cited in ICG 2003: 1)

In 1999 an international arbitration tribunal granted Brčko District autonomous status with high levels of international control (Bieber 2005: 426) amounting to a fully fledged international trusteeship (ICG 2003: 9). The creation of the district was due in part to its strategic position between the FBiH and SR which meant it was difficult to agree which entity could lay claim to the territory, and in part to allow the large numbers of displaced Bosniaks and Bosnian-Croats to return to their pre-war homes (ICG 2003: 7). Rates of return did indeed exceed rates in other parts of the country (Heimerl 2005: 384) with an above-average economic recovery rate (Bieber 2005: 430–431). Mujkić, in work which continues the development of his ethnopolis thesis, describes Brčko District as a potential multi-ethnic oasis capable of driving a stake through the heart of the ethnopolitical vampire of Bosnia (Mukic 2008b). This echoes comments from the former High Representative Paddy Ashdown who said, 'The message from Brčko should be loud and clear – co-operation and reintegration pay off' (cited in Bieber 2006: 135).

Institutional reform has been key to distinguishing Brčko District as the 'vampire's stake'. A multi-ethnic government was established under the auspices of the Brčko District Supervisor Robert William Farrand on 8 March 2000 (Government 2006: 14). The District Supervisor is a position reserved for a member of the international community, until now always an American.[7] Until 2004 the members of the District Assembly were appointed by the District Supervisor, and Assembly members now representing the main political parties in Bosnia-Herzegovina (Bieber 2006: 136). There is no formal power-sharing arrangement as there is for the rest of the country, and there is no reference to ethnicity in the structure of the assembly or administration, except a proviso that it shall reflect the composition of the population (Bieber 2006: 137). As claimed in a speech by the then District Supervisor:

> Since its establishment, Brčko District has gone from being a symbol of social and physical devastation to one of progress and interethnic cooperation, as well as an incubator for reforms in the transition from a communist command economy to a democratic market economy. Today, Brčko is a prosperous, multi-ethnic community ... Brčko District has become a post-conflict success story studied by many, envied by some, and copied unfortunately by none. That could be because its

success has depended first and foremost on the efforts and willingness of the people of Brčko, who decided to live together, and in peace.[8]

This is a clear statement of the importance of the 'willingness' of Brčko District citizens to play the role expected of them, placing the responsibility on *their* shoulders for the success of the return of internally displaced persons, reintegration of the different ethnic groups, and reconciliation. The citizen who has a place in Brčko District is someone who has decided to live with other ethnicities in peace. Implicit in this is a citizen who is also willing to accept the terms of the transition and the justice on offer through the multi-ethnic reform. One key area in which multi-ethnic reform was implemented is that of education. In the following section of the chapter, I outline the education reform logic and implementation before moving on, in section 7.3, to the citizenship acts of students who decided to protest the multi-ethnic integration of their secondary schools.

7.2 EDUCATION REFORM IN BRČKO DISTRICT

The special status of Brčko District and high levels of funding for the territory opened up possibilities for reforms not feasible elsewhere in Bosnia-Herzegovina. Education reform in Brčko District was treated as a method by which to solve the problem of segregated education that had emerged during the war, and to promote this as a model for the rest of the country. Published and official accounts of the reform process thus tend to present it as a linear progression from the problematic state of less modern and segregated education towards an end point depicted as modern, integrated, and successful. Any problems encountered on the way, such as the student protests which are the focus of this chapter, are side stories in the more accepted version of events.

The influence of the prior education system of the SFRY is important to note. Education at this time was high quality and broad based (Perry 2003: 19), with good levels of access to pre-school, primary and secondary education (Fischer 2006a: 298). However, it was also these same socialist values that led to a system encouraging conformity and dedication to the political regime (Perry 2003: 20). Education during this period was designed to engineer a socialist youth with a degree of shared Yugoslav identity and to emphasise pride in the country's ability to incorporate diverse linguistic and cultural groups into a multi-coloured Yugoslav nation (Hromadzic 2008: 544). This led to a style of education which prioritised facts and collective solidarity over analytical skills, and which entrenched political interference and outdated organizational and pedagogical structures (Fischer 2006a: 298-300). For Stabbak, '[m]oving from "socialist" education (with the interests of the state as its underpinning ideology) to "ethnic-nationalist" education (with the interests of an ethno-national group as its underpinning ideology) has been a conceptually simple matter' (Stabback 2004: 49). The socialist self-management system controlled individual decision making within a framework of centralised control, and education as an instrument for political control was established. This has continued in the post-war era as nationalist politicians have sought to manipulate curricula as part of a struggle for political and territorial control.

According to Hromadžić, the post-war education system in Bosnia-Herzegovina reflects the consequences of the destruction of the war, the paradoxes of the Dayton Peace Accords, and the weaknesses of the Bosnian Constitution (Hromadzic 2008: 544). After 1995, and the establishment of consociational democracy with the two-entity and autonomous district structure, education in Bosnia-Herzegovina has been decentralised with 13 education policy-making authorities: the government of the SR; the government of the FBiH; the ten cantons within the FBiH; and Brčko District. This has made the system difficult to coordinate at the state level (Smith and Vaux 2002: 24) and vulnerable to ethno-national capture by leaders who in many cases see education as a means of promoting ideologies linked to politico-cultural identities (Stabback 2004: 44). This can be seen in the three separate national curricula which the decentralised system maintains: the Bosniak National Plan and Programme, the Croatian National Plan and Programme, and the Serbian National Plan and Programme (Becker 2017: 127). The manipulation of education as a political tool includes among other methods the design of curricula to reflect nationalist myth and propaganda, the encouragement of the sole use of either the Latin or Cyrillic script,[9] and the support of cultural activities associated with a particular ethnic identity. While education has become a sphere in which nationalist forces oppose reform to ensure the protection and transfer of certain cultural and religious principles across generations, it has also been seen by international players as one of the layers of reform underpinning the transition towards peace and democracy. A Peace Implementation Council[10] meeting in Bonn in December 1997 called on:

> the competent authorities to work together to ensure that all persons are educated according to their needs and in a manner which also contributes to tolerance and stability within a multi-ethnic Bosnia-Herzegovina and to develop without delay an education programme consistent with these principles. (cited in Perry 2003: 47)

Clearly education reform is seen by such actors as vital for ensuring peace and stability in Bosnia-Herzegovina, by educating citizens with values that can support a multi-ethnic country. This is a clear example of the framing of citizenship discussed in Chapter 4 where virtues associated with the transitional justice citizen are those which meet the criteria and needs of transition. Indeed, the segregation of classrooms, mono-ethnic schools, and parallel schools treat students as part of an ethnic group and thus stand in contrast to concepts of democratic citizenship (Fischer 2006a: 300). The assumption of integrated schooling is that increased contact time between students from different groups will promote values of tolerance, respect for diversity, and coexistence (Perry 2003: 37, Hughes 2007: 421, Becker 2017). Despite questions being raised about such assumptions in the literature on education and reconciliation (Smith and Vaux 2002: 19), in Brčko District integrated education was seen as key for educating tolerant multi-ethnic citizens, who in turn could promote and sustain the transition and lend credence to the success story of the District. The physical mixing of students from different ethnic groups in the same classes was supported by a new subject on democracy and human rights (Jones 2012: 138).

This is multi-ethnicity by design, where students are taught to be multi-ethnic in their outlook and to see themselves as joint citizens within a multi-ethnic society. By delegitimizing ethno-national affiliation and emphasizing demo-cratic norms, students are encouraged to share a (liberal democratic) vision of political and moral community which requires mixing between ethnonational groups and the public acceptance of an overarching civic identity (Jones 2012: 138). It also suggests that the only relevant cleavages between the popula-tion are those based on ethno-national identity, and that the justice issues of relevance in the district are those associated with relationships between the different ethno-national groups.

Prior to the establishment of the special legal status for Brčko District in 1999, the territory had been split into three parts during the war, both in terms of geography and in terms of schooling. In the territory controlled by the Bosniaks the syllabus of the Tuzla canton was used; in the territory controlled by Bosnian-Croats the syllabus of the Posavina canton was used; and in the territory controlled by Bosnian-Serbs the SR syllabus was used (OSCE 2007: 6). Due to displacement dynamics during the war the Bosniak and Bosnian-Croat populations were mainly living in the rural areas of the District and the Bosnian-Serb population were mainly in the town, each being served by their own school system. The establishment of Brčko District in 1999, however, changed the political and financial context, making reform possible. Segregated education became a key issue in improving relationships between the three main ethno-national groups and promoting development in the District, as well as promoting a multi-ethnic citizen consistent with the values of a multi-ethnic district. Brčko District now has an integrated education system with students and teachers sharing and attending all classes together, except that of mother-tongue language classes (Becker 2017: 129). Estimates are that students in Brčko District spend less than 25 to 30 per cent of their lesson time separated by nationality, which contrasts significantly with the rest of the country, leading to Brčko District education reform being seen as a model for potential wider reform (Clark 2010: 354–355). However, the changes had to be forced on the population by the District Supervisor (Becker 2017: 129) and it was at this moment that the students at the schools began to protest. While these protests passed and the schools were eventually integrated, analysing them as an act of citizenship is helpful for drawing out the tensions inherent in processes intended to mould certain values and virtues of the transitional justice citizen. It demonstrates the importance of acts of disruption which counter any simplified notion of the 'good' transitional justice citizen. It is also another empirical example of the way in which the acts of the transitional justice citizen can seek to expand the scope of justice, or indeed what counts as justice, beyond that which is included in the transitional justice process.

7.3   STUDENT PROTESTERS AND THEIR ACTS OF CITIZENSHIP

Education offers the chance to shape minds, hearts and behaviours of succeeding generations. Educational responses [to intergroup conflict] express this hope: if we can educate young people to respect others, to understand the costs of group hatreds, to avoid stereotypes, to develop tools for resolving disputes, to choose to stand up to demagogues, and to be peacemakers, we might hope to prevent future violence. (Minow 2003: 214)

[...] the Supervisor will integrate the District's educational system, harmonize curricula within the District, and ensure the removal of teaching material which the Supervisor considers to be inconsistent with the objective of creating a democratic, multi-ethnic society within the District.[11]

At the time when Brčko District was established the first thing that was multi-ethnic was the government and we had a multi-ethnic assembly, but the first thing that was of major importance for the people was the education system. (Interview 120308)

In July 1999 the Brčko District Supervisor established an education department within his office, intent on pursuing education reform (Perry 2003). However, the new education law was unable to gain a majority in the District Assembly due to opposition from the Serb Democratic Party (*Srpska Demokratska Stranka*, SDS)[12] and the Serb Orthodox Church (ICG 2003). It only became law after intervention from the District Supervisor, who used his powers to impose the Single Law on Education and Harmonized Curriculum on 5 July 2001 (Perry 2003: 78). This law provided a strict framework for integrated schooling including specific provisions for language[13] (OSCE 2007: 7); increased contact time between students (Perry 2003: 80) including in some national subject lessons (OSCE 2007: 15); and a new subject lesson of Democracy and Human Rights (OSCE 2007: 16).

The ethno-national integration of the high school in Brčko District is particularly interesting. After the Final Award in 1999 returnee Bosniaks and Bosnian-Croats joined those who had been forcibly displaced into the rural parts of the District while Brčko Town was mostly inhabited by Bosnian-Serb stayee residents and newcomers. Parallel education systems developed which served the different populations. In 2000/2001 the mainly Bosniak school system operating in the rural parts of the District started to be integrated with the mainly Bosnian-Serb school system operating in Brčko Town. This happened in two distinct phases for secondary schools. In the first phase there was a two-shift system whereby the pupils from the two different school systems would use the same school buildings in Brčko Town but at different times. Students were brought by bus into the town according to a carefully regimented schedule so that there was a limited and controlled time during which the two student bodies were able to interact. The aim was to enable contact between the different ethnic groups of students and to normalise the use of the same school space in the afternoon or the morning.[14] The second phase of integration occurred through the ethnic mixing of classes and teaching staff, except in the national subjects such as language, on a year-by-year basis until all years were mixed. At the time of the implementation of the two-shift system in 2000, protests were held by students which lasted for four days. This was followed by a previously unplanned period of approximately one month when the schools were closed before the second phase of integration began.

On the first day of the protests, Bosniak students who had been displaced from Brčko Town during the war gathered in a group in the centre of town and walked through the main pedestrian area, chanting and carrying banners. On the following day Bosnian-Serb students abandoned their classes and left their schools, marched towards each other from two different schools at opposite sides of town, and met in the centre. Once at the centre they staged a demonstration with chanting and banners. This was repeated on two other days. There was also some destruction of property, and the police intervened in the afternoon of the last day to break up the group of Bosnian-Serb protesters. Following these four days of protest the high schools were closed by the Office of the High Representative (OHR) for approximately one month before fully integrated classrooms were introduced incrementally on a year-by-year basis. There is limited published or available material which mentions these protests, and the official accounts take a particular view which contrasts with students' own accounts of the events. In an Organization for Security and Cooperation

in Europe (OSCE) report on education reform in Brčko District the protests are
mentioned in relation to legal reform and the actions of the supervisor:

> Although this [Final Award] gave the Supervisor a clear and robust mandate to
> reform education in the District, it was not until after student riots in 2000 that
> multi-ethnic or 'integrated' education became a more immediate concern. In these
> riots secondary school students had protested against the introduction of such
> multi-ethnic schooling. It was widely suspected that politicians had orchestrated this
> protest and that it was only nominally about education. The riots took place just 15
> days before municipal elections in the rest of the country. (OSCE 2007: 7)

Here the 'riots' are constructed as acts of deviance interrupting the pace
and structure of educational reform. The use of the term 'riots' conjures up
images of chaos and violence, in contrast to the term 'protests' which implies
a focused message, a coherent aim, and a sense of contributing to debate rather
than seeking to disrupt it. In another account of the protests in a working paper
of the European Centre for Minority Issues, the students are again dismissed
as taking part in 'riots' and are framed as pawns manipulated by nationalist
forces:

> The need for reform became very clear in the riots of October 2000 as over 1,000
> Bosnian Serb students (widely assumed to have been incited by nationalist Serb
> agitators) protested and demanded separate schools, rather than the already segre-
> gated morning/afternoon shift system in place. Bosniak students were injured in the
> melee and demanded better protection from the local and international authorities
> working to mediate the situation. This was not a riot based simply on educational
> issues; rather the incident reflected the opposition among hardliners to integration in
> the district and the animosity that lingered after the decision to make Brčko a special
> autonomous district. (Perry 2003: 78)

Teachers also shared accounts with me of the presumed influence of nationalist
politicians on the actions of the students:

> [G]enerally the demonstrations didn't have any effect, seeing as they had been
> implemented by the political leaders, meaning that somebody has given them the
> green light to do something they should do and they were manipulated by those
> people, then they went out on the streets.[15]

> [A]t the time they decided to join the education system there were protests, and the
> worst thing about these protests was the children didn't really feel that they had to
> fear anything because they have to go to school with other nationalities, but they
> were manipulated and somebody used the children to achieve his goals or aim.[16]

Nationalist politicians did protest in response to multi-ethnic reform and in
October 2001, when the second phase of integration was underway, SDS
politicians staged a boycott of the District Assembly (Jeffrey, 2006: 217).

However, explaining the protests exclusively by referencing to nationalist political agitation essentially erases the accounts of the students who protested and dismisses the content of the protests as irrelevant for justice claims that should be part of the transition. The students' motivations, actions and responses are absent, reduced as they are to a stage of reform; a problem which required an institutional solution through an imposed education law. This can be illustrated in an account offered by a government official from the Brčko District Department for Education of the incremental, planned, and controlled process of reintegration in schools:

> [W]e had a strike of students so the school stops for about a month and all the things have been done between the political parties in order to solve the situation ... They did it step by step, first mixing the first graders, then second, third, and fourth were mixed.[17]

There is a clear sense of control in this account, of not recognizing any need to address the content of the protests or the justice claims that were being made. This is a sense of order, which has been discussed in earlier chapters, in the face of illegitimate claim-making by the students. In addition, the association of the protests with political views considered to be non-legitimate makes it too easy to dismiss them, missing the analytical richness of the students' own accounts. These accounts demonstrate their attempts to claim a 'disruptive' space as a means by which to debate and contest the justice on offer. For the students I interviewed, the protests were central to their ability to express themselves in a rapidly changing society. In the official accounts of the protests the assumption is that the students were manipulated by Bosnian-Serb politicians. However, in the students' accounts they explain that in fact it was the Bosniak students who protested first:

> [T]here was a lot of fear and we were pretty scared calling each other by our names so that someone might recognize that we are Bosniaks...The incident that caused the demonstration in general was the fact that two of our friends were beaten up by a boy and his sister, they were beaten up by a group of Serb students and that happened on a Friday and as a result we protested. And then after that for several days came the Serb protests.[18]

> First the day before we came out on the streets Bosniaks came out from the technical school near OHR, and they demonstrated by going to the Catholic Church through the whole town and in the end, they burnt a Serbian flag and that probably made many people angry. Serbs, all kids from all Serbs, came out onto the streets and they started demonstrating against integrated schools.[19]

Indeed, in the student accounts they were keen to emphasise the spontaneous and organic nature of *their* protest:

> The protest itself wasn't something that was planned. We actually gathered in front of the school and then we heard what happened [to the two fellow students who were beaten up] and we started gathering and decided to protest to draw the attention of the authorities [...] The authorities did not really notice the protests until they were happening, nobody was aware there were going to be protests, they just reacted when they saw a crowd of people walking down the city [...] nobody planned it.[20]

> [T]hose pupils from the technical school came to the grammar school and let's say they called us out, but the Director locked the school so we couldn't go out, but most of the students went out of the window and after that the doors were unlocked when almost no-one was left in school. So when all students were in one big crowd we started.[21]

The spontaneous nature of the protests in the students' account is in stark contrast with the tone of the official accounts that I have quoted. These latter accounts describe a manipulated (and deviant) student body who were later moulded into being 'good' transitional justice citizens through a controlled, managed and incremental reform process. The binary between acceptance of reform and illegitimate claim-making is stark and cannot capture the justice claims which were part of the student protests. This is perhaps not surprising given the importance placed on Brčko District as a 'success' story which I described earlier in this chapter. The success story rests on a framing of the 'good' multi-ethnic citizen who receives the justice on offer and does not seek to disrupt it or introduce other justice claims. Significantly, in a context of limited political agency, the act of protest was an important vehicle for contesting these framings and for voicing discontent with the justice on offer. Before the protests no elections had been held for the District Assembly and the education reform itself had been forced through by the internationally appointed District Supervisor. There was a clear concern among the students that the reform itself was being pursued too fast and too aggressively and without adequate consultation:

> That's the idea of Brčko District, complete integration. These are ideas I completely agree with, but it went too fast. One day you're told okay, you're going to Brčko, we didn't even feel comfortable being there.[22]

> Any integration cannot be done very fast, and each integration makes lots of changes and for some people who are stuck in one system it's a big change for them and that's how I and my generation felt at that time.[23]

There is a sense of needing to be heard in a changing environment. This was an environment in which the students were not always able to define the 'right' ways to make claims. As students they were told that they had to start going to school under conditions that were not of their choosing and were halted in their protests which were dismissed for being against the values of integration and multi-ethnicity. The momentum of reform was supplied by institutions of the international community, the District Government and the master-narrative of needing to 'solve' the 'problem' of segregated education. This seemed to take away from the students any sense of being able to question the process itself in light of other concerns; life in Brčko District and multi-ethnic education came as a package. As one former student told me:

> They [the OHR] closed school for three weeks, a reaction, and basically for the first two or three days of demonstration they just left it. They were very quiet about it but after they said you do whatever you want, multi-ethnic school will happen and that was it.[24]

The insistence on a certain pace and content of reform, with no consultation with students or teachers, meant that the broader context of multi-ethnic education was not taken into account. The act of protest communicated this gap and tried to bring to the attention of officials other potential justice concerns and claims. In parallel to education reform, and in line with the multi-ethnic ambitions of the District, the return of Bosniak residents had been encouraged and supported. But this return process generated significant anxiety:

> [T]his integration process had also to do with getting to know each other for the first time.[25]

> [P]eople were crashing windows of the stores that were belonging to Bosniaks because at that time some of the people were coming back and opening their stores in the town...you know Bosnians were coming back to the town, Croats were coming back to the town, so living together started in those times.[26]

It was the Bosniak students who had started the protests even though they were the students being returned to Brčko Town. The act of protest was an expression of a right to be in that town; to reclaim their part of that space politically, economically, and socially: 'we did chant some things like 'this is Bosnia this is Brčko we're from Brčko we have the right to be here' and so on 'we want to live where we're born' and stuff like that.[27] The return process was extremely sensitive. During the war, while Brčko had been under the control of the Bosnian-Serb forces, Bosnian Serbs who had been displaced from other parts of the country were welcomed into Brčko and given homes. The return of displaced former Bosniak and Croat residents generated a lot of anxiety among those Bosnian Serbs who were then to be displaced a second time. The protests expressed such anxiety, both in terms of security and return among the Bosnian Coats and Bosniaks, and in terms of housing and job security among the

Bosnian Serbs. It was not just a case of saying 'no' to multi-ethnic education, but of trying to engender a debate and raise concerns about the multi-ethnic 'package' and pace of reform in the District. This cannot be captured in the idea of Brčko District as a 'model' and 'success' – an idea which underpins accounts dismissing the 'deviant' protests as mere ethno-national manipulation. We can see this in the following report:

> Upon the imposition and implementation of educational reform in 2001, politicians claimed that 'them' and 'theirs' would not succumb to multi-ethnic schools with 'the other'. To the contrary, the majority of people were willing to learn about the reforms and were comfortable enough with the changes to send their children to the newly reconstituted schools. Marginalizing the spoilers, whether through elections, removal from office or temporary establishment of a transitional authority, can provide space in which the peace and progress that the average people want can take root. (Perry 2003: 95)

The narrative here is clearly one which marginalises and delegitimises the protests as a 'bad' element in an otherwise 'good' population willing to play their part in making the reforms a success. A split is presented: on the one side is the pre-integration system captured by nationalist elites who manipulated popular opinion, while on the other is the post-integration system where people embrace what they have really wanted all along. The politics of Brčko District recognise as legitimate the actions of a transitional justice citisen which are consensual, non-conflictual and supportive of multi-ethnic institutions. This implies a dichotomy between pre and post integration and a passivity on the part of the citizens of Brčko District. However, the students were not passive and used protest as a way of contesting the neat, linear 'success' narrative.

7.4 DISRUPTIVE CLAIM-MAKING: WHERE CONTEXT MEETS JUSTICE

The transitional justice citizen as imagined and framed through transitional justice discourse and practice is a virtuous one. They must hold certain virtues associated with the neoliberal dominant script of transitional justice to play the role expected of them. This includes an acceptance of the terms of justice on offer, an acceptance of the ordering of society through institutional reform to manage conflict, and not seeking more radical social change and transformation. As discussed in Chapter 4, spontaneous, popular and collective action for justice is delegitimized in the 'lasting normative imprint' of the emergence of the field of transitional justice as a legalistic, liberal and state-centric set of policies and practices (Zunino 2019: 231). Accordingly, more 'disruptive' modes of making claims are also delegitimized. The 'rupture' of acts of citizenship (Isin 2008: 27) does not fit well with the transitional justice citizen as elaborated in Part 1 of this book. But it does fit well with the transitional justice citizen as an active seeker of justice, as an interlocutor in what counts as legitimate claim-making at times of transition.

The acts of the students analysed in this chapter can be dismissed as the result of manipulation by nationalist politicians, as a momentary lapse in the inevitable progress towards a democratic and multi-ethnic citizenry of Brčko District. They can be, and they have been, in the official accounts of the protests. However, interviews with those who took part tell a different story and remind us of the importance of the transitional justice citizen as an active *seeker* of justice. While the multi-ethnic reform imposed 'from above' by the international community forms a cornerstone of a success narrative that justifies the mode of transition pursued in Brčko District, the protests demand a conversation and engender a debate about the multi-ethnic 'package'. They also importantly represent the agency of the students in a context in which politicians, policy makers and indeed researchers have failed to understand this. In analysis of protests in 2017 by high-school students in Jajce and Travnik, this time against ethnically segregated schooling, Piersma observes that

> much less scholarly attention has been devoted to the ways in which the students themselves deal with their own everyday experience of this school situation. The ethno-political projects of the ruling political class are shaping much of Bosnian society, but the students are equally political agents in an environment in which their ethnic status appears to determine many of their actions. (Piersma 2019: 935–936)

The students in Brčko were not necessarily opposed to integrated education, but they had not been consulted on the pace, the timing, or the manner of integration. It was assumed that they would play their role as 'good' citizens of Brčko, the model District. We can see this in how the official accounts compare the 'bad' students to the 'good' population at large who support the multi-ethnic reforms. The protests as acts of citizenship contest ideas of what 'good' and 'success' look like. But there is limited room for such nuance in the process which carefully managed and mandated the transition. Their acts prompt us to wonder whether the virtuous citizen might be the one who is disruptive, unsatisfied, and searching for answers and accountability. This manner of claim-making was visible, arresting, and effective, even if the integrated schooling was eventually implemented. It was only through the protests that the students were able to raise questions about the larger context of the transition, of the relevance of the patterns of the return of internally displaced people, of fears over jobs and housing, and of feelings of disempowerment, in a District run by an internationally appointed District Supervisor with a reform agenda agreed by others elsewhere.

The act of protest also makes clear the ongoing contested nature of justice as a concept and practice, echoing other work by Lai whose book on socioeconomic justice in Bosnia-Herzegovina 'redefines justice processes as characterised by contestation and social mobilization, involving struggles over who is considered the bearer of justice claims, and how these claims are put forward in processes of public deliberation' (Lai 2020: 15). This contestation and struggle are written out in the dominant script of transitional justice, as we can see clearly in the account of the student protests elaborated in this chapter. Writing about later popular protests in different cities across Bosnia-Herzegovina in 2014, Lai identifies the tendency for international actors either to dismiss progressive and transformative politics as nostalgia for the socialist past (Lai 2020: 145) or to re-package and de-politicise them as part of the same transition agenda (Lai 2020: 166), thereby subordinating any justice claims which fall outside of those offered by the formal transitional justice process (Lai 2020: 155). This is strikingly similar to the official accounts of the student protests in this chapter, whereby the justice concerns of the students were dismissed as backwards-looking nationalism and a refusal to accept the multi-ethnic future of Brčko District. In contrast, the response by the OHR and the OSCE in Europe to the 2017 student protests in Jajce and Travnik, against segregated schooling, was publicly supportive (Piersma 2019: 942).

As we can also see in this chapter, the importance of the act of protest, according to Lai, was that 'people recognised themselves as bearers of justice claims and gave shape to a new, more meaningful and holistic conception of post-war justice' (Lai 2020: 162). The students that I interviewed had different reasons for protesting, but their act gave them a voice, reminded wider society and the international actors that justice is contested, and actively sought a more disruptive and confrontational space in which to speak back to the transitional justice agenda.

NOTES

1.   This chapter builds on work I have published previously and which I cite throughout the chapter, namely Jones, B. (2012) 'Exploring the Politics of Reconciliation through the case of Education Reform in Brčko District, Bosnia-Herzegovina', *International Journal of Transitional Justice* 6: 126–148; Jones, B. (2015) Educating Citizens in Bosnia-Herzegovina: Models, Claims and Experiences in Post War Education Reform. Fischer, M. Ed. *Twenty Years after Dayton: The Western Balkans between Transitional Justice and Reconciliation.* Routledge; and Jones, B. (2011). Understanding Responses to Postwar Education Reform in the Multiethnic District of Brčko, Bosnia-Herzegovina. Paulson, J. ed. *Education and Reconciliation, Exploring Conflict and Post-Conflict Situations.* London/ New York: Continuum.

2.   See https://www.icty.org/en/press/new-war-demographics-feature-icty-website (last accessed 31 March 2022).

3. It is important to note that the DPA recognizes group rights only of Bosniaks, Bosnian-Croats and Bosnian-Serbs, causing significant issues and political marginalisation for minority groups in the country. The *Sejdic and Finci v. Bosnia-Herzegovina* case illustrates this. The European Court of Human Rights found that the exclusion of members of the 14 minority groups in the country from running for election to the House of Peoples or Presidency amounted to discrimination. For more information see https://www.justiceinitiative.org/litigation/sejdic-and-finci-v-bosnia-and-herzegovina#:~:text=By%20a%20vote%20of%2014,Article%2014%20taken%20in%20conjunction (last accessed 31 March 2022).

4. *Federacija Bosne i Hercegovine.*

5. Serb Republic.

6. The High Representative and the District Supervisor were created by the Dayton Peace Agreement in 1995 in order to oversee the civilian implementation of the agreement. Appointed by the international community they have wide-ranging powers over Bosnian politics with an effective veto on political decisions.

7. The position of the District Supervisor still exists but since 2012 its functions have been suspended.

8. Speech 8 March 2009. Available at: http://www.ohr.int/supervisor-raffi-gregorians-speech-at-the-central-ceremony-at-the-brcko-district-anniversary-celebration-on-march-8-2009/ (last accessed 12th November 2021.

9. Speech 8 March 2009. Available at: http://www.ohr.int/supervisor-raffi-gregorians-speech-at-the-central-ceremony-at-the-brcko-district-anniversary-celebration-on-march-8-2009/ (last accessed 12th November 2021.

10. The Peace Implementation council was established in 1995 and comprises 55 countries and agencies that support the peace process in many different ways. For more information see: http://www.ohr.int/international-community-in-bih/peace-implementation-council/.

11. Annex to Final Award, 18 August 1999, point 11.

12. *Srpska Demokratska Stranka* was founded by Radovan Karadžić, a former politician convicted of genocide, crimes against humanity, and war crimes by the ICTY. The party is associated with nationalist Bosnian-Serb politics.

13. Four rules on the use of language were stipulated in the law: the student has freedom of expression in their own language; school documents will be issued in the language and alphabet requested by the student or parent; the ethnic composition of teachers should reflect that of teachers in the school; and existing textbooks can be used if they are harmonised with the curriculum.

14. Interview 190607 and Interview 130308.

15. Interview 140308a.

16. Interview 120308.

17. Interview 190607.

18. Interview 250308.

19. Interview 260308.

20. Interview 230308.

21. Interview 260308.

22. Interview 030707b.

23. Interview 290308.

24. Interview 150308.

25. Interview 120308.

26.   Interview 130308.
27.   Interview 230308.

8. Conclusion to *The Transitional Justice Citizen*

> After April the eleventh all, those, doors, were, shut […] so there was a tacit boycott of anything that would be representing the views or dissenting views. (Côte d'Ivoire)[1]

> What is the image of a Black Tunisian? It is always that they are in second place, not a citizen. (Tunisia)[2]

> That's the idea of Brčko District, complete integration. These are ideas I completely agree with, but it went too fast. One day you're told okay, you're going to Brčko, we didn't even feel comfortable being there. (Bosnia-Herzegovina)[3]

Transitional justice has the potential to be many different things. It is a discourse, a set of policies, a set of practices, an opening and a closing, an opportunity for change, and a moment of reckoning. However, the conditions of the emergence of the field and its evolution through time have crystallised a particular transitional justice norm (Nagy 2008) which now dominates how societies respond to large-scale human rights violations of the past. As outlined in the early chapters of this book, the question is not whether but *when* transitional justice will be implemented. I would also add that the question of *how* it is to be implemented has retreated into the distance. The international norm of transitional justice reads from the liberal-legalist script that Sharp (2018) and others have identified.

Critical scholarship on transitional justice, as well as reflexive practice, has opened the field in the last decade and pushed the boundaries of its reach. Lively debates bring in socio-economic crimes (Waldorf 2012), propose transformative justice ideas (Gready and Robins 2014), deconstruct the neo-colonialism of the field (Maddison and Shepherd 2014), and highlight the fact that transitional justice may not be that just after all (Jones 2017). As Miller reflects, transitional justice 'developed a robust industry out of scattered histories of makeshift bargains, trials, and truths and then made habitual a combination of certainty (about the need for justice) and uncertainty (about whether justice could be achieved, particularly through these practices)' (2020: 357). It is to this broad body of work that this book speaks, offering a framework for understanding what I believe to be a central problematic of the field: the disconnect between long-term historical struggle and the justice on offer through a transitional justice process. This disconnect underpins a series of critiques which have been developed in the wider literature which I draw on in this book. These critiques identify a lack of history or context in the way transitional justice processes are designed and implemented, they identify a lack of satisfaction among victims with the justice they are offered, and they raise the question of whether transitional justice should be abandoned for its failure to transform deeply rooted structures of injustice and inequality. The disconnect between longer-term historical struggle and the justice on offer through a transitional justice process also fails to acknowledge the agency of those living in societies where there is a transitional justice process. This failure, in turn, contributes to the increasing concentration of transitional justice expertise in the Global North, in think tanks, in internationally mobile experts and entrepreneurs, and away from those who have experienced the violence and who have the greatest stake in its resolution and repair.

These threads of critique, these multi-faceted problems with the global norm of transitional justice, and the alternative lenses which have been used to rethink and reframe the transitional justice project in more recent critical scholarship, have been brought together in this book, in which I have tried to do two simple things. Firstly, I have tried to demonstrate that transitional justice is a citizenship question. Both regimes of citizenship and the individual acts of citizens are pertinent for understanding the empirical unfolding of transitional justice. Moreover, insights from citizenship studies are helpful for framing, probing, and advancing our knowledge about the problems of transitional justice as well as alternative ways in which it can be imagined and practiced. The most pressing contemporary debates of the field are advanced if we can draw on citizenship studies and study 'the citizen' in transitional justice contexts. Secondly, I aimed to show that the figure of the transitional justice citizen who is constructed and illuminated through transitional justice discourse, policy and practice, as well as through citizenship acts, is not only a justice receiver but also an active seeker of justice. Such an understanding de-naturalizes transitional justice and rightly places an emphasis on the people themselves as pre-existing agents with agendas that intersect with transitional justice but do not necessarily flow from it. By focusing on these two simple aims I have tried to respond to the critical scholarship which demands more context, more history, more local voices. I have suggested that if we consider the transitional justice citizen in their fullest form as a receiver and seeker of justice then we can offer a substantial response and potential ways forward.

8.1   EXPERTS, CITIZENS, AND CLAIMS TO JUSTICE

Despite the tendency of the field of transitional justice to extol its technical and non- or a-political nature (McGill 2002: 66), transitional justice is clearly an act of intervention. An intervention into the lives of people; into the contexts in which they live; into a passage of time; into a landscape of morality and virtues; and into an ongoing debate about the meaning of justice and how it may be realised. The problem is that this intervention is too often made based on a series of false assumptions. It assumes that experts and entrepreneurs of transitional justice have adequate knowledge to design, implement and advocate for certain forms of justice. It assumes that a particular version of transitional justice is what is needed to respond to the injustice of the past. It also assumes that disagreements over the kind of justice needed indicates a 'lack' in those who disagree – a lack of knowledge or a lack of virtue – rather than a problem with the transitional justice process and the justice that it offers.

Bell has described the trajectory of the field of transitional justice as a trajectory which has profoundly altered the original justice claims of the field as practitioners responded to oppression and violence. She writes that:

> Across this trajectory, something quite profound seemed to happen to the original justice claim: the more it moved from local claim, to expert discourse, to established fieldhood, the more it became divorced from the social commitments that had driven its genesis in the first place. In fact, to state things strongly, full emergence as a credible academic field often almost equated to severance from the social movement that had driven its genesis as a practice, sometimes in the name of 'objectivity' and sometimes in the name of 'proper scholarship'. (Bell 2002: 91)

Her work calls on us to ask what the label of transitional justice obscures or makes clear (Bell 2002: 93–94); and in this book I claim that the transitional justice label obscures the long-term historical struggles for justice by placing boundaries around who can make claims, what claims can be made, and how claims should be made.

In each of the case study chapters, acts of citizenship are analysed as windows onto the intersection between historical struggle and contemporary transitional justice processes. These acts of justice – in Côte d'Ivoire, Tunisia, and Bosnia-Herzegovina – are expanding who can be included in the process of making claims, expanding what (in)justice can be included in claim-making, and about expanding the manner and arenas in which claims can be made. In the chapter on Côte d'Ivoire, citizenship struggles underpin political violence and a landscape of contested identity and belonging. The transitional justice process has not grappled with this complex history and instead divides the population neatly into the 'good' and the 'bad' according to who supports the transitional justice on offer. The elite-led process with limited consultation has been dominated by the victors with an international audience in mind – it has ticked the boxes of the global norm, allowing Ouattara to pursue what has been described as a victor's justice. This has been possible because of the framing of the 'Gbagbo camp' as being associated with a morally corrupt and violent past, unable to accept that justice must prevail. The citizenship acts of individuals from this camp urge us to question such simplistic analysis as they push the boundaries placed around who can make justice claims. While it is important not to fall foul of the same simplistic analysis which I critique, by suggesting that all those in the 'Gbagbo camp' have the same motivation, the acts which make justice claims and which demand a rethinking of the approach to justice expose the limitations of a transitional justice process which includes those who agree and excludes those who do not. Transitional justice experts and entrepreneurs expect a homogeneity of views, or at least to produce one through the transitional justice process; and when there is diversity, the acts and actors can too easily be dismissed as being associated with the violent past and therefore less legitimate as interlocutors of justice.

In the chapter on Tunisia, I wrote about how Black Tunisian activists use their acts of citizenship to expand the justice on offer through transitional justice by demanding recognition of the injustice of racism, its historical presence in the country, and the need to transform social, economic, and legal structures beyond those envisaged by the transitional justice experts and entrepreneurs. They do not passively accept the boundaries placed around what justice claims can be made; and through their participation in the process, advocacy outside of the process, and capturing of the opportunity presented by an opening of public space and dialogue, they changed the content of the report of the IVD and were instrumental in the establishment of a new law against racial injustice. The transitional moment presented an opportunity for Black Tunisian activists to connect historical injustices with contemporary claims to justice and to bring the issue of racism to the fore, an issue which was not an intended focus of the transitional justice process. Indeed, as described in the chapter, these acts of citizenship are neither well recognised nor understood by transitional justice experts and entrepreneurs, a blind spot which illustrates a tendency for transitional justice advocates and experts to acknowledge as injustices those which are recognizable in the context of previous work and the international norm of transitional justice. Despite this, the Black Tunisian activists were able, through their acts, to utilise spaces inside and outside of the process to expand the remit of justice claims addressed by transitional justice and to make the process work for them. Racism as a historical and ongoing injustice was not on the transitional justice agenda until the Black activists themselves acted to expand what claims could be made.

In the chapter on Bosnia-Herzegovina students, acts of citizenship were seen by political elites as disruptive and illegitimate. This fits with the framing of the virtuous transitional justice citizen who is supposed to accept the justice on offer and make justice claims through the formal transitional justice process. While the multi-ethnic reform imposed 'from above' by the international community formed a cornerstone of a success narrative that justified the mode of transition pursued in Brčko District, the student protests demanded a conversation and engendered a debate about the multi-ethnic 'package' of transitional justice. The students in Brčko were not necessarily opposed to integrated education, but they had not been consulted on the pace, the timing, or the manner of integration. It was assumed that they would play their role as 'good' citizens of Brčko, the model District, but their acts disrupted this division between the 'good' and the 'bad' citizen. They prompt us to ask whether the 'good' citizen might be the one who disrupts, who challenges the mode of claim-making, and who pushes the boundaries placed around how claims to justice can be pursued as part of a transitional justice process. The acts also remind us that justice is contested, and continues to be so before, during and indeed after any transitional justice process.

The transitional justice citizen is thus the place where historical struggle meets contemporary claims to justice. In Côte d'Ivoire, the transitional justice process encountered a long history of struggle over identity and belonging encapsulated in the concept of *Ivoirité*. Patterns of political exclusion and political violence all informed the acts of Gbagbo supporters who wanted to connect justice with histories of colonialism, exclusion, and competition over who belongs. In Tunisia, the transitional justice process encountered a long history of racial injustice perpetuated by the very silence of transitional justice on the issue. The transitional moment provided an opportunity for Black Tunisian activists to seek acknowledgement of their experiences of long standing. In Bosnia-Herzegovina, the formation and mobilization of ethno-national identity long before the war led to a complex picture which was not captured in the transitional justice approach, which sought a multi-ethnic blank slate. The marginalization of any concerns which would question the integration of the schools forced the hands of the students who took to the streets.

The citizenship acts in each of the chapters are made by those who are actively seeking justice. This justice that they seek may be counter to the justice on offer through the transitional justice process, and it may also overlap with but seek to extend the justice on offer. The sense of agency in each of the chapters is a powerful illustration of the dual nature of the transitional justice citizen – as framed through discourse and practice and as made through acts. We see the two elements interact and shape each other in the case studies. The citizenship acts respond to, and change in response to, the boundaries established around claim-making by the transitional justice process. We see this in the pivoting between the refusal to participate and the proposal of alternatives by Gbagbo supporters in Côte d'Ivoire. In turn, the transitional justice experts, entrepreneurs, and advocates adjust in response to the citizenship acts. We see this in the inclusion of a section on racism in the report of the Tunisian IVD. The transitional justice citizen is the sum of both the framing of the passive and virtuous citizen and the acts of the active seeker of justice who makes different and more expansive claims to justice.

There are, of course, differences between the cases. Not all acts are successful in certain senses. While in Tunisia the activists were able to expand the justice on offer, the legal changes are threatened by the political changes and lack of resources for training and implementation. In Côte d'Ivoire the supporters of Gbagbo have not been fully integrated as interlocutors in the transitional justice debate. In Bosnia-Herzegovina the student protests delayed but did not change the mode of multi-ethnic integration. Not all acts of citizenship are easily accepted or understood. In Côte d'Ivoire the 'bad' guys are making claims; while in Tunisia, it is the historically marginalized and, in Bosnia-Herzegovina, disempowered youth. Not all acts are articulated by the transitional justice citizen as a direct question of citizenship. The Black Tunisian activists are very clear that their struggle is a struggle for equal citizenship; while the Ivoiriens who support Gbagbo frame their struggle as connected to voice, to democracy, and to the fight against neo-colonialism; while the Bosnian students see their acts as agency and claiming the right to determine how multi-ethnic integration should take place. Not all acts take the same form or have the same trajectory. In Tunisia, we see an opportune moment and the opening of public space which allows for the gradual building of discontent to manifest in intense activism targeted at participating in the transitional justice process as well as lobbying for additional legal reform. In Côte d'Ivoire, we also see a collection of different acts of boycott and lobbying coming together to place pressure on the Ivoirien government and to rally support among those who feel politically excluded and marginalized. In Bosnia-Herzegovina, we see a focused act of protest, a moment of collective action which seemed to be spontaneous and then end relatively quickly. Some of these acts across the cases are ongoing, building momentum and leading to new acts. Others take place at a moment in time.

Citizenship acts, according to the approach taken in this book, are 'deeds that rupture social-historical patterns' and 'claim rights and impose obligations in emotionally charged tones' which then disrupt established order, offer new possibilities, and shift established order (Isin and Nielsen 2008: 2 and 10). Importantly they bring 'into being political subjects that did not exist previously' (Squire 2016: 265). Across the differences that can be identified between, and indeed within, the cases, these red threads are present. Despite varied levels of success in materially changing the transitional justice process and redrawing the boundaries placed around claim-making, in each act of citizenship analysed there are claims, obligations, new possibilities, new subjects and shifts in the established order which are evoked and visible. This renders them relevant and worthy of analysis. In each case the acts of citizenship claim rights. In Côte d'Ivoire, this is the right to be included in the transitional justice debate and process. In Tunisia, it is the right to include other claims to justice. In Bosnia-Herzegovina, it is the right to protest and to be heard. In each case we also see the associated obligations; of the government to lead a more inclusive process; of the transitional justice experts and entrepreneurs to consider a wider range of relevant injustices; and of the political elites to listen to more voices and consider their own fallibility. It is also inspiring to see the new possibilities, subjects and shifts in the acts of citizenship. In Côte d'Ivoire, alternative road maps for transitional justice are presented as part of a lobby against victor's justice; in Tunisia, legal reform paves the way for new cases and improved justice; and in Bosnia-Herzegovina, alternative modes of articulating claims lay bare the elite and closed nature of a transitional justice process which is supposed to benefit the whole of society. The shifts in established order are more or less perceptible depending on the case and may also only have been planted as seeds ushering in future shifts and changes which either are not possible immediately or cannot currently be imagined by the actors themselves.

The case studies all speak to each other through these acts of citizenship but also through the red threads of the book as a whole. Part 1 of the book is about the boundaries placed around claim-making by mainstream transitional justice: boundaries around who can make claims, what claims can be made, and how claims should be made. Who can make claims is about who is seen as being virtuous and what claims are considered to be legitimate. Part 2 pushes these boundaries and demonstrates the problematic assumptions which underpin them as well as the possibilities for them to be overcome. The interplay between the transitional justice citizen as imagined through the transitional justice norm, and the transitional justice citizen as framed through acts of citizenship is enlightening. Taken together the two parts of the book constitute the transitional justice citizen, and demonstrate that this citizen – both imagined and enacted – can bring history, context and struggle back into transitional justice.

8.2   THE TRANSITIONAL JUSTICE CITIZEN AND TRANSITIONAL JUSTICE

This book fits squarely in the transitional justice literature which recognises justice as a contested concept and practice (Lai 2020 and others), and which sees the transitional justice mainstream as limited. This fourth generation of transitional justice scholarship is 'characterized by a willingness to interrogate some of the foundational blindspots and limitations of the field' (Sharp 2019: 570). These limitations have been outlined in Chapter 1, but I return to them here in order to connect the transitional justice citizen with these key critiques. The purpose of doing this is to demonstrate both how the transitional justice citizen can speak back to these critiques, and how work on the transitional justice citizen can improve our understanding of important dynamics and outcomes in transitional justice processes. This is an approach which does not seek to do away with transitional justice or to deconstruct it beyond use but, instead, to capture some of its potential to respond to harms and to improve lives.

As outlined in Chapter 1, the book responds to a series of questions: how is the citizen constructed through transitional justice? How does the citizen connect historical struggle with contemporary calls for justice as part of a transitional justice process? What do these citizenship acts tell us about the empirical unfolding of transitional justice? What struggles are most important at times of transitional justice and what happens to them as a transitional justice process unfolds? Employing acts of citizenship as a lens has allowed me to answer these questions in ways which highlight the interplay between rupture and change, between order and disorder, between historical struggle and contexts of contemporary transitional justice processes. It has allowed me both to describe the transitional justice citizen and to demonstrate how analysis of this citizen and their acts adds value to the transitional justice field. In this section I thus return to the organising themes with which I set up the book: looking from the inside out; order and closure; and the non-linearity of struggle.

8.2.1   Looking from the Inside Out

The power of looking from the inside out is that it decentres transitional justice as an intervention. One of the major shortcomings of the field has been its reliance on jurisprudence 'rather than detailed empirical studies of people's experiences of violence or the social context in which crime is embedded' (McGill 2002: 66). It has also gained, through its status as a global norm (Nagy 2008), a sense of naturalness (Sharp 2018) which places it at the centre of our view, displacing the people themselves from the centre of our analysis (McGill 2002: 67). This is problematic because it limits both our understanding of the very harms which transitional justice is supposed to address and our understanding of how transitional justice unfolds empirically and with which it impacts. Work on decentring interventions in general highlights how 'The failure to consider equally at least the perspectives and perceptions of those who face the potentially adverse effects of interventions in their everyday lives leaves a crucial part of intervention dynamics unexplored' (Schroeder 2018: 144). This is particularly pertinent and problematic for transitional justice which promises many things to those who have been harmed, traumatised, and marginalised by violence. As Schroeder suggests, 'In a world where interventions have become the norm, we hold that research must engage meaningfully with the ways in which new types of globalized interventions transform and are themselves transformed by their encounters with complex domestic situations' (2018: 146). And by taking an inside–out approach this means starting with the domestic situation as a way of understanding the encounters, rather than beginning with the intervention itself.

If we consider the three case studies, we can appreciate how the transitional justice citizen and their acts undertake this process of decentring transitional justice as an intervention. In Côte d'Ivoire the acts of boycott and lobbying are framed as reminders of factors which have been ignored by the transitional justice process. A complex history of colonialism, political exclusion, and ongoing political violence, and complex intersections between political identity and autochthony, all form the historical and contemporary domestic situation in which the transitional justice processes intervened. This context directly shaped the content and manner of the transitional justice process, as well as its inability to bring together Ivoiriens in the aftermath of violence. In Tunisia we see a similar process whereby the acts of Black Tunisian activists demanded that the history of racial injustice be included as part of the transitional justice offer, working within but also outside of the formal transitional justice process. While the transitional justice intervention was itself an opportunity, demonstrated by the submission of a dossier to the IVD, it was also in many ways beside the point. The social media presence, public debate, and lobbying for legal reform were a culmination of a long-standing sense of injustice and previous attempts to bring racism into the public mind. These acts of citizenship were part of a trajectory which was at one point in time punctuated by transitional justice, with each shaping the other. In Bosnia-Herzegovina the student protests were dismissed as nationalist sour grapes in response to multi-ethnic reform. However, the students were also trying to make their voices heard – voices which spoke of concerns over housing, jobs, and the daily experiences of segregation and integration. By refusing to see this, the political elite continued with their reforms, falsely assuming that the protests were only in response to their policies and programme of change.

The decentring of transitional justice through citizenship acts also has implications for notions of expertize. Miller has written that we need to decentre the intervention of peace 'experts' if we want to achieve the goal of supporting peace (Miller 2018: 271), moving away from the previously accepted mode of technocratic solutions of technocrats for post-conflict dilemmas (Miller 2018: 261). The peace studies literature has gone quite some way towards this decentring in theory with notions of everyday or emancipatory peace which began 'to theorize how peace might be built not for those living in postconflict contexts by intervention experts, but through *interaction and exchange*' (Miller 2018: 261). In the transitional justice field this has been seen in work which focuses on the local and different standpoints (Shaw and Waldorf 2010) and in calls to pay attention to what local populations demand (Anders and Zenker 2014) in contrast to what transitional justice entrepreneurs are prepared to offer. However, these approaches, which are essentially about the empowerment of communities, need to be linked to political space and capabilities to be 'relevant to the task of creating better governance structures and state-society relationships that are vital to transitional efforts to overcome legacies of authoritarianism and armed conflict' (McGill 2002: 67). This is about agency, and agency that we can see clearly in the citizenship acts analysed in Part 2 of the book.

Peace governance literature, in similar ways to that of the transitional justice field, has tended towards ideas of inclusion as a way of speaking to the need to decentre intervention. As Pospisil describes it:

> The inclusion paradigm, currently dominating the liberal peacebuilding discourse, is the unmistakable call of conducting peace as a whole-of-society effort that should increase social cohesion at the national level. Nobody shall be left behind in this effort; everybody needs to be associated with one another and integrated into the transitional process. (Pospisil 2020: 338–339)

This is seen as the 'the "normalcy" of the ultimate relational equalizer of joint citizenship' (Pospisil 2020: 338–339) which has echoes in the framing of the transitional justice citizen from Part 1 of the book, as a participatory, virtuous agent responsible for holding up their side of the democratic peace pact (Henderson 2006: 199). The process of inclusion thus ends in a state of consensus, an equaliser that is harmonious and closes a lid on the discord of the past. But these approaches run the risk of not in fact acknowledging the richness and agency present in the local, or indeed not actually decentring the expertise on which the intervention is based. A lack of understanding or acknowledgement of actors 'on the ground' adopting widely diverging standpoints with regard to interventions renders the local (Birkholz et al., 2018: 175) less powerful as a counterweight to the heavy technocratic expertise of the transitional justice intervention.

This is an expertise which, at the same time as eschewing 'basic political analysis', manages to 'practically and normatively' contribute to 'an intensely political framing of the issues involved' (McGrattan 2009: 164). In Côte d'Ivoire the victor's justice imposed aligned the new President's power with the 'good' of transitional justice and his opponents with the 'bad' of violence. In Tunisia the blind spots of the transitional justice process framed certain claims as valid and others as not relevant. In Bosnia-Herzegovina multi-ethnic education was elevated as the only legitimate way of pursuing justice, with other voices dismissed as spoilerism. In each case the transitional justice process was led by a set of elites and transitional justice entrepreneurs who claimed expertise for themselves. Despite invitations to participate, and indeed expectations of participation, the openness to local voices was limited. The local population was consulted through the transitional justice process, or invited to submit certain claims, but these local experiences were pitted against elite and foreign expertise. Supporters of Gbagbo in Côte d'Ivoire were excluded from public debate if they refused to reproduce the transitional justice narrative about the violence; Black Tunisian activists had to fight to have their expertise regarding their own experience of injustice recognised by the transitional justice process and wider society; Bosnian students had to shout louder to demonstrate that they were not just puppets of the nationalist political parties, but were experts of their own lives and the implications on the version of multi-ethnic integration pursued by elites.

An underlying dynamic that can be observed in each case is that of embedded ambivalence. As described by Miller, this means that:

> The practices, institutions, and conceptualisation of justice that defined the enterprise appeared to be both absolutely necessary and largely unachievable. Thus, even if experts were uncertain about the field's practices, they remained confident about its objectives. Embedded ambivalence denotes certainty about outcomes and the necessity of the project while routinising doubts about means and application. That combination stabilized the enterprise as a whole, since it had the effect of detaching its consensual, noble ends from disputed or questionable means. Critiques that could be answered by expanding the transitional justice field rose to the fore while those that struck at foundational assumptions – such as linear temporality, (neo)liberal political and economic structures, or unequal power relations – often receded. (2020: 354)

This embedded ambivalence can explain the seeming contradiction between a move to the local in both policy discourse and transitional justice practice while at the same time the core beliefs of the field in terms of what it does and why are strengthened. Miller goes on to write:

> That confidence and unease can characterize the same enterprise – and sometimes the same practice or person – reflects how 'virtue fields' are particularly well-positioned to enact what Lang and Desai call global ungovernance. Virtue fields, defined as enterprises organized explicitly around social justice and progress objectives achieved through specific practices, consolidated and professionalized in the name of humanity in the late twentieth century. They are generally marked by a simultaneous commitment to the construction of formal, often legal, institutions and the production of flexible, site-specific practices. Moreover, they are particularly amenable to 'ungoverning' because the virtuous nature of their core object makes it both centrally important and all but impossible to attain. The transformation from certainty to ambivalence may have happened more quickly in transitional justice – telling a 'history' of the field can feel like watching a time-lapse video in which a seed grows into a tree in mere seconds – but it is not unique to this particular enterprise. As in other virtue fields, practitioners, scholars, and experts in transitional justice maintain certainty about the necessity of their objectives even while questioning the capacity of their specific practices and projects to achieve them. (Miller 2020: 355)

This somewhat lengthy quote is useful for tying together the assumed 'goodness' of transitional justice with its crystallization of certain forms of expertise and the careful boundaries that are placed around who can make claims, what claims can be made, and how claims should be made. These are boundaries which are rendered visible by acts of citizenship which at the same time demonstrate that alternatives exist. Citizenship acts are thus important windows onto the relevant experiences and contexts of (in)justice which include but are not contained by transitional justice. Citizenship acts can decentre transitional justice as an intervention and strike at the foundational assumptions described in the Miller quote above.

8.2.2   Order and Desire for Closure

The transitional justice citizen comprises two parts. The first is framed through mainstream transitional justice discourse, policy, and practice, as a passive justice receiver. This part of the transitional justice citizen participates in the ways invited by transitional justice experts and entrepreneurs and maintains their claims to justice inside the boundaries which are set by the transitional justice process. The second part of the transitional justice citizen is the active seeker of justice who, through their citizenship acts, pushes and contests the boundaries set by the transitional justice process. These two parts certainly interact, with the transitional justice citizen moving between more passive and more active encounters with justice and claim-making. What is important about this movement between the two parts of the transitional justice citizen is that it helps us to understand that transitional justice is necessarily incomplete in the justice it offers and the claims it allows. As highlighted in Chapter 1, transitional justice is caught between its lofty aims to bring justice and peace and the limitations and compromizes that form the reality of its design and implementation. At the same time as offering hope and possibility, transitional justice seeks closure and order in ways which limit claim-making. The transitional justice citizen brings this to life in ways seen in the case study chapters.

There are numerous studies which show that law and the pursuit of legal justice may not be people's priorities in the aftermath of conflict, and that in fact economic needs, security and rehabilitation are often deemed to be more important (Davidovic 2020: 299). This underpins the crises of legitimacy and effectiveness in the contemporary mainstream transitional justice field, as critical scholars demand that transitional justice be fundamentally transformative of social order (Sharp 2019: 571). As Sharp writes,

> The trouble is, while transformation may be a useful conceptual prism for thinking about the limitations of the mainstream goals and modalities of the field, taken liter-

ally it is an improbable outcome in most transitional justice scenarios, and perhaps especially in fragile postconflict states. (Sharp 2019: 571)

If we reflect on this in the context of the three case studies, we can see the tension between more radical demands for transformation and the constraints of the limits that transitional justice in practice places around more transformative claim-making. In Côte d'Ivoire the supporters of the former President want a discussion about the involvement of the former colonial power, France, in the management of the violence as well as the future of Ivoirien democracy. They lobbied around rethinking political dialogue and organization in the country and how the political community could be inclusive of dissenting voices. In Tunisia the Black activists sought to dismantle a history of racial injustice embedded in the economy, society and culture, as well as to reform the legal system. In Bosnia-Herzegovina, the student protesters wanted to make multi-ethnic integration also a question of job and housing security.

An observation by Bell is pertinent here when she poses the question:

[A]re transitional justice mechanisms the key to social justice and transformation? Undoubtedly not. That will be achieved by a responsive reconstruction of political and legal institutions and social infrastructure and relationships, over time. Transitional justice provides some answer to only one piece of a more complex job of moving incrementally from conflict. Conflict resolution will be likely to require different mechanisms dealing with different justice claims, across different stages of that journey. (Bell 2002: 97)

The challenge is that, as described in Part 1 of this book, the transitional justice global norm that has crystallised around toolkits, pillars, and large numbers of entrepreneurs and experts over-promises. The discourse has come, over time, to present transitional justice as *the* necessary response to violence of the past. This has hardened the boundaries about what kinds of claims can be made and foregrounded liberal, linear, and neat teleology from the violent past to the peaceful future. The citizenship acts analysed in Part 2 of this book are an important reminder and illustration of the limitations of transitional justice in this regard and the need for transformation to at least intersect with transition in the pursuit of justice. But this is a debate which is not at all settled in the transitional justice literature:

Whether transitional justice ought to be defined by the mainstream toolkit of (predominantly legal and quasi-legal) mechanisms, such as truth commissions, trials, reparations, and institutional reforms, or by wider notions of societal repair, and whether its focus ought to be narrowly on responding to periods of conflict or authoritarian rule, or more widely on a range of historical and contemporary societal injustices – including those affecting ostensibly peaceful and democratic societies – remain live issues. (Evans 2022: 3)

Some are wary of overburdening an already stretched field or see value in keeping the aims distinct (Waldorf 2012), while others claim that the field will not survive unless it adapts to incorporate more radical transformations capable of tackling root causes of violence (McAuliffe 2017). Responding to these debates, Hoddy and Gready observe that:

> What is missing from this literature is the place of critical theorising in transform-
> ative practice, that is, where new knowledge is developed about the social systems
> where change is sought, and how these systems disempower and constrain, and how
> these features might be challenged. (2020: 563)

I would suggest that the transitional justice citizen is one such place where new knowledge can be gleaned about the how and what of the transformations being sought. Acts of citizenship are direct windows onto demands for trans-formation, and the responses to them can tell us how systems react and seek to constrain.

In Côte d'Ivoire, we saw that by framing citizenship acts as democratic, as anti-colonial, and as liberating, the transitional justice citizens were inserting themselves into a debate which revealed the weakness of the government response – a victor's justice with no intention of addressing the legacy of political violence and identity politics. Ouattara's focus on reconciliation through economic prosperity closes the option of addressing more transform-ative change in political culture, identity and community. In Tunisia we saw that multiple interventions were needed in education, economy and law for the society to acknowledge and address racial injustice. Lack of inclusion of racial injustice in the transitional justice process, as well as resistance from the government in institutionalising and implementing legal reform, tried to avoid opening up the possibility for such new and far-reaching changes. But windows of opportunity were leveraged as networks of civil society actors worked together to submit dossiers and lobby for legal reform. In Bosnia-Herzegovina we saw that basic needs around jobs and housing informed citizenship acts of protest, while the political elite closed down the schools and pursued with renewed rigour and speed their pre-determined multi-ethnic reintegration process.

The impulse to order and the desire for closure, as discussed in Chapter 1, find their roots in the conditions of the emergence and consolidation of the field of transitional justice. The liberal-legal paradigm (Sharp 2018) around which the field has developed prizes linear, institutional reform based on rule-of-law and liberal democracy. It individualises the victim and the perpetrator and works against more solidaristic forms of community, identity and action (Bowsher 2018). In Part 1 of the book I described how the transitional justice citizen is framed according to the boundaries placed around claim-making. In

Part 2 of the book I argued that the transitional justice citizen offers insights into the kinds of transformations at stake and the inevitable limitations of any transitional justice process. This is not to suggest that transitional justice is doomed, but rather to assert that the transitional justice citizen is one important window into understanding the what and how of transformation, and the points at which such transformations intersect, more or less harmoniously, with transitional justice.

8.2.3 The Non-Linearity of Struggle

The impulses towards closure discussed above stem from the tendency and acceptance within peace governance in general to seek closure, a return to 'normal' politics and the resolution of root causes (Pospisil 2020: 330). These 'three pillars' of peace governance are nonetheless widely seen in critical scholarship as having 'failed in realising [their] vision' of settled, managed post-conflict states (Pospisil 2020: 330). Instead, 'the reality of peace governance is that it is often only able to stabilise and institutionalise the contestation that underpins an ongoing conflict. What formalises is not settlement or closure, but political unsettlement' (Pospisil 2020: 342). We see this clearly in transitional justice, as a part of this peacebuilding governance architecture, where unsettlement continues. Despite this being understandable, and even enriching, such unsettlement is too easily dismissed as problematic for the closure sought by the process. McEvoy has written of the 'respectabilization' of transitional justice, which dulls the dilemmas and ambiguities inherent to it as a site of political, legal, and cultural struggle (McEvoy 2018: 187–188). This process of respectabilization runs as a thread throughout both parts of the book, beginning with the crystallization of the global norm and the dulling of certain struggles brought into the frame by the acts of citizenship in Part 2.

The transitional justice citizen performs an important function of connecting historical struggle with that of contemporary transitional justice. This is important because, despite the previously discussed ordering and closure of mainstream transitional justice discourse and practice, '[o]ften the very process of transitional justice design and implementation will involve contestation that is itself a process of contending with the past' (Bell 2002: 97). Recognizing such contestation with the past acknowledges the importance of historical struggle in putting transitional justice on the agenda in the first place (McEvoy and McGregor 2008), and sheds light on how transitional justice plays out in context and with different effects. Building on the previous section, such historical struggle is often associated with more radical transformative demands coming from a desire to address the root causes of conflict. These are demands and transformations which are too often side-lined by transitional justice processes, to their detriment. For as Davidovic reminds us: 'We can neither deal with the past nor ensure non-recurrence of conflict if we reinforce the same patterns of discrimination and marginalization (albeit perhaps towards different groups) that existed pre- and during conflict' and that we need to be alert to the "network of factors" that lead to armed conflict, the "most common suspects would be inequality, poverty, exclusion and marginalisation"' (2020: 295).

Thinking of this unsettlement as historical struggle, we can see the interplay between closure and unsettlement in all the case studies. In Côte d'Ivoire attempts by Ouattara to close and resolve the conflict led to lack of dialogue, an elite-led process, and a problematic victor's justice. The acts of citizenship analysed were a direct attempt to continue the struggle by unsettling the transitional justice process and questioning its assumptions, compromises, and effects. In Tunisia the nonetheless wide-reaching transitional justice process did not engage with racial injustice and the historical marginalization and disempowerment of Black Tunisians. Continuing political destabilization, and ongoing protests about poor living conditions and economic opportunities have blunted the progress made by their activism and legal successes. In Bosnia-Herzegovina, the student protests unsettled the simplistic analysis of the conflict and of reconciliation, communicating that closure and constraint might, in fact, be damaging for individual wellbeing and community healing. The quick and uncompromising response by political elites ensured that the protests were shut down and policies pursued as planned. These processes of intervention, response and change are non-linear, with some moments in time and some contexts offering an opening for radical demands and others closing them down.

Turning again to peace governance literature, such unsettledness is to be expected, with 'The everyday practices of conflict transitions [...] habitually embracing practices of non-closure, political unsettlement, a multiplicity of transitional processes ongoing in parallel referring to a multitude of conflictscapes' (Pospisil 2020: 351). What is surprising then is not that there is ongoing struggle, but that transitional justice entrepreneurs and experts might ever expect it to be otherwise. Members of societies which are reckoning with large-scale violations of human rights and histories of violence will not understand conflict in the same way or be seeking to respond to the same conflict or violence; they will also not have the same or compatible understandings of the past, the future, or theory of change (Pospisil 2020: 344). While the erasure of struggle might suit the logic of the transitional justice global norm, it does little to ensure an inclusive, transformative and effective justice. What we can learn from struggle is that history matters – whether it is the history of colonial invasion and political exclusion, or the history of racial discrimination. We can learn that context matters – whether it is the living conditions of those supposed to integrate and reconcile, or the exclusion from public dialogue.

It is not only a question of historical struggle that is ignored, marginalised and made invisible in the pursuit of order, but also an inability to see, learn from, and respond to changes in struggle. Drawing from the South African case, Kerr and Dixon identify what they refer to as 'a conundrum to the transitional justice paradigm', meaning how to 'understand new forms of post-transitional violence and victimization which are not simply a straight-forward continuation of the violence of the old era, but in fact draw on some of the languages and practices of liberation struggle and transitional justice' (2022: 94). Thinking beyond South Africa, and to the case studies in Part 2 of this book, we can see the dynamic nature of struggle, as it takes on new forms in its encounter with transitional justice. In Côte d'Ivoire, the long-standing struggle over autochthony, political belonging, and political exclusion encoun-tered a transitional justice process which demarcated perpetrators and victims, prized political stability above political inclusion, and delegitimised certain voices and certain struggles. In Tunisia, the long-standing struggle for racial equality encountered a reluctant transitional justice process which sent the struggle into different forms of participation and lobbying targeted at the windows of opportunity. In Bosnia-Herzegovina, the long-standing struggle over what multi-ethnic living looks like and how ethno-national identity is to be understood encountered a transitional justice process which categorised people and groups and marginalised identities and everyday life contexts which fell outside of the frame of multi-ethnic reconciliation. In each case, in each of the acts of citizenship the struggle evolved and partly used – as well as partly rejected – transitional justice.

Acts of the transitional justice citizen are thus not about the citizen's *lack* – lack of knowledge, lack of virtue – but about a lack in how a given transitional justice process has been designed and implemented. Perhaps the most con-cerning of assumptions is that of closure, meaning that any transitional justice process marks a distinct break from the past and therefore from violence. In fact, transitional justice can only reach its goals if it is seen as an ongoing process of contestation and negotiation, recognizing and learning from his-torical struggle in its previous and new forms. The transitional justice citizen brings this ongoing and unsettled reality to the fore and gives it a purpose.

8.3   CONCLUSION

[T]ransitional justice is a discourse that is shaped by power and articulated very differently depending on who frames the debates and who owns and presents the knowledge. (Lykes and van der Merwe 2019: 412)

In many ways the story of this book is one of encounters between different articulations of justice. These different articulations do not meet on a level

playing field, nor do they have an equal chance of shaping the kind of transitional justice process that is put in place. A central actor in these encounters
is the transitional justice citizen. This is a figure both imagined and framed by
policy and discourse and made through acts which push boundaries, rewrite
scripts, and demand more than the justice on offer. This figure connects historical struggle with contemporary calls to justice and brings context back in
as a way of understanding what justice could and should be. The transitional
justice citizen is thus real, imagined, and also not yet in existence.

While critical studies of transitional justice have gathered in strength and
impact in recent years, Sharp warns against painting too broad a brush in critiques of mainstream transitional justice as hegemonic, neoliberal, or neocolo-
nial (Sharp 2019: 579). While this book certainly draws from and speaks to this
more critical literature, the intention has been to engage thoughtfully with such
critiques to find new entry points into a better understanding and better practice of transitional justice. While it is true that the citizenship acts analysed in
Part 2 seem to occur when other options have been closed off, delegitimised by
the framings and priorities of the increasingly monolithic transitional justice
norm, they also offer windows of opportunity for change, for disruption, and
for the writing of new scripts. In simple terms the transitional justice citizen
seeks rather than only receives justice, reminding all actors of the possibility
of different forms, content and effects of transitional justice.

While acts of the transitional justice citizen are indeed about the opening
up of possibilities across a range of potential justice options, it is also true to
say that the acts analysed in this book tend towards demands which are more
transformative of structures and of standards of living. We know that populations in transitional-justice-affected countries seek socio-economic redress,
are interested in broader human development and do not necessarily prioritise
the more dominant pillars of the transitional justice global norm. Citizenship
acts articulate these demands, insert them into the transitional justice process
and push back against transitional justice entrepreneurs and experts who have
a narrow vision of the past, the present and the priorities for the future. The
kinds of disruption and contestation which we see in such acts are thus points
of learning; indicators that the transitional justice offer may be incomplete,
unjust in its implementation, or inadvertently slowing down a more comprehensive set of transformations with a linear beginning and end to transition.
Too often the political order, elite interests, or inequalities are not altered
as much as the term 'transition' would imply; indeed we know that political
resistance can occur if reports and recommendations around justice delve too
deeply into structural change (Miller 2020: 375). We need to be reminded that
a break with the past does not mean that all injustice is ended, and acts of the
transitional justice citizen do just that.

Acts of the transitional justice citizen are also enriching in their diversity and in their divergence from the prevailing justice norm. As explored at length throughout both parts of this book, it should not be a surprize that different points of view are present at times of transitional justice. This is not only a product of the divisions generated by conflict and violence but also a natural facet of a vibrant political community – something towards which one should strive, particularly in the face of violence which has included some and excluded others from such community. Political identity is transformed by violence and citizenship itself may have been denied to particular groups or individuals as part of a previous regime or through targeted human rights violations. Transitional justice is thus a question of citizenship. This means it is more than a case of adding in citizenship to the field of transitional justice. It is about recognizing how transitional justice evokes citizenship questions at the same time as citizenship struggles intersect with and shape transitional justice. This keeps diversity and divergence at the forefront of the search for justice, something which is not closed by transitional justice but continually open. This breaks with the evolution of the transitional justice field in which

> radically disparate events of multiple societies around the world over the course of five decades were incorporated into commensurate problems. To understand different sites of conflict and violence as comparable helped make common applications of justice seem plausible and thus a common peace attainable. (Miller 2020: 359)

I hope that this book, through the figure of the transitional justice citizen, has given a face to the agency which we already know to be so vital at times of transitional justice. Conceptualizing the transitional justice citizen in the way I have done here provides a way of bringing together the different threads of critical scholarship that is hopefully productive and optimistic. I hope that this approach will encourage other scholars to work on and with the transitional justice citizen, to go beyond a snapshot approach of a society reckoning with a violent past to probe more deeply into what might seem like failings or problematic processes and outcomes, as well as to interrogate more closely and ask different questions to different actors about what counts as justice, what counts as success. Inevitably this will connect the aims of transitional justice processes with the everyday polity, citizens, and their grievances which might not otherwise be considered transitional justice concerns. This is a continual movement between the possibility of contestation, the redefinition of claim-making, and the actual foreclosure of options. The transitional justice citizen offers a productive way of capturing it.

There will, of course, be limitations to what the transitional justice citizen can do for the field of transitional justice. There are perhaps limits to how far we can take such contestation, such opening, such invitation to disruption and divergence. We might want to ask ourselves whether we can or should ever keep boundaries around who can make claims, around what claims can be made and around how claims can be made. These are reasonable words of caution. However, we are perhaps so far from the danger of a transitional justice 'free for all' that it is not worth limiting the explorations that we can undertake now in good faith: explorations of the origins, effects, and justice around such boundaries. If we care about justice, and it is certain that we should, it is precisely those boundaries that we must continuously challenge, pushing them back to include other voices until a new path opens before us. For if transitional justice is about anything, it should be about bearing witness, about listening, and about amplifying those voices which violence and injustice have muffled. We owe a debt of gratitude to the transitional justice citizen for all their efforts to do so.

NOTES

1.   Interview 290514.
2.   Interview TA02.
3.   Interview 030707b.

Bibliography

Adou, D. D. F. (2018). Resistance to Transitional Justice in the Context of Political Violence in Cote d'Ivoire. Resistance and Transitional Justice. Abingdon and New York, Routledge: 17–34.

Adou, D. D. F. and B. Jones (forthcoming a). National Commission for Reconciliation and Compensation of Victims. Encylopedia of Transitional Justice: Second Edition. L. Stan and N. Nedelsky. Cambridge, Cambridge University Press.

Adou, D. D. F. and B. Jones (forthcoming b). Cote d'Ivoire. Encyclopedia of Transitional Justice: Second Edition. L. Stan and N. Nedelsky. Cambridge, Cambridge University Press.

Adou, D. D. F. and B. Jones (forthcoming c). Commission of Dialogue, Truth and Reconciliation. Encyclopedia of Transitional Justice: Second Edition. L. Stan and N. Nedelsky. Cambridge, Cambridge University Press.

Akindes, F. (2004). The Roots of the Military-Political Crises in Cote d'Ivoire. Uppsala, Nordiska Afrikainstitutet. Research Report No. 128.

Alcoff, L. M. (2009). The Problem of Speaking for Others. Challenging Conventional, Interpretive, and Critical Conceptions in Qualitative Research. A. Y. Jackson and L. A. Mazzei. Abingdon and New York, Routledge: 117–135.

Almas, G. (2007). The Political Implications of Economic Adjustment: Crisis, Reform and Political Breakdown in Cote d'Ivoire. Perspectives on Cote d'Ivoire: Between Political Breakdown and Post-Conflict Peace. C. I. Obi. Uppsala, Nodiska Afrikainstitutet: 10–29.

Amstutz, M. (2006). Restorative Justice, Political Forgiveness and the Possibility of Political Reconciliation. The Politics of Past Evil. D. Philpott. Indiana, University of Notre Dame Press.

Anders, G. and O. Zenker (2014). "Transition and Justice: An Introduction." Development and Change 45(3): 395–414.

Andrieu, K. (2010). "Civilizing Peacebuilding: Transitional Justice, Civil Society and the Liberal Paradigm." Security Dialogue 41(5): 537–558.

Arenhövel, M. (2008). "Democratization and Transitional Justice." Democratization 15(3): 570–587.

Arthur, P. (2009). "How 'Transitions' Reshaped Human Rights: A Conceptual History of Transitional Justice." Human Rights Quarterly 31: 321–367.

Arthur, P., Ed. (2011). Identities in Transition: Challeges for Transitional Justice in Divided Societies. Cambridge and New York, Cambridge University Press and International Center for Transitional Justice.

Arthur, P. and C. Yakinthou (2018). Changing Contexts of International Assistance to Transitional Justice. Transitional Justice, International Assistance, and Civil Society. P. Arthur and C. Yakinthou. Cambridge, New York, Melbourne, New Delhi, Cambridge University Press: 1–24.

AU (2019). Transitional Justice Policy. Addis Ababa, African Union.

Bah, A. B. (2010). "Democracy and Civil War: Citizenship and Peacemaking in Cote d'Ivoire." African Affairs 109(437): 597–615.

Baldo, S. (2011). Ivory Coast Must Avoid Victor's Justice: Podcast with Suliman Baldo. In Focus, International Centre for Transitional Justice.

Balibar, E. (2015). Violence and Civility: on the Limits of Political Philosophy. New York, Columbia University Press.

Barma, N. H. (2017). The Peacebuilding Puzzle: Political Order in Post-Conflict States. Cambridge, New York, Melbourne, New Delhi, Singapore, Cambridge University Press.

Becker, M. T. (2017). "Socializing with the Out-Group: Testing the Contact Hypothesis among School Students in Bosnia and Herzegovina." Croatian Political Science Review **54**(4): 126–142.

Bell, C. (2009). "Transitional Justice, Interdisciplinarity and the State of the 'Field' or 'Non-Field'." The International Journal of Transitional Justice **3**: 5–27.

Bell, C. (2022) Transitional Justice: Understanding the Field in Evans, Matthew ed. Beyond Transitional Justice: Transformative Justice and the State of the Field (or Non Field) London and New York: Routledge.

Belloni, R. (2005). "Peacebuilding at the Local Level: Refugee Return to Prijedor." International Peacekeeping **12**: 434–447.

Bennet, T., et al., eds. (2012). African Perspectives on Tradition and Justice. Antwerp and Cambridge, Intersentia.

Bernath, J. (2016). "'Complex Political Victims' In the Aftermath of Mass Atrocity: Reflections on the Khmer Rouge Tribunal in Cambodia." The International Journal of Transitional Justice **10**(1): 46–66.

Besson, S. (2015). "The Bearers of Human Rights' Duties and Responsibilities for Human Rights: A Quiet (R)evolution?" Social Philosophy and Policy **21**(1): 244–268.

Bieber, F. (2005). "Local Institutional Engineering: A Tale of Two Cities, Mostar and Brčko." International Peacekeeping **12**: 420–433.

Bieber, F. (2006). Post War Bosnia: Ethnicity, Inequality and Public Sector Governance. Basingstoke and New York, Palgrave Macmillan.

Birkholz, S. Scherf. T. and Schroeder, U. C. (2018). "International interventions seen from the 'Middle': Perceptions of intermediary actors in Côte d'Ivoire and Lebanon". Cooperation and Conflict 53 (2): 173–192

Blaise, L. (2018). Est-ce que tu vis dans un arbre? : Chronique d'un Racisme Ordinaire en Tunisie. https://www.middleeasteye.net/fr/reportages/est-ce-que-tu-vis-dans-un-arbre-chronique-dun-racisme-ordinaire-en-tunisie, Midde East Eye

Bliesemann de Guevara, B. and R. Kostić, Eds. (2018). Knowledge and Expertise in International Interventions: The Politics of Facts, Truth and Authenticity. London and New York, Routledge.

Bosire, L. K. and G. Lynch (2014). "Kenya's Search for Truth and Justice: The Role of Civil Society." The International Journal of Transitional Justice **8**: 256–276.

Bougarel, X., et al., eds. (2007a). The New Bosnian Mosaic: Identities, Memory and Moral Claims in Post-War Society. Aldershot, Ashgate.

Bougarel, X., et al. (2007b). Introduction. The New Bosnian Mosaic: Identities, Memories and Moral Claims in a Post-War Society. X. Bougarel, E. Helms and G. Duijzings. Aldershot, Ashgate: 1–38.

Bowsher, J. (2018). "'Omnus et Singulatim': Establishing the Relationship between Transitional Justice and Neoliberalism." Law Critique **29**: 83–106.

Bringa, T. (1995). 'Being Muslim the Bosnian Way': Identity and Community in a Central Bosnian Village. Princeton, Princeton University Press.

Brinton Lykes, M. and van der Merwe, H. (2019). "Critical Reflexivity and Transitional Justice Praxis: Solidarity, Accompaniment and Intermediarity". The International Journal of Transitional Justice **13**: 411–416

Brudholm, T. (2008). Resentment's Virtue: Jean Amery and the Refusal to Forgive. Philadelphia, Temple University Press.

Buckley-Zistel, S. (2006). "Dividing and Uniting: The Use of Citizenship Discourse in Conflict and Reconciliation in Rwanda." Global Society **20**: 101–113.

Buckley-Zistel, S. (2011). Narration und Transition. Vom Umgang mit der Vergangenheit in Warheitskommissionen nach extremer Gewalt. Bürgerkrieg Erzählen. S. Ferhadbegović and B. Weiffen. Konstanz, University of Konstanz Press.

Buckley-Zistel, S., et al. (2014). Transitional Justice Theories: An Introduction. Transitional Justice Theories. S. Buckley-Zistel, T. K. Beck, C. Braun and F. Mieth. Abingdon and New York, Routledge: 1–16.

Campbell, C. and C. Turner (2008). "Utopia and the Doubters: Truth, Transition and the Law." Legal Studies **28**(3): 374–395.

Carla, A. (2005). "Community Security: Letters from Bosnia. A Theoretical Analysis and its Application in the Case of Bosnia-Herzegovina." Peace, Conflict and Development **7**: 217–250.

Chambers, S. and J. Kopstein (2001). "Bad Civil Society." Political Theory **29**(6): 837–856.

Clark, N. J. (2010). "Education in Bosnia-Herzegovina: The Case for Root-and-Branch Reform." Journal of Human Rights **9**(3): 344–362.

Colvin, C. J. (2008). "Purity and Planning: Shared Logics of Transitional Justice and Development." The International Journal of Transitional Justice **2**(3): 412–425.

Commission, T. a. D. (2019). Truth And Dignity Commission. The Final Report: Executive Summary. T. a. D. Commission. Tunis, Truth and Dignity Commission.

Dali, I. M. (2015). "Les Mobilisations des 'Nors Tunisiens' au Lendemain de la Revolte de 2011: Entre Affirmation d'une Identite Historique er Defense d'une 'Cause Noire'." Politique Africaine **140**: 61–81.

Darling, J. (2017). "Acts, Ambiguities, and the Labour of Contesting Citizenship." Citizenship Studies **21**(6): 727–736.

Davidovic, M. (2020). "Transform or Perish? The Crisis of Transitional Justice." Conflict, Security and Development **20**(2): 293–302.

de Greiff, P. (2009). Articulating the Links Between Transitional Justice and Development: Justice and Social Reintegration. Transitional Justice and Development: Making Connections. P. de Greiff and R. Duthie. New York, Social Science Research Council: 28–75.

de Greiff, P. (2013a). Report of the Special Rapporteur on the Promotion of Truth, Jusitce, Reparation and Guarantees of Non-Recurrence A/68/345, Geneva, United Nations.

de Greiff, P. (2013b). Report of the Special Rapporteur on the Promotion of Truth, Jusitce, Reparation and Guarantees of Non-Recurrence A/HRC/24/42. Geneva, United Nations.

de Greiff, P. (2014). Report of the Special Rapporteur on the Promotion of Truth, Justice, Reparation and Guarantees of Non-Recurrence A/69/518. Geneva, United Nations.

de Greiff, P. (2015). Report of the Special Rapporteur on the Promotion of Truth, Justice, Reparation and Guarantees of Non-Recurrence A/HRC/30/42. Geneva, United Nations.

de Greiff, P. (2016). Report of the Special Rapporteur on the promotion of truth, Justice, Reparation and guarantees of non-recurence A/71/567 Geneva, United Nations.

de Greiff, P. (2017). Report of the Special Rapporteur on the Promotion of Truth, Justice, Reparation and Guarantees of Non-Recurrence A/HRC/34/62. Geneva, United Nations.

de Greiff, P. (2017). Report of the Special Rapporteur on the Promotion of Truth, Justice, Reparation and Guarantees of Non-Recurrence A/HRC/34/62. Geneva, United Nations.

de Waardt, M. (2010). "Naming and Shaming Victims: The Semantics of Victimhood." The International Journal of Transitional Justice 10(3): 432–450.

Deiana, M.-A. (2016). "To Settle for a Gendered Peace? Spaces for Feminist Grassroots Mobilisation in Northern Ireland and Bosnia-Herzegovina." Citizenship Studies 20(1): 99–114.

Diallo, Y. (2005). From Stability to Uncertainty: a Recent Political History of Cote d'Ivoire. Halle, Saale, Max Planck Institute for Social Anthropology. Working Paper 74.

Diaz, C. (2008). Challenging Impunity from Below: The Contested Ownership of Transitional Justice in Colombia. Transitional Justice from Below: Grassroots Activism and the Struggle for Change. K. McEvoy and L. McGregor. Oxford and Portland, Hart Publishing.

Donia, R. J. and J. V. A. Fine Jr (1994). Bosnia and Herzegovina: A Tradition Betrayed. London, Hurst.

Duffield, M. (2002). "Social Reconstruction and the Radicalization of Development: Aid as a Relation of Global Liberal Governance." Development and Change 33(5): 1049–1071.

Duthie, R. (2009). Building Trust and Capacity: Civil Society and Transitional Justice from a Development Perspective. New York, International Center for Transitional Justice.

Duthie, R. and P. Seils (2017). Justice Mosaics: How Context Shapes Transitional Justice in Fractured Societies. New York, International Center for Transitional Justice.

Dzaja, S. M. (2005). Bosnian Historical Reality and its Reflection in Myth. P. Kolsto. London, Hurst and Company: 106–129.

Eastmond, M. and J. M. Selimovic (2012). "Silence as Possibility in Everyday Life." The International Journal of Transitional Justice 6(3): 502–524.

Edyvane, D. (2017). "The Passion for Civility." Political Studies Review 15(3): 344–354.

Eisikovits, N. (2013). "Peace versus Justice in Transitional Settings." Politica and Societa 2: 221–236.

EU (2015). The EU's Policy Framework on Support to Transitional Justice. Brussels, European Union.

Evans, M. (2016). "Structural Violence, Socioeconomic Rights, and Transformative Justice." Journal of Human Rights 15(1): 1–20.

Evans, M. (2022) In, Against, and Beyond Transitional Justice: Themes and Dilemmas for the Field (or Non-Field), in Evans, Matthew ed. Beyond Transitional Justice: Transformative Justice and the State of the Field (or Non Field) London and New York: Routledge.

Fassatoui, O. (2021). Tunisia's Law Against Racial Discrimination: The Mixed Results of a Pioneering Legislation. https://www.arab-reform.net/publication/tunisias-law

-against-racial-discrimination-the-mixed-results-of-a-pioneering-legislation/, Arab Reform Initiative. 2021.

Faure, Y. A. (1982). Le Complexe Politico-Economique. Etat et Bourgeoisie en Cote d'Ivoire. Faure and Medard. Paris, Karthala: 21–60.

Findlay, M. (2009). "Activating a Victim Constituency in International Criminal Justice." The International Journal of Transitional Justice **3**: 183–206.

Fischer, A. (2006a). Integration or Segregation? Reforming the Education Sector. Peacebuilding and Civil Society in Bosnia-Herzegovina Ten Years After Dayton. M. Fischer. Berlin, Lit.

Fletcher, L. and H. Weinstein (2018). "How Power Dynamics Influence the North-South Gap ini Transitional Justice." Berkeley Journal of International Law **36**(2): 190–217.

Fletcher, L., et al. (2009). "Context, Timing and the Dynamics of Transitional Justice: A Historical Perspective." Human Rights Quarterly **31**: 163–220.

Fullard, M. and N. Rousseau (2011). Truth Telling, Identities, and Power in South Africa and Guatemala. Identities in Transition: Challenges for Transitional Justice in Divided Societies. P. Arthur. Cambridge, New York, Melbourne, Madrid, Cape Town, Singapore, Cambridge University Press: 54–86.

Glasius, M. (2009). "What is Global Justice and Who Decides? Civil Society and Victim Responses to the International Criminal Court's First Investigations." Human Rights Quarterly **31**: 496–520.

Govantes, B. and M. H. de Larramendi (2021). "The Tunisian Transition: A Winding Road to Democracy." The Journal of North African Studies https://doi/10.1080/13629387.2021.1963238.

Government, B. (2006). Brčko District of BiH 2000–2007. Brčko, Brčko District Government.

Gready, P. and S. Robins (2014). "From Transitional to Transformative Justice: A New Agenda for Practice." The International Journal of Transitional Justice **8**(3): 339–361.

Hamber, B. and R. A. Wilson (2002). "Symbolic Closure Through Memory, Reparation and Revenge in Post-Conflict Societies." Journal of Human Rights **1**(1): 35–53.

Hansen, T. O. (2014). The Vertical and Horizontal Expansion of Transitional Justice. Transitional Justice Theories. T. B. Susanne Buckley-Zistel, C. Braun and F. Mieth. Abingdon and New York, Routledge: 105–124.

Heimerl, D. (2005). "The Return of Refugees and Internally Displaced Persons: From Coercion to Sustainability?" International Peacekeeping **12**: 377–390.

Henderson, G. P. (2006). "The Public and Peace: The Consequences for Citizenship of the Democratic Peace Literature." International Studies Review **8**(2): 199–224.

Hoddy, E. T. and P. Gready (2020). "From Agency to Root Causes: Addressing Structural Barriers to Transformative Justice in Transitional and Post-Conflict Settings." Contemporary Social Science **15**(5): 561–576.

Hoffman, J. (2004). Citizenship Beyond the State. London, Sage.

Holder, R. (2018). Just Interests: Victims, Citizens and the Potential for Justice. Cheltenham and Northampton, Edward Elgar Publishing.

Hooks, B. (1990). Yearning: Race, Gender, and Cultural Politics. Cambridge, MA, Southend Press.

Hovil, L. and M. C. Okello (2011). "Editorial Note." The International Journal of Transitional Justice **5**(3): 333–344.

Howell, E. and A. Schaap (2014). The Aboriginal Tent Embassy and Australian Citizenship. Routledge Handbook of Global Citizenship Studies. I. Isin and P. Nyers. Abingdon, Routledge: 568–580.

Hromadzic, A. (2012). "'Once we had a House' Invisible Citizens and Consociational Democracy in Post-War Mostar, Bosnia and Herzegovina." Social Analysis **56**(3): 30–48.

Hromadzic, J. (2008). "Discourses of Integration and Practices of Reunification at the Mostar Gymnasium, Bosnia-Herzegovina." Comparative Education Review **52**: 541–563.

Hughes, C. (2009). 'We Just Take What They Offer': Community Empowerment in Post-War Timor-Leste. New Perspectives on Liberal Peacebuilding. E. Newman, R. Paris and O. P. Richmond. Tokyo and New York, United Nations University Press.

Hughes, J. (2007). "Mediating and Moderating Effects of Inter-Group Contact: Case Studies from Bilingual/Bi-National Schools in Israel." Journal of Ethnic and Migration Studies **33**: 419–437.

Human Rights Watch (2015). Making Justice Count: Lessons from the ICC's Work in Cote d'Ivoire. United States of America, Human Rights Watch.

Human Rights Watch (2019). Tunisia: Truth Commission Outlines Decades of Abuse. https://www.hrw.org/news/2019/04/05/tunisia-truth-commission-outlines-decades-abuse, last accessed 24.02.23

ICG (2003). Bosnia's Brčko: Getting In, Getting On and Getting Out. Sarajevo and Brussels, International Crisis Group. Balkans Report No. 144.

ICG (2007). Ensuring Bosnia's Future: A New International Engagement Strategy. Sarajevo and Brussels, International Crisis Group. Europe Report 180.

ICG (2011). A Critical Period for Ensuring Stability in Cote d'Ivoire, International Crisis Group. Africa Report 176.

ICTJ (2013). "ICTJ Program Report: Tunisia." Retrieved 29 August 2019.

Ilif, A. R. (2012). "Root and Branch: Discourses of 'Tradition' in Grassroots Transitional Justice." The International Journal of Transitional Justice **6**: 253–273.

Isin, I. (2008). Theorizing Acts of Citizenship. Acts of Citizenship. I. Isin and G. Nielsen. London and New York, Zed Books.

Isin, I. and G. Nielsen (2008). Acts of Citizenship. London and New York, Zed Books.

Isin, I. and G. Nielsen (2008). Introduction. Acts of Citizenship. I. Isin and G. Nielsen. London and New York, Zed Books.

Jankowitz, S. (2018). "The 'Hierarchy of Victims' in Northern Ireland: A Framework for Critical Analysis." The International Journal of Transitional Justice **12**(2).

Jebli, H. (2020). Tunisia Still Has Much to do to Eliminate Racism. https://www.al-monitor.com/originals/2020/06/tunisia-racism-black-people-consitution-rights.html, Al-Monitor: https://www.al-monitor.com/originals/2020/2006/tunisia-racism-black-people-consitution-rights.html.

Jeffrey, A. (2008). "Adjudications of 'Civility': Gentrifying Civil Society." Geopolitics **13**(4): 740–744.

Jeffrey, A. and M. Jakala (2015). "Using Courts to Build States: The Competing Spaces of Citizenship in Transitional Justice Programmes." Political Geography **47**: 43–52.

Jones, B. (2012). "Exploring the Politics of Reconciliation through Education Reform: The Case of Brčko District, Bosnia and Herzegovina." The International Journal of Transitional Justice **6**(1): 126–148.

Jones, B. (2015). Educating Citizens in Bosnia-Herzegovina: Models, Claims and Experiences in Post War Education Reform. Transitional Justice and Reconciliation: Lessons from the Balkans. M. Fischer and O. Simic. Abingdon and New York, Routledge: 193–208.

Jones, B. (2015). "Stories of 'Success'. Narrative, Expertise and Claims to Knowledge." Canadian Journal of Law and Society **30**(2): 293–308.

Jones, B. (2017). Seeking a 'Just Justice': Discursive Strategies of Resistance to Transitional Justice in Côte d'Ivoire. Resistance and Transitional Justice. B. Jones and J. Bernath. Abingdon and New York, Routledge.

Jones, B. and J. Bernath (2017). Introduction: Resistance and Transitional Justice. Resistance and Transitional Justice. B. Jones and J. Bernath. Abingdon and New York.

Jones, B. and J. Bernath, Eds. (2017). Resistance and Transitional Justice. Abingdon and New York, Routledge.

Jones, B. and A. D. D. Fatogoma (2018). "Reading the 'Uncivil' in Civil Society Resistance to Transitional Justice in Cote d'Ivoire." Political Geography **67**.

Jones, E. and J. Gaventa (2002). Concepts of Citizenship: A Review. Brighton, Brighton Institute of Development Studies.

Kabeer, N. (2005). Introduction: The Search for Inclusive Citizenship, Meanings and Expressions in an Interconnected World. Inclusive Citizenship: Meanings and Expressions. K. Naila. London and New York, Zed Books.

Kaplan, R. D. (2014). Balkan Ghosts: A Journey Through History. New York, Picador.

Keil, S. (2014). Whatever Happened to the Plenums in Bosnia?, www.balkaninsight .com/en/article/whatever-happened-to-the-plenums-in-Bosnia.

Kelsall, T. (2006). "Politics, Anti-Politics, International Justice: Language and Power in the Special Court for Sierra Leone." Review of International Studies **32**(4): 587–602.

Kennedy, D. (2018). A World of Struggle: How Power, Law, and Expertise Shape Global Political Economy. Princeton and Oxford, Princeton University Press.

King, S. J. (2021). Democracy and Progress Towards Racial Equality in Tunisia: Interview with Zied Rouine. https://www.arab-reform.net/publication/democracy -and-progress-towards-racial-equality-in-tunisia-interview-with-zied-rouine/, Arab Reform Initiative: https://www.arab-reform.net/publication/democracy-and -progress-towards-racial-equality-in-tunisia-interview-with-zied-rouine/.

Kostić, R. (2008). "Nationbuilding as an Instrument of Peace? Exploring Local Attitudes towards International Nationbuilding and Reconciliation in Bosnia Herzegovina." Civil Wars **10**: 384–412.

Kothari, U. and B. Cooke (2001). The Case for Participation: The New Tyranny? Participation: The New Tyranny? U. Kothari and B. Cooke. London, Zed Books: 1–15.

Lacerda, T. (2010). "'Victim': What is Hidden Behind this Word?" The International Journal of Transitional Justice **10**(1): 179–188.

Lai, D. (2020). Socioeconomic Justice: International Intervention and Transition in Post-War Bosnia and Herzegovina. Cambridge, New York, Melbourne, New Delhi, Singapore, Cambridge University Press.

Lambourne, W. (2012). Outreach, Inreach and Civil Society Participation in Transitional Justice. Critical Perspectives in Transitional Justice. N. Palmer, P. Clark and D. Granville. Cambridge, Antwerp, Portland, Intersentia: 235–261.

Lamont, C. K. and H. Boujneh (2012). "Transitional Justice in Tunisia." Politicka Misao **49**(5): 32–49.

Lefranc, S. (2002). Politiques du Pardon. Paris, Presses Universitaires de France.

Leuffen, D. (2011). Case Selection and Selection Bias in Small-n Research. Research Design in Social Science: How to Practice What They Preach. London, Palgrave Macmillan: 145–160.

Lister, R. (2003). Citizenship: Feminist Perspectives. Hampshire and New York, Palgrave Macmillan.

Little, A. (2009). The Northern Ireland Paradox. The Politics of Radical Democracy. A. Little and M. Lloyd. Edinburgh, Edinburgh University Press.

Lynch, G. (2018). Performances of Injustice: The Politics of Truth, Justice and Reconciliation in Kenya. Cambridge and New York, Cambridge University Press.

Mac Ginty, R. (2018). Key Concepts in Political Transitions. The Elgar Companion to Post-Conflict Transition. H.-J. Giessmann and R. Mac Ginty. Cheltenham and Northampton, Edward Elgar Publishing.

Maddison, S. and L. Shepherd (2014). "Peacebuilding and the Postcolonial Politics of Transitional Justice." Peacebuilding 2(3): 253–269.

Madlingozi, T. (2010). "On Transitional Justice Entrepreneurs and the Production of Victims." Journal of Human Rights Practice 2(2): 208–228.

Mahmoud, Y. and A. Ó Súilleabháin (2020). "Improvising Peace: Towards New Social Contracts in Tunisia." Journal of Intervention and Statebuilding 14(1): 101–118.

Malcolm, N. (1994). Bosnia: A Short History. London, Basingstoke and Oxford, Pan Books.

Mamdani, M. (2009). Saviors and Survivors: Darfur, Politics and the War on Terror. London and New York, Verso.

Marie, A. (1998). Pas de Societie Civile sans Democratie. Contre l'Etat et sa Societie, l'Existence Democratique des Jeunes Chomeurs Abidjanais Engages dans l'Opposition. Individualisations Citadines et Developpement d'une Societie Civile. Leimdorfer and Marie. Abidjan, Dakar and Paris, Universite de Paris-I, Gescivia-ledes: 63–111.

Marshall-Fratani, R. (2006). "The War of 'Who Is Who': Autochthony, Nationalism, and Citizenship in the Ivoirian Crisis." African Studies Review 49(2): 9–43.

Mazzei, L. A. and A. Youngblood Jackson (2009). Introduction: The Limit of Voice. Voice in Qualitative Inquiry: Challenging Conventional, Interpretive, and Critical Conceptions in Qualitative Research. A. Y. Jackson and L. A. Mazzei. Abingdon and New York, Routledge: 1–13.

McAuliffe, P. (2017). Transformative Transitional Justice and the Malleability of Post-Conflict States. Cheltenham and Massachusetts, Edward Elgar Publishing.

McEvoy, K. and K. McConnachie (2013). 'Victims and Transitional Justice: Voice, Agency and Blame.' Social and Legal Studies 22(4): 489–513.

McEvoy, K. and L. McGregor (2008). Transitional Justice from Below: An Agenda for Research, Policy and Praxis. Transitional Justice from Below: Grassroots Activism and the Struggle for Change. K. McEvoy and L. McGregor. Oxford and Portland, Hart Publishing.

McEvoy, K. and L. McGregor, eds. (2008). Transitional Justice from Below: Grassroots Activism and the Struggle for Change. Oxford and Portland, Hart Publishing.

McEvoy, K. (2018). "Travel, Dilemmas and Nonrecurrence: Observations on the 'Respectabilisation' of Transitional Justice". International Journal of Transitional Justice 12:185–193.

McGill, D. (2022). Transforming Experiences of Citizen Security? in Evans, M. ed. Beyond Transitional Justice: Transformative Justice and the State of the Field (or Non Field) Routledge: London and New York.

McGrattan, C. (2009). "'Order Out of Chaos': The Politics of Transitional Justice". Politics 29(3): 164–172.

Meister, R. (2002). "Human Rights and the Politics of Victimhood." Ethics and International Affairs 16: 91–108.

Mendez, J. E. (2016). "Victims as Protagonists in Transitional Justice." The International Journal of Transitional Justice 10(1): 1–5.

Miller, P. B. (2006). "Contested Memories: The Bosnian Genocide in Serb and Muslim Minds." Journal of Genocide Research **8**(3): 311–324.

Miller, Z. (2008). "Effects of Invisibility: In Search of the 'Economic' in Transitional Justice." The International Journal of Transitional Justice **2**: 266–291.

Miller, Z. (2020). "Embedded Ambivalence: Ungoverniong Global Justice." Transnational Legal Theory **11**(3): 353–381.

Minow, M. (2003). Education for Coexistence. Imagine Coexistence: Restoring Humanity after Violent Ethnic Conflict. A. Chayes and M. Minow. San Francisco, Jossey-Bass.

Moffett, L. (2016). "Reparations for 'Guilty Victims': Navigating Complex Identities of Victim-Perpetrators in Reparation Mechanisms." The International Journal of Transitional Justice **10**(1): 146–167.

Mukic, A. (2008a). We The Citizens of Ethnopolis. Sarajevo, Centar za Ljudska Prava Univerziteta u Sarajevu.

Mukic, A. (2008b). "Marginalizacija Oaze Multietnicnosti u BiH: Pravni i Politicki Status Distrikta Brčko u Predstojecim Ustavnim Promjenama." http://www .pulsdemokratije.ba/index.php?a=pdf&l-bs&id-824.

Murphy, C. (2017). The Conceptual Foundations of Transitional Justice. Cambridge, New York, Melbourne, Delhi, Cambridge University Press.

Mutua, M. (2001). "Savages, Victims and Saviors: The Metaphor of Human Rights." Harvard International Law Journal **42**(1): 201–246.

Mutua, M. (2009). Politics and Human Rights: An Essential Symbiosis. The Role of Law in International Politics: Essays in International Relations and International Law. M. Byers. Oxford, Oxford University Press: 149–176.

Mzioudet, H. (2018a). Mobilizing for Social Justice: Black Tunisian Activism in Transitional Justice. Transitional Justice Process in Tunisia: A Series of Published Articles. Justice Info and the University of Warwick: 3–7.

Mzioudet, H. (2018b). Termination with Prejudice. https://carnegie-mec.org/diwan/ 75786, Carnegie Middle East Centre: https://carnegie-mec.org/diwan/75786.

N'Da, S. A. Y. and G. Fokou (2021). Knowledge Asymmetry and Transitional Justice in Cote d'Ivoire. Knowledge for Peace: Transitional Justice and the Politics of Knowledge in Theory and Practice. B. Jones and U. Luhe. Cheltenham and Northampton, Edward Elgar Publishing: 75–98.

Nader Nadery, A. (2007). "Peace or Justice? Transitional Justice in Afghanistan." The International Journal of Transitional Justice **1**: 173–179.

Nagy, R. (2008). "Transitional Justice as Global Project: Critical Reflections." Third World Quarterly **29**(2): 275–289.

Newman, E. (2002). Transitional Justice: The Impact of Transnational Norms and the UN. Recovering from Civil Conflict: Reconciliation, Peace and Development. E. Newman and A. Schnabel. Portland, Cass.

Ní Aoláin, F. and C. Campbell (2005). "The Paradox of Transition in Conflicted Democracies." Human Rights Quarterly **27**(1): 172–213.

Njeru, S. and T. Masiya (2021). The Politics of Knowledge in the Emergence of the Transitional Justice Industry in Zimbabwe: The Case of Taking Transitional Justice to the People Programme, 2009–2011. Knowledge for Peace: Transitional Justice, Epistemic Communities and the Politics of Knowledge. B. Jones and U. Luhe: 120–143.

Nouwen, S. M. H. (2014). "As You Set Out for Ithaka: Practical, Epistemological, Ethical and Existential Questions About Socio-Legal Empirical Research in Conflict." Leiden Journal of International Law **27**(1): 227–260.

O'Connor, K. (2013). Repatriation. The Politics of (Re)-Constructing and Contesting Rwandan Citizenship. Refugees Studies Centre Working Paper 92. Oxford, Refugees Studies Centre.

Obi, C. I. (2007). Introduction. Perspectives on Cote d'Ivoire: Between Political Breakdown and Post-Conflict Peace. C. I. Obi. Uppsala, Nordiska Afrikainstitutet: 5–9.

Observer, T. and F. 24 (2018). Ivorian Man Who Spoke Out Against Racist Violence in Tunisia is Murdered. https://observers.france24.com/en/20181228-tunisia-ivory -coast-falikou-coulibaly-migration, The Observer and France 24.

Oglesby, E. (2007). "Educating Citizens in Post-War Guatemala: Historical Memory, Genocide and the Culture of Peace." Radical History Review **97**: 77–98.

OHCHR (2009). Rule-of-Law Tools for Post-Conflict States: National Consultations on Transitional Justice. New York and Geneva, United Nations.

Ohlin, J. D. (2007). "On the Very Idea of Transitional Justice." The Whitehead Journal of Diplomacy and International Relations **8**(1): 51–68.

Okello, M., C. and L. Hovil (2011). "Editorial Note." The International Journal of Transitional Justice **5**: 333–344.

Olivius, E. (2019). "Claiming Rights in Exile: Women's Insurgent Citizenship Practices in the Thai-Myanmar Borderlands." Citizenship Studies **23**(8): 761–779.

Oommen, T. K. (1997). Citizenship, Nationality and Ethnicity: Reconciling Competing Identities. Cambridge, Polity Press and Blackwell.

OSCE (2007). Lessons from Education Reform in Brčko. Brčko, OSCE Mission to BiH Education Department.

Oualdi, M. H. (2021). "Commemorating the Abolition of Slavery in Tunisia. The Rights of Black Citizens and the History of Slaves of European Origin." Esclavages et Post-Esclavages **4**: 1–17.

Palmer, N., et al. (2015). "Introduction: Ways of Knowing Atrocity: A Methodological Enquiry into the Formulation, Implementation, and Assessment of Transitional Justice." Canadian Journal of Law and Society **30**(2): 173–182.

Payne, L., et al. (2010). "The Jusitce Balance: When Transitional Justice Improves Human Rights and Democracy." Human Rights Quarterly **32**(4): 980–1005.

Pearce, J. (2007). Violence, Power and Participation: Building Citizenship in Contexts of Chronic Violence. IDS Working Paper 274. Brighton, Institute of Development Studies.

Pensky, M. (2012). Commentary on Critiquing Core Transitional Justice Concepts. Critical Perspectives in Transitional Justice. N. Palmer, P. Clark and D. Granville. Cambridge, Antwerp, Portland, Intersentia: 91–99.

Pentelovitch, N. H. (2008). "Seeing Justice Done: The Importance of Prioritizing Outreach Efforts at International Criminal Tribunals." Georgetown Journal of International Law **39**(3): 445–494.

Perry, V. (2003). Reading, Writing and Reconciliation. Flensburg, European Centre for Minority Issues.

Peskin, V. (2005). "Courting Rwanda: The Promises and Pitfalls of the ICTR Outreach Programme." Journal of International Criminal Justice **3**(4): 950–961.

Piccolino, G. (2012). "David Against Goliath in Cote d'Ivoire? Laurent Gbagbo's War Against Global Governance." African Affairs **111**(442): 1–23.

Piccolino, G. (2018). "Peacebuilding and Statebuilding in Post-2011 Cote d'Ivoire: A Victor's Peace?" African Affairs **117**(468): 485–508.

Piersma, M. J. (2019). "'Sistem te laže!': The Anti-Ruling Class Mobilisation of High School Students in Bosnia and Herzegovina." Nations and Nationalism **25**(3): 935–953.

Pillay, S. (2016). "The Impossible Machine: A Genealogy of South Africa's Truth and Reconciliation Commission. By Adam Sitze." Law and Society Review **50**(3): 802–804.

PNUD (2004). Raport National sue la Cohesion Sociale.

Porter, N. (2003). The Elusive Quest: Reconciliation in Northern Ireland. Belfast, The Blackstaff Press.

Pospisil, J. (2020). "The Ungovernance of Peace: Transitional Processes in Contemporary Conflictscapes." Transnational Legal Theory **11**(3): 329–352.

Pouessel, S. (2016). "The Democratic Turn in Tunisia: Civic and Political Redefinition of Canons of Cultural Diversity." Nationalism and Ethnic Politics **22**(1): 50–70.

Pouessel, S. (2018). Pourquoi les Tunisiens se mobilisent contre le racisme. https://www.middleeasteye.net/fr/opinion-fr/pourquoi-les-tunisiens-se-mobilisent-contre-le-racisme, Middle East Eye: https://www.middleeasteye.net/fr/opinion-fr/pourquoi-les-tunisiens-se-mobilisent-contre-le-racisme.

Preysing, D. (2016). Transitional Justice in Post-Revolutionary Tunisia (2011–2013): How the Past Shapes the Future. Wiesbaden, Springer VS.

Pugh, M. (2009). Towards Life Welfare. New Perspectives on Liberal Peacebuilding. E. Newman, R. Paris and O. P. Richmond. Tokyo, New York, Paris, United Nations University Press: 78–96.

Pykett, J., et al. (2010). "Framing the Good Citizen." The British Journal of Politics and International Relations **12**: 523–538.

Quattrini, S. (2020). "Religion, Identity and Ethnicity: The Quest of Tunisian Religious Minorities for Full Citizenship." Rpwaq Arabi **25**(2): 67–82.

Renner, J. (2012). A Discourse Theoretic Approach to Transitional Justice Ideals. Critical Perspectives in Transitional Justice. N. Palmer, P. Clark and D. Granville. Cambridge, Antwerp, Portland, Intersentia: 51–71.

Riehl, V. (2007). New War – Old Peace: About the Descent into Civil War in Cote d'Ivoire and its Absence in Ghana. Perspectives on Cote d'Ivoire: Between Political Breakdown and Post-Conflict Peace. C. I. Obi. Uppsala, Nordiska Afrikainstitutet: 30–49.

Rousseau, J. J. (1968). The Social Contract (Cranston Translation). London and New York, Penguin Books.

Rubli, S. (2012). Transitional Justice: Justice by Bureaucratic Means? Swisspeace Working Paper Series. Bern, Swisspeace.

Rubli, S. (2016). Transitional Justice as an Instrument for Political Struggles: Dealing with the Past and State-Formation in Burundi Political Science, University of Basel. PhD.

Salehi, M. (2021). "Trying Just Enough or Promising Too Much? The Problme-Capacity-Nexus in Tunisia's Transitional Justice Process." Journal of Intervention and Statebuilding DOI: 10.1090/17502977.2021.1882756.

Salvioli, F. (2018a). Report of the Special Rapporteur on the Promotion of Truth, Justice, Reparation and Guarantees of Non-Recurrence A/HRC/39/53. Geneva, United Nations.

Salvioli, F. (2018b). Report of the Special Rapporteur on the Promotion of Truth, Justice, Reparation and Guarantees of Non-Recurrence A/73/336. Geneva, United Nations.

Sassen, S. (2006). The Repositioning of Citizenship and Alienage: Emergent Subjects and Spaces for Politics. Displacement, Asylum, Migration. K. E. Tunstall. Oxford and New York, Oxford University Press.

Saward, M. (2013). "The Dynamics of European Citizenship: Enactment, Extension and Assertion." Comparative European Politics 11(1): 49–69.

Scaglioni, M. (2020). Becoming the 'Abid': Lives and Social Origins in Southern Tunisia. Milano, Ledizioni.

Schaap, A. (2006). "Agonism in Divided Societies." Philosophy and Social Criticism 32(2): 255–277.

Schaap, A. (2007). The Time of Reconciliation and the Space of Politics. Law and the Politics of Reconciliation. S. Veitch. Aldershot and Burlington, Ashgate.

Sharp, D. (2018). Rethinking Transitional Justice for the Twenty-First Century. Beyond the End of History. Cambridge, New York, Melbourne, New Delhi, Cambridge University Press.

Sharp, D. (2019). "What Would Satisfy Us? Taking Stock of Critical Approaches to Transitional Justice". International Journal of Transitional Justice 13: 570–589

Shaw, R. and L. Waldorf, eds. (2010). Localizing Transitional Justice: Interventions and Priorities after Mass Violence. Stanford, Stanford University Press.

Shinko, R. E. (2008). "Agonistic Peace: A Postmodern Reading." Millennium: Journal of International Studies 36(3): 473–491.

Simić, O. (2016). "Feminist Research in Transitional Justice Studies: Navigating Silences and Disruptions in the Field." Human Rights Review 17(1): 210–222.

Sisk, T. D. (1996). Power Sharing and International Mediation in Ethnic Conflicts. Washington D.C., United States Institute of Peace.

Skilbeck, R. (2008). "Funding Justice: The Price of War Crimes Trials." Human Rights Brief 15(3): 1–5.

Smith, A. and T. Vaux (2002). Education, Conflict and International Development. London, Department for International Development.

Smooha, S. (2002). "Types of Democracy and Modes of Conflict Management in Ethnically Divided Societies." Nations and Nationalism 8: 423–431.

Sprenkels, R. (2017). 'Restricted Access' Promises and Pitfalls of Victim Participation in Transitional Justice Mechanisms: A Comparative Perspective. Research Report, Impunity Watch.

Squire, V. (2016). "Unauthorised Migration Beyond Strucure/Agency? Acts, Interventions, Effects." Politics 37(3): 254–272.

Sriram, C. (2007). "Justice as Peace? Liberal Peacebuilding and Strategies of Transitional Justice." Global Society 21(4): 579–591.

Sriram, C. (2009). Transitional Justice and the Liberal Peace. New Perspectives on Liberal Peacebuilding. E. Newman, R. Paris and O. P. Richmond. Tokyo and New York, United Nations University Press: 112–130.

Stabback, P. (2004). Curriculum Development, Diversity and Division in Bosnia and Herzegovina. Education, Conflict and Social Cohesion. S. Tawil and A. Harley. Geneva, UNESCO IBE.

Staeheli, L. (2010). "Political Geography: Democracy and the Disorderly Public." Progress in Human Geography 34(1): 67–78.

Staeheli, L. (2011). "Political Geography: Where's Citizenship?" Progress in Human Geography 35(3): 393–400.

Stubbs, P. (1999). Displaced Promises: Forced Migration, Refuge and Repatriation in Croatia and Bosnia-Herzegovina. Uppsala, Life and Peace Institute.

Subotic, j. (2014). Bargaining Justice: A Theory of Transitional Justice Compliance. Transitional Justice Theories. S. Buckley-Zistel. New York, Routledge: 128–143.

Subotić, J. (2012). "The Transformation of International Transitional Justice Advocacy." The International Journal of Transitional Justice 6(1): 196–125.

Tawa, N. P. and A. Engelsdorfer (2017). Acceptance of the International Criminal Court in Cote d'Ivoire: Between the Hope for Justice and the Concern of 'Victor's Justice'. After Nuremberg. Exploring Multiple Dimensions of the Acceptance of International Criminal Justice. S. Buckley-Zistel, F. Mieth and M. Papa. Nuremberg, International Nuremberg Principles Academy.

Theidon, K. (2003). "Justice in Transition: The Micropolitics of Reconciliation in Peru." Journal of Conflict Resolution 50(3): 433–457.

Triponel, A. and S. Pearson (2010). "What Do You Think Should Happen? Public Participation in Transitional Justice." Pace International Law Review 22(1): 103–144.

Tunisia, R. O. (2013). Organic Law on Establishing and Organizing Transitional Justice. Tunis, Ministry of Human Rights and Transitional Justice, Technical Commission Organizing the National Dialogue on Transitional Justice.

Turner, C. (2013). "Deconstructing Transitional Justice." Law and Critique 193: 203–206.

UN (2004). The Rule of Law and Transitional Justice in Conflict and Post-Conflict Societies. U. N. S. Council. S/2004/616.

UN (2016). Report of the Special Rapporteur on the Promotion of Truth, Justice, Reparation and Guarantees of Non-Recurrence. Geneva, United Nations.

Van De Merwe, H., et al. (2009). Introduction. Assessing the Impact of Transitional Justice: Challenges for Empirical Research. H. Van De Merwe, V. Baxter and A. Chapman, R. Washington D.C., United States Institute of Peace Press: 1–11.

Vandeginste, S. (2012). "Burundi's Truth and Reconciliation Commission: How to Shed Light on the Past while Standing in the Dark Shadow of Politics?" The International Journal of Transitional Justice 6: 355–365.

Venema, D. (2012). Transitions and States of Exception: Towards a More General Theory of Transitional Justice. Critical Perspectives in Transitional Justice. N. Palmer, P. Clark and D. Granville. Cambridge, Antwerp, Portland, Intersentia: 73–89.

Vetlesen, A. J. (2005). Evil and Human Agency: Understanding Collective Evildoing. Cambridge, Cambridge University Press.

Vinck, P. and P. N. Pham (2010). "Outreach Evaluation: The International Criminal Court in the Central African Republic." The International Journal of Transitional Justice 4: 421–442.

Waldorf, L. (2012). "Anticipating the Past: Transitional Justice and Socio-Economic Wrongs." Social and Legal Studies 21(2): 171–186.

Waters, T. W. (2015). "Clearing the Path: The Perils of Positioning Civil Society in Conflict and Transition." Israel Law Review 48(2): 165–187.

Weine, S. M. (1999). When History is a Nightmare: Lives and Memories of Ethnic Cleansing in Bosnia-Herzegovina. New Brunswick, New Jersey, London, Rutyers University Press.

Wilmer, F. (1997). "Identity, Culture and Historicity: The Social Construction of Ethnicity in the Balkans." World Affairs 160(1): 3–16.

Wilson, R. A. (2011). Writing History in International Criminal Trials. Cambridge, Cambridge University Press.

Wilson, R. A. (2016). "Expert Evidence on Trial: Social Researchers in the International Criminal Courtroom." American Ethnologist **43**(4): 730–744.

Woodward, S., L. (1999). Bosnia after Dayton: Transforming a Compromise into a State. After the Peace: Resistance and Reconciliation. R. L. Rothstein. London, Lynne Reiner: 139–164.

Yere, H.-M. (2007). Reconfiguring Nationhood in Cote d'Ivoire? Perspectives on Cote d'Ivoire: Between Political Breakdown and Post-Conflict Peace. C. I. Obi. Uppsala, Nordiska Afrikainstitutet: 50–65.

Yin, R. K. (2009). Case Study Research: Design and Methods. Thousand Oaks and London, SAGE.

Zaum, D. (2007). The Sovereignty Paradox: The Norms and Politics of International Statebuilding. Oxford, Oxford University Press.

Zunino, M. (2019). Justice Framed: A Genealogy of Transitional Justice. Cambridge, New York, Melbourne, New Delhi, Singpore, Cambridge University Press.

Index